DATE DUE

AUG 3 77			
MAR 17 '84			
OCT 24 '84			
NOV 28 '84			

THE DISCOVERY
OF THE
PACIFIC ISLANDS

THE DISCOVERY
OF THE
PACIFIC ISLANDS

BY

ANDREW SHARP

OXFORD
AT THE CLARENDON PRESS

Oxford University Press, Ely House, London W.1

GLASGOW NEW YORK TORONTO MELBOURNE WELLINGTON
CAPE TOWN SALISBURY IBADAN NAIROBI LUSAKA ADDIS ABABA
BOMBAY CALCUTTA MADRAS KARACHI LAHORE DACCA
KUALA LUMPUR SINGAPORE HONG KONG TOKYO

© OXFORD UNIVERSITY PRESS 1960

FIRST PUBLISHED 1960
REPRINTED LITHOGRAPHICALLY IN GREAT BRITAIN
AT THE UNIVERSITY PRESS, OXFORD
FROM CORRECTED SHEETS OF THE FIRST EDITION
1962, 1969

PREFACE

THE main basis for our modern knowledge of the Pacific Islanders at the time of European contact is of necessity the records of the early European explorers. The first fruits of my research over many years in these fields were embodied in a previous study entitled *Ancient Voyagers in the Pacific*.[1] It became obvious during this research that many of the identifications of islands allegedly seen by various explorers were suspect or speculative. My further inquiries indicated that these defects arose from the fact that the classical hydrographers of the past, from whom most of the identifications had been inherited, did not have the advantage of systematic access to authoritative records, a number of which have furthermore come to light in comparatively recent times, or to the copious topographical and nautical data which are contained in modern hydrographic authorities and charts. I found that by abstracting objectively from the original records the relevant topographical and nautical data and comparing it with the modern material, the identity of most of the islands that were encountered in the exploration period could be established, and that the remaining uncertainties were reduced to comparatively small proportions. This in its turn made a tracing of the sequence of discovery possible. I do not mean by this that any marked degree of error or doubt has existed concerning the identity of most of the islands discovered by the more systematic later explorers, but even in their case the credit for first discovery of any given island is of course dependent on the disposal of the possible claims of predecessors. This book, therefore, is a study *ab initio* of the discovery of the various Pacific Islands, with full recognition of uncertainties, coupled with summaries of the ethnological observations of the discoverers before European influence could have been material.

A word is due on the relationship of the present book to other

[1] Sharp, A., *Ancient Voyagers in the Pacific* (Polynesian Society, 1956; reprinted by Penguin Books, 1957).

modern works on Pacific exploration, either general or regional. J. C. Beaglehole's *The Exploration of the Pacific* (London, 1934) gives excellent summaries of the political and geographical backgrounds, main events, and personalities of the main voyages of the exploration of the Pacific as a whole without attempting a systematic examination of the sequence of discovery of the Pacific Islands or of the ethnological data of the discoverers. I regard the present study and a study such as Beaglehole's as being complementary. P. H. Buck's *Explorers of the Pacific* (Honolulu, 1953) summarizes the main voyages in Polynesia without attempting a rigorous analysis of its discovery. E. W. Dahlgren's *The Discovery of the Hawaiian Islands* (Uppsala, 1917) is specifically devoted to the demonstration that there is no evidence of the discovery of the Hawaiian Islands before Cook. G. C. Henderson's *The Discoverers of the Fiji Islands* (London, 1933) traces impressively the first sighting of almost every island and rock in the Fiji group. E. A. Stackpole, in *The Sea-Hunters* (Philadelphia–New York, 1953), gives numbers of gleanings from newspaper accounts and logs of American whaling voyages. A. Krämer, H. Nevermann, and O. Reche, in the relevant volumes of *Ergebnisse der Südsee-Expedition 1908–1910* (Hamburg, 1917–54), give valuable notes on the discovery of the Caroline Islands, the Marshall Islands, the Admiralty Islands, and the Bismarck Archipelago, subsuming Kubary, Coello, Meinicke, Wichmann, and other older authorities.

In the case of sources contained in an extended collection comprising a number of volumes published at different times, I have cited the relevant volume, followed by the place and year of publication.

I have followed the example of Amherst, Thomson, Markham, and other translators and editors of Spanish texts in omitting accents from Spanish proper names, except in the case of a few traditional names of islands.

I am indebted to the Librarian and staff of the Alexander Turnbull Library, Wellington, for assistance in the manifold demands I have made on its Pacific collection over a long period, and to the Librarian of the Royal Geographical Society, London, the

Librarian of the Hocken Library, Dunedin, and Mr. A. G. Bagnall, of the New Zealand National Library Service, for providing or arranging for copies of references which were not immediately available to me. Photographs of the Herrera and Prado maps, Bougainville's chart, and Bligh's plan were provided by the Alexander Turnbull Library.

A. S.

CONTENTS

CONTENTS xi

LIST OF ILLUSTRATIONS

MAPS

PLATES

Map 1. The Pacific Basin

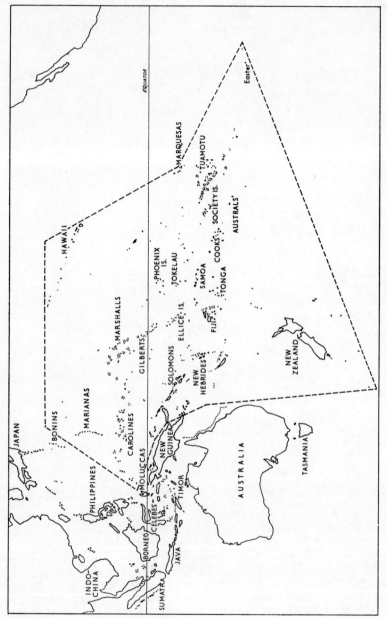

MAP 1. The Pacific Islands

1. Introduction

THE objects of this book are to trace the first European or American discovery of the various Pacific Islands, or the first firm report where the possibility of previous contact arises, so far as these issues can be determined from known records; and to summarize the factual observations of the discoverers and their associates on the ways of life of the islanders.

The exploration of the Pacific Islands is of considerable interest in itself, recalling as it does the historic ventures of a long succession of voyagers into unknown seas. The settling of doubts about the identity of the islands referred to by those voyagers also opens up the way to the shedding of interesting light on the islands and their inhabitants at the time of discovery.

By 'Pacific Islands' is meant the islands of Polynesia, Micronesia, and Melanesia. They are defined by the dotted line on the map The Pacific Islands. Encounters with Australia, New Guinea and its coastal islands, the Japanese islands including the Bonins, and the islands relatively near the western coast of the Americas are included only so far as this is desirable as background to the elucidation of the exploration of the Pacific Islands as defined.

A systematic review of the history of previous opinion on the identity of the various islands that were encountered by the ships that played a part in the exploration of the Pacific is not attempted. It is only in comparatively recent times that many vital clues in the topographical and other hydrographic data of the Pacific Islands have been systematically assembled in modern authorities such as the British Admiralty's *Pacific Islands Pilot*,[1] and that numbers of first-hand records of Pacific exploration have come to light. The hindsight which these advantages give the modern researcher was denied to the geographers of earlier centuries. The records of Pacific exploration have accordingly been examined *ab initio* in order to trace the sequence of discovery or possible discovery.

In the ensuing sections the topographical and nautical details in

---

[1] Hydrographic Department, Admiralty, *Pacific Islands Pilot* (London, 1931–57).

the accounts of those voyages which made, or might have made, a discovery are summarized in small type. The summarized data are then compared with the data in modern maps and hydrographic authorities such as the *Pacific Islands Pilot* in order to demonstrate the discovery or possible discovery. Where some specific point of topography which is not ascertainable from a detailed map is stated, the appropriate reference in the *Pacific Islands Pilot* is stated. Where alternative identifications of islands are possible they are stated, the first firm reports of such islands being traced in later sections.

As far as possible first-hand records are cited, namely the diaries, journals, reports, logs, and charts of the navigators of the vessels concerned, and of the senior officers who had access to the navigators' information. For the most part authoritative printed sources are used. These are relatively accessible to students, and sample checks with such original manuscripts as are available appear to indicate that little is usually added by them to the printed sources. Some gleanings on the discoveries of Bougainville and Duclesmeur, derived from unpublished logs and diaries through microfilms supplied to the Alexander Turnbull Library by courtesy of the French National Archives, are given in the relevant sections.

For the identifications of islands reliance is mainly placed on the topographical descriptions, particularly of sequences of islands, together with the times of the passages as compared with the feasible sailing times, and the observations of latitude. In reference to latitude, a comparison of a large number of latitudes of known points in the data of navigators up to the last three decades of the eighteenth century with the modern figures shows a margin of error of a degree, a degree representing a distance of 60 geographical miles or 69 statute miles. The tendency until the middle of the seventeenth century was to make these observations of latitude too high, i.e. too far south in the southern hemisphere and too far north in the northern. Even in later times, when improved instruments gave more accurate readings, latitudes must be treated as subject to some error through indifferent observation or, when the sky was obscured, through reliance on estimation from the previous observation. Calculations of longitude after Cook's second voyage, when combinations of methods using lunar observations and chronometers came into use, give a broad indication of area in conjunction with latitudes, and have been systematically quoted in conjunction with latitudes in accordance with the conventional maritime practice from about that time. Longitudes in the earlier accounts, while subject to a large margin of error in most cases, are occasionally of use where there is a demonstrated persistent standard error. The figures of distance traversed in the earlier accounts, while often subject to a large margin of error, are sometimes helpful as guides to comparative distances within one given account where the conditions of wind and current are recorded or determinable. Estimations in the accounts of the extent of coastlines and islands are also occasionally of use as a broad guide to the relative sizes of coastlines or islands within one given account.

The length of the league in the early Portuguese and Spanish accounts was usually at the rate of $17\frac{1}{2}$ leagues to the degree,[1] i.e. about 3·43 geographical or sea miles, or slightly under 4 statute or land miles. The league or mile in the Dutch accounts may be taken as about 4 geographical miles. References to miles in the present book, apart from passages in small type, are to geographical miles.

The summaries of the ethnological data recorded by the discoverers are confined to their factual observations of the appearance, dress, ornaments, arts and crafts, canoes, fishing, cultivations, foods, livestock, houses, statues, and burial places of the Pacific Islanders. It has been a frequent and justified reproach against the interpretations placed by the Pacific explorers on the customs and beliefs of the islanders that these opinions were for the most part prejudiced and unscientific. On the other hand there is ample evidence, as the summaries will indicate, that in their factual observations the plain blunt sailors of the exploration period were consistent, realistic, and objective. The great significance of the observations of the discoverers derives of course from the fact that they were recorded at the time of European contact.

For a number of reasons dates have been repeated as given in the

[1] Burney, J., *Discoveries in the South Sea*, vol. i (London, 1803), p. 52.

cited accounts. In many cases the dates in those accounts are
reckoned by sea-days measured from noon to noon, not in civil
time measured from midnight to midnight. Since it is not always
clear whether the event in question happened before or after midnight, it would seldom be practicable to translate the dates systematically to civil time. Occasionally there is reason to believe
that in a published narrative the recounter changed his times to the
civil equivalent, as Cook said he did in his journal of his second
voyage, and Bligh in his published narrative of his first voyage.
Here the contrary difficulty of deciding whether an event happened before or after noon would arise if one tried systematically
to translate all such dates into sea-days in conformity with the
practice in most of the accounts. In some cases, again, it is not
clear whether the days are given in sea-days or civil time. Nor in
the exploration period was there any general agreement on when
or where to add or lose a day with easting or westing, or on other
variations in the calendar.

The place-names used in the *Pacific Islands Pilot* have been
adopted, apart from minor changes such as the use of the more
usual Pukapuka for Danger Islands, Anuta for Cherry Island,
Tongatabu for Tongatapu, and the like.

2. The Expedition of Ferdinand Magellan

IN 1513 Nuñez de Balboa crossed the Isthmus of Darien and discovered the Pacific Ocean. Already Francisco de Serrano had
penetrated eastward as far as the Moluccas. A Portuguese, Ferdinand Magellan, to give him his anglicized name, aspired to cross
the unknown portion of the globe that lay between, thereby
establishing a passage to the East Indies from the east. He interested
Charles I of Spain in his project, and set sail from Seville in 1519
as the commander of an expedition of five ships. After rounding
South America through the Strait of Magellan, the surviving three
ships, the *Trinidad*, the *Victoria*, and the *Concepcion*, struck out on

their epic traverse of the Pacific. The ships were fortunate enough not to encounter any storms. Magellan was in the *Trinidad*.

Of Magellan's voyage across the Pacific, the only extant account with nautical detail is that of Francisco Albo,[1] who left Spain as a senior officer of the *Trinidad* and was later transferred as pilot to the *Victoria*, which was the only ship to reach Europe again. Albo's report, found in the Spanish archives, was published as late as 1837, by which time much mystification had arisen from previous and less authoritative accounts. Albo's report gives daily notes of the *Victoria*'s course, readings of latitude, and the islands which were encountered.

After quoting latitudes in the Strait of Magellan which agree closely with the modern ones, Albo goes on to record details of a course across the Pacific bearing for the most part to the north-west. The ships encountered two uninhabited islands in the South Pacific. The first was discovered on 24 January 1521, the reading of latitude on this day being 16¼ degrees south. It was fringed with trees and was uninhabited, and since bottom could not be found on account of the depth of water, the expedition proceeded on its way, the island being named San Pablo because it was discovered on the day of St. Paul's conversion. The second island was estimated to be 9 degrees farther on (i.e. about 540 geographical miles). Its latitude, according to Albo, was 10⅔ degrees south. Here they caught a large number of sharks, for which reason they called the island Los Tiburones. The date of this discovery was 4 February 1521. On 12–13 February the expedition crossed the equator. On 26 February the course was changed to west. On 6 March 1521, while proceeding west in latitude 13 degrees north, the ships arrived in sight of two islands, which were named Los Ladrones (The Thieves), because the skiff of the *Trinidad* was stolen by the islanders. The latitude given for the more southerly, which looked to be 20 leagues broad in the direction of the north, was 12⅔ degrees north, the other island being judged to be in 13 degrees and more. The ships departed from the southern of these islands on 9 March, going to the west-south-west in 12⅔ degrees when they left. On 16 March 1521 they came to a number of islands in and about latitude 9 degrees north, which from numerous details were the Philippines.

The only islands which conform with Albo's detail of the two islands south of the equator are either Fangahina or Angatau or Pukapuka for San Pablo, and Caroline Island or, less probably,

[1] Navarrete, M. F., *Colección*, vol. iv (Madrid, 1837), pp. 12, 96, 209–47.

Vostok, for Los Tiburones. Fangahina, Angatau, and Pukapuka
are in the north-eastern sector of the Tuamotu Archipelago, their
latitudes being 16, 15¾, and 14¾ degrees south respectively. Raroia
and Takume, to the west of Angatau, being two islands close
together, may be ruled out, since Albo's details indicate that the
island in question was seen at close quarters. Caroline Island and
Vostok Island are two isolated islands close to latitude 10 degrees
south some 600-odd miles beyond Fangahina, Angatau, and Pukapuka. Caroline Island has a bay on the western or lee side from the
south-east trade wind, and is noted for its fish.[1] Los Ladrones were
Guam and Rota, the southernmost islands of the Marianas. The
latitude of the southern part of Guam is 13½ degrees north, as
compared with Albo's reading of 12⅝ degrees at his stopping place
off the south of the island, and Rota lies close to the north side of
Guam. Guam lies broadly north and south over a distance of some
30 miles. Albo's statement that on the 9th, when they left, they
were in the same latitude of 12⅝ degrees, at which time no other
islands were apparently visible to the south, again conforms with
Guam. The subsequent course to the Philippines confirms the
identification.

The well-known narrative of Antonio Pigafetta, one of the
personnel of the *Trinidad*, gives an interesting and at times droll
picture of the people of Guam, and no less of the European sailors,
at the time of this first European contact in 1521:

'On Wednesday, the 6th of March, we discovered a small
island in the north-west direction, and two others lying to the
south-west. One of these islands was larger and higher than the
other two. The captain-general wished to touch at the largest of
these islands to get refreshments of provisions; but it was not
possible because the people of these islands entered into the ships
and robbed us, in such a way that it was impossible to preserve
oneself from them. Whilst we were striking and lowering the
sails to go ashore, they stole away with much address and diligence
the small boat called the skiff, which was made fast to the poop of
the captain's ship, at which he was much irritated, and went on
shore with forty armed men, burned forty or fifty houses, with

[1] *Pacific Islands Pilot*, vol. iii, pp. 201-2.

several small boats, and killed seven men of the island; they re-
covered their skiff. After this we set sail suddenly, following the
same course. Before we went ashore some of our sick men begged
us that if we killed man or woman, that we should bring them
their entrails, as they would see themselves suddenly cured.

'It must be known that when we wounded any of this kind of
people with our arrows, which entered inside their bodies, they
looked at the arrow, and then drew it forth with much astonish-
ment, and immediately afterwards they died. Immediately after
we sailed from that island, following our course, and those people
seeing that we were going away followed us for a league, with a
hundred small boats, or more, and they approached our ships,
showing to us fish, and feigning to give it to us. But they threw
stones at us, and then ran away, and in their flight they passed with
their little boats between the boat which is tied at the poop and
the ship going at full sail; but they did this so quickly, and with
such skill that it is a wonder. And we saw some of these women,
who cried out and tore their hair, and I believe that it was for the
love of those whom we had killed. These people live in liberty and
according to their will, and some of them wear beards, and have
their hair down to their waist. They wear small hats, after the
fashion of the Albanians; these hats are made of palm leaves. The
people are as tall as us, and well made. They adore nothing, and
when they are born they are white, later they become brown, and
have their teeth black and red. The women also go naked, except
that they cover their nature with a thin bark, pliable like paper,
which grows between the tree and the bark of the palm. They are
beautiful and delicate, and whiter than the men, and have their
hair loose and flowing, very black and long, down to the earth.
They do not go to work in the fields, nor stir from their houses,
making cloth and baskets of palm leaves. Their provisions are
certain fruits named Cochi, Battate; there are birds, figs a palm
long, sweet canes, and flying fish. The women anoint their bodies
and their hair with oil of cocho and giongioli. Their houses are
constructed of wood, covered with planks, with fig leaves, which
are two ells in length: they have only one floor; their rooms and
beds are furnished with mats, which we call matting, which are

made of palm leaves, and are very beautiful, and they lie down on palm straw, which is soft and fine. These people have no arms, but use sticks, which have a fish bone at the end. They are poor, but ingenious, and great thieves, and for the sake of that we called those three islands the Ladrone Islands. The pastime of the men and women of this place, and their diversion, is to go with their little boats to catch those fish which fly, with hooks made of fish bones. The pattern of their small boats is painted here-after, they are like the fusileres, but narrower. Some of them black and white, and others red. On the opposite side to the sail, they have a large piece of wood, pointed above, with poles across, which are in the water, in order to go more securely under sail: their sails are of palm leaves, sewed together, and of the shape of a lateen sail, fore and aft. They have certain shovels like hearth shovels, and there is no difference between the poop and the prow in these boats, and they are like dolphins bounding from wave to wave. These thieves thought, according to the signs they made, that there were no other men in the world besides them.'[1]

Pigafetta, in mentioning three islands where Albo mentions two, no doubt had in mind Guam's small islet close to its southern point.

It was not long after Magellan's discovery of Guam and Rota that the *Trinidad* again visited the Marianas. Magellan had died and the *Concepcion* had been burned for want of manpower. The *Victoria* returned to Spain via the Cape of Good Hope. The *Trinidad* set out from the Moluccas under the command of Gonzalo Gomez de Espinosa across the North Pacific in an attempt to reach North America. After encountering several islands the ship returned to the Moluccas, where it was wrecked.

An account of this phase of the expedition is extant in three copies in Portuguese. It includes a statement that it is a transcription from the paper-book of a Genoese pilot of the *Trinidad*, who reached Portugal in 1524. This was no doubt Leon Pancaldo, a Genoese who was described in an official report by Antonio Brito,

---

[1] The passage from Pigafetta is taken from the English translation in *The First Voyage round the World, by Magellan*, ed. Lord Stanley (London, 1874), pp. 68–71.

the Portuguese commander in the Moluccas who rescued the survivors of the *Trinidad*, as 'pilot of the ship'. Pancaldo, who was interviewed as one of the three known survivors of the *Trinidad* who finally got to Spain, himself says in a sworn deposition in the Spanish archives that he had made accounts of the voyage in Italian which were seized by the Portuguese in the Moluccas, and that he got to Portugal at a later date. Carvalho, the regular pilot of the *Trinidad*, had died in the Moluccas before the *Trinidad* set out on its attempt to sail to North America. The narrative is obviously a Portuguese paraphrase rather than a transcription in the literal sense, since it includes a statement of the return of the *Victoria* to Europe and speaks of the Portuguese as 'we' and the members of the *Trinidad*'s company as 'they'.[1]

After travelling 12 days from a port on the east side of the modern Halmahera in $1\frac{1}{4}$ degrees north, the winds being contrary all the time, the *Trinidad*, on 6 May 1522, came on two small islands, which 'might be in five degrees more or less', named the islands of San Juan. Thence Espinosa navigated farther to the north-east, and arrived at an island named 'Chyquom', which was 'in fully nineteen degrees', making this island on 11 June 1522. From this island they took a man, whom they carried away with them, and navigated farther on, tacking about with contrary winds until they reached latitude 42 degrees north. Being then in great distress they put back for the Moluccas. They desired to make the 'island which is named Magrague', but could not fetch it, whereupon the 'man whom they carried with them, and whom before they had carried from that island', told them to go farther on and they would make three islands, where there was a good port. On arriving at these three islands, they fetched them with some danger, and anchored in the middle of them in 15 fathoms. Of these islands, the largest was inhabited by twenty persons. It was named Mao, and was 'in twenty degrees more or less'. Here 'the black man and three Christians ran away'.

The visit of the *Trinidad* to 'Mao' had a sequel, which serves as a check on the authenticity of the foregoing account, and throws some more light on the location of Mao. In 1526 the *Santa Maria de la Victoria*, under the command of Toribio Alonso de Salazar, following the path of Magellan, came to an island which was undoubtedly Guam (see section 3). At Guam the *Santa Maria de la Victoria* picked up a Spaniard named Gonzalo de Vigo. He told them he was the sole survivor of

[1] Navarrete, M. F., *Colección*, vol. iv (Madrid, 1837), pp. 12, 305, 311, 383–6; *The First Voyage round the World, by Magellan*, ed. Lord Stanley (London, 1874), pp. lvi, 1–29 (the Paris variants have been preferred).

three men who had deserted from the *Trinidad* at a place called 'Mao' which lay to the north, and that the islanders had later brought him to Guam, there being some thirteen islands altogether.

The combined evidence of Pancaldo and Vigo therefore shows that Mao was one of three islands lying to the north of Guam in somewhere around latitude 20 degrees north, and that the islands were close enough together for Pancaldo to speak of the ship's having dropped anchor in the middle of them. These data fit the islands in the north of the Marianas known as the Maug Islands, and there are no others which conform to the details. The latitude of the Maug Islands is·20 degrees north. The *Pacific Islands Pilot* describes them as consisting of three rocky islands lying in a circle, and records that in 1906 the German warship *Condor* entered the channel between two of these islands and anchored inside.[1] It is obvious that the *Trinidad* did the same in 1522.

The island 'Magrague', described as being the same as the place called 'Chyquom', which was 'in fully nineteen degrees, was either Agrigan, as the name seems to suggest, or Asuncion. These two islands lie to the south-east of the Maug Islands in latitudes 18¾ and 19½ degrees north respectively.

It remains to identify the 'two small islands in five degrees more or less' which were discovered by the *Trinidad* on the outward leg of her last journey, between the modern Halmahera and the northern islands of the Marianas. The Sonsorol Islands, on the western fringe of the Caroline Islands, consist of two islands, Sonsorol and Banna, about a mile apart, in latitude 5⅛ degrees north. Other islands in the vicinity of 5 degrees are Pulo Anna and Merir, but the thought that two out of Pulo Anna, Merir, and the Sonsorol Islands viewed as one island could have been covered in sufficiently quick succession to be described as the discovery of two small islands on the same day would be unrealistic. The winds were contrary and the *Trinidad* had taken 12 days to cover 300 to 350 miles. The Sonsorol Islands were well situated to be the only islands seen between Halmahera and the northern sector of the Marianas.

The date of the discovery of the Sonsorol Islands is corroborated

[1] *Pacific Islands Pilot*, vol. i, p. 547.

by the fact that they were called San Juan, and the day dedicated to St. John is 6 May. One of the manuscript copies of the narrative of the voyage gives the date as 3 May and says the name given to the islands was St. Antony, but the correlation of 6 May with the Church festival of St. John puts the date 6 May 1522 for the discovery beyond doubt.

It is evident, therefore, that the Spanish were the first to discover islands in the Caroline group.

The achievements of Magellan's expedition in Pacific discovery may be summarized as follows: Fangahina or Angatau or Pukapuka in the Tuamotu Archipelago was discovered on 24 January 1521. Caroline Island or, less probably, Vostok Island in the mid-Pacific area was discovered on 4 February 1521. Guam and Rota, the two southernmost islands of the Marianas, were discovered on 6 March 1521. These discoveries were made by Ferdinand Magellan himself. After Magellan's death the Sonsorol Islands, on the western fringe of the Caroline Islands, were discovered by Gonzalo Gomez de Espinosa on 6 May 1522; an island which was either Agrigan or Asuncion in the northern sector of the Marianas was discovered by Espinosa on 11 June 1522; and the Maug Islands, also in the northern sector of the Marianas, were discovered by Espinosa in the latter part of 1522, a landing being made. Gonzalo de Vigo, a deserter from the *Trinidad*, traversed the Marianas from the Maug Islands to Guam at some time prior to 1526.

3. Toribio Alonso de Salazar

IN 1525 a second expedition set out from Spain for the Pacific under the command of Garcia Jofre de Loiasa. First-hand accounts of this expedition by Hernando de la Torre and by Andres de Urdaneta, two officers of the flagship *Santa Maria de la Victoria*, are extant.[1] That of Hernando de la Torre includes day-to-day nautical observations.

[1] Navarrete, M. F., *Colección*, vol. v (Madrid, 1837), pp. 241–313; *Colección . . . de Indias*, vol. v (Madrid, 1866), pp. 5–67.

Of the seven ships of Loiasa which left Spain, only four entered the Pacific, on 26 May 1526. A few days later they were separated by a storm. One of the vessels, the *Santiago*, made its way to Mexico. Another, the *San Lesmes*, was not heard of again. Only two of the ships, the *Santa Maria de la Victoria* and the *Santa Maria del Parral*, crossed the Pacific independently.

The only thing that is known of the course of the *Santa Maria del Parral* is that eventually she reached the Philippines, where she was wrecked. The story of the voyage was not preserved. It is hard to believe that the *Santa Maria del Parral* could have passed from the Strait of Magellan to the Philippines without encountering any islands. Perhaps also the *San Lesmes* encountered some island or islands before she met her fate. But such islands as these two ships may have seen or visited remained unknown to the outside world.

The story of the flagship, the *Santa Maria de la Victoria*, therefore tells the sum of the ascertainable discoveries of the remnants of Loiasa's expedition. Loiasa himself did not live to see the outcome, dying in mid-Pacific. Four days later his second-in-command, Juan Sebastian del Cano, also died. It fell to Toribio Alonso de Salazar to command the *Santa Maria de la Victoria* during that part of the voyage when land was discovered in the Pacific.

On 21 August 1526 land was discovered to the north. De la Torre said they stood off for the night, and in the morning came close to the island without finding bottom. The latitude on the south side was taken as 14 degrees 2 minutes north. Two of the sides appeared to be about 10 and 9 leagues long. In the interior of the west part there was a big lagoon, the water of which looked very green, with big trees to the east. To this island they gave the name San Bartolomé. They could not land because of the current. Leaving San Bartolomé on 23 August, the *Santa Maria de la Victoria* proceeded west in search of Magellan's Ladrones, which they reached 12 days later, being hailed from a canoe by Gonzalo de Vigo (see section 2).

The only island anywhere near 14 degrees at 12 days' sailing from the Ladrones is Taongi, the detached northernmost atoll of the Marshall group. Its configuration is much as described. The *Pacific Islands Pilot* comments specifically on the green colour of the lagoon.[1] Its latitude is 14½ degrees north.

[1] *Pacific Islands Pilot*, vol. ii, p. 458.

The only original discovery of the *Santa Maria de la Victoria* in the Pacific Islands was that of Taongi in the Marshall Islands, on 21 August 1526, by Toribio Alonso de Salazar.

4. The Portuguese Discoveries

JORGE DE MENESES, Portuguese Governor-designate of the Moluccas, in 1526, while *en route* to the Moluccas to take up his command, was blown past Halmahera and down to the New Guinea area. He came upon islands judged to be 200 leagues distant from the Moluccas, inhabited by a people called Papuas. In a port named Versija, south of the equator, he spent some time waiting for the wind to change. He then came to the Moluccas, passing south of Halmahera, finally arriving in the Moluccas in May 1527. The Moluccas were the five 'spice islands' lying close to the western side of Halmahera.[1]

It is evident that Meneses made no discoveries of Pacific Islands as defined for the purposes of the present study, his course being confined to western New Guinea. This encounter was, however, of great significance for Pacific discovery, since the knowledge of lands to the south-east of the East Indies induced later Spanish ships to follow the New Guinea coast into the Pacific area to the north and east.

There are no known first-hand accounts of Portuguese voyages into the area of the Pacific Islands as defined. There are, however, several indirect references by contemporary writers who had access to such accounts, either verbal or written. The following evidence is taken from these contemporary writers.

(a) DIOGO DA ROCHA

Andres de Urdaneta, a survivor of Loiasa's expedition (see section 3), was in the Moluccas until 15 February 1535. He eventually got back to Spain via the Cape of Good Hope. In a report to the Spanish Emperor after his return, he gave a summary of the geography of the

[1] Barros, J. de, *Asia*, Decade 4 (Madrid, 1615), pp. 53–54.

islands in and around the Moluccas.[1] In this he stated that 'to the north-east of the Moluccas is an archipelago of islands which are very close together, which a fusta of the Portuguese discovered 200 leagues from the Moluccas, and they are from 3 to 9 leagues north'.

The account of this discovery by Antonio Galvano, a Portuguese historian who was himself Governor of the Moluccas for a time, states that in 1525 Jorge de Meneses, Captain of the Moluccas, sent a vessel under the command of Diogo da Rocha, with Gomez de Sequeira as pilot, and that they came upon islands east of the Philippines in 9 or 10 degrees. They sailed between the islands which were close together. They returned to the Moluccas via the island of Batochina (i.e. Halmahera).[2]

Barros, another sixteenth-century Portuguese historian, who had access to the official records of Portuguese exploration, says that the islands named after Gomez de Sequeira were discovered in Antonio de Brito's time in the Moluccas, apparently towards the end of 1525; that the fusta remained there for 4 months; and that the islanders indicated that there was metal 'contra o ponente da ilha em hūa serra muy alta', which appears to mean that there was a high mountain ridge towards the west of the island. The islanders were simple friendly people who did not know the language of the islands near the Moluccas and appeared to be unaware of the outside world, but said their island had been inhabited for many centuries.[3]

Couto, another sixteenth-century Portuguese historian, says that Jorge de Meneses sent Gomez de Sequeira to Mindanao, that the latter missed the way because of the weather, and discovered many islands close together in 9 to 10 degrees north, which were called Isles of Gomez de Sequeira.[4]

It is probable that the Islands of Sequeira were those of Yap Atoll, on the north-western fringe of the Caroline group, in 9½ degrees north. Yap Atoll consists of four or five main islands lying within a large reef structure. The *Pacific Islands Pilot* says that the south-westernmost of these islands has a good harbour and is hilly inland, and that there are two passages between the islands within the reef which small craft can pass through at certain states of the tide.[5] This gives particular point to Galvano's statement that the

[1] *Colección . . . de Indias*, vol. v (Madrid, 1866), pp. 5, 52, 63.
[2] Galvano, A., *Tratado* (London, 1862), p. 168.
[3] Barros, J. de, *Asia*, Decade 3 (Lisbon, 1563), pp. 259–61.
[4] Couto, D. do, *Asia*, Decade 4 (Lisbon, 1602), p. 67.
[5] *Pacific Islands Pilot*, vol. i, pp. 508–10.

ship was able to pass between the islands which were very close, while the presence of a hill and the easily detected channel and harbour on the south-west side of the atoll, which are rare features in the case of the atolls in the vicinity, support the tentative identification.

Since Urdaneta refers to islands extending from 3 to 9 degrees, and Galvano says that Rocha returned via Halmahera, it is possible that other islands on the fringe of the western Carolines were seen by Rocha.

Galvano states that Rocha's discovery occurred in 1525 during Meneses's governorship. However, Urdaneta[1] and Barros both say that Meneses arrived at the Moluccas in May 1527. The date can therefore be given only as at some time prior to Urdaneta's departure from the Moluccas on 15 February 1535, probably about 1525–7.

(b) FRANCISCO DE CASTRO

We shall see in section 7 hereafter that the ships of Villalobos's expedition in 1543 passed close to Fais and either Yap or possibly Ulithi, in the western Carolines. At Fais the local people came out in canoes making the sign of the cross and saying 'Buenos dias, matelotes' (Good day, sailors). At Ulithi or Yap the same thing happened. Galvano says that this was because he had sent one Francisco de Castro as commander of a ship on a proselytizing mission to the islands discovered by Rocha and that a number of the islanders had been baptized.[2]

It is unlikely that this incident could be explained by the view that Christian teaching had been remembered from the time of Rocha or from some of the lost ships of previous expeditions. The existence of islands in this area was known to the Portuguese from Rocha's discovery, and Galvano was a vigorous spreader of Christianity and of the Portuguese dominion. There is no good reason to doubt Galvano's statement, which is the most natural explanation of the incident. It does not, however, follow that Francisco de Castro visited Ulithi and Fais himself, since these islands are close to Yap, and the teaching may have been spread from there.

---

[1] *Colección . . . de Indias*, vol. v (Madrid, 1866), p. 27.
[2] Galvano, A., *Tratado* (London, 1862), pp. 231–3.

(c) SUMMARY

Jorge de Meneses discovered western New Guinea in 1526, thereby opening the way for later Spanish expeditions to follow the north coast of New Guinea and so find some of the Pacific Islands to the north and east of New Guinea.

Diogo da Rocha discovered some islands on the western fringe of the western Carolines which were probably those of Yap Atoll, at a date prior to 15 February 1535, probably about 1525–7. He may also have discovered other islands on the western fringe of the western Carolines.

It is probable that Francisco de Castro again made contact with islands in the Yap–Ulithi–Fais area in 1537–8.

5. Alvaro de Saavedra

ALVARO DE SAAVEDRA was the first explorer to cross the Pacific from North America to the East Indies. He subsequently made two unsuccessful attempts to get back to North America from west to east. He died on the second of these attempts.

Cortes, conqueror of Mexico, having been commanded to dispatch an expedition to try to ascertain the fate of the remnants of Magellan's company and to support Loiasa's expedition (see sections 2 and 3), accordingly sent Saavedra from Mexico in 1527 with three ships.

The primary authority for Saavedra's voyage is an account in the first person which, from internal evidence, is obviously by Saavedra himself, although traditionally attributed to Francisco Granada, who was presumably the scribe and preserved it after Saavedra's death.[1] This account stops shortly before Saavedra's death. It gives a day-by-day record with references to detailed nautical information secured from the pilots, and with statements in the first person of action of an authoritative character taken by the author. It is unfortunately illegible in the portion dealing with

---

[1] Navarrete, M. F., *Colección*, vol. v (Madrid, 1837), pp. 465–75.

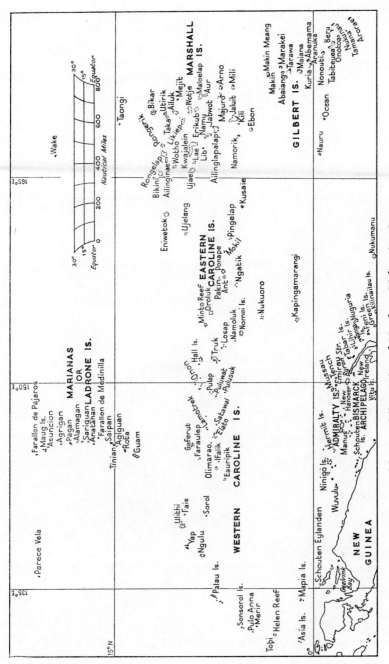

MAP 2. Micronesia and Northern Melanesian Groups

the first attempt to return to North America. Two other accounts, both by Vicente de Napoles, one of the few survivors of the expedition, are extant.[1] Where details are given from Napoles, his name is specifically stated.

Saavedra's three ships left Mexico on 31 October 1527. Napoles says that the flagship, the *Florida*, had a crew of 12 and 38 landsmen, that the *Santiago* had 45 crew and landsmen, and that the *Espiritu Santo* had 15 crew and landsmen. The expedition bore to the south-west for a time and then took a westerly course, being at that time, according to Napoles, in latitude 11 degrees. On the 41st day out the latitude was still 11 degrees. A few days later the *Florida* had to shorten sail as a result of a temporary misadventure, and the two other ships were borne out of sight by the high wind and never seen again by the people of the *Florida*. The *Florida* continued to the west, and on the 59th day out the course was changed from the west to the south-west. The following morning an island which the pilot thought was one of Magellan's Ladrones was sighted. This was on 29 December 1527. They spent 2 days trying to find an anchorage, but could not on account of the depth of the water. Some islanders appeared in five or six boats, but would not come near the Spaniards. Napoles says that there appeared to be a dozen islands and more, that they were well peopled, that they were in 11 degrees, and that they could not make port because of many shoals. Resuming the course to the west the following day, Saavedra two days later, on 1 January 1528, came to an island with two small islands and low land extending as far as 30 leagues. They arrived in the evening, found anchorage, and rode to anchor for the night. The following day, being unable to land on account of the adverse wind, they moved to a small island 4 leagues away, where they found water and remained for 6 days. This island was uninhabited, but some people came from another island and some friendly exchanges took place until the people took fright and fled. The pilot went ashore and took the latitude at 11 degrees. The *Florida* set out again to the west on 8 January, and 23 days later, without encountering any other land, reached the Philippines.

Napoles says that Saavedra gave the first island that was seen the name Los Reyes because they saw it on the day of Los Reyes. This day is 6 January, which was actually passed at the second island. The two lots of islands encountered by the *Florida* on Saavedra's

[1] *Colección . . . de Indias*, vol. v (Madrid, 1866), pp. 68–96; Navarrete, M. F., *Colección*, vol. v (Madrid, 1837), pp. 476–86.

traverse of the Pacific were the two atoll complexes of Utirik–
Taka and Rongelap–Ailinginae, in the northern Marshalls. Both
these lots of islands are close to the 11th parallel of latitude, and
Saavedra's narrative indicates that all the islands seen during the
traverse were relatively close together east and west of one another in or close to this parallel, according with Napoles's statement that the first lot of islands were in 11 degrees, whereas Guam
is in 13 degrees. Saavedra's pilot's identification of the first lot of
islands with the Ladrones is comparable to a dozen similar 'wild
surmises' on the part of early Spanish pilots. The description of
the second lot of islands fits in with Rongelap–Ailinginae, which
extend over some 60 miles, Ailinginae being some 10 miles west
of Rongelap on the south side. The statement that the pilot went
ashore at these islands and took the latitude in 11 degrees fits in
with the fact that the southern islands are only a few miles north
of the 11th parallel and that anchorage can be found in the lee or
south-west side of Rongelap and again at Ailinginae close to it on
the west. Utirik and Taka are two almost conjoined atolls with
many islets, and the entrances through the reefs are small and
difficult to distinguish. They are, as the map shows, in a position
befitting an expectation that they and then Rongelap–Ailinginae
would be the only islands seen as the ship passed through the
Marshalls near the 11th parallel, particularly after changing direction to the south-west shortly before coming to Utirik–Taka.
Saavedra and Napoles are thus in entire accord.[1]

Only a few brief words were exchanged with the uncompre-
hending natives. They had cloaks and mats made from palm
leaves, the mats being so fine that from a distance they appeared
like gold. They used charred lances for weapons.

In due course Saavedra made contact with the remnants of
Loiasa's expedition in the Moluccas. After various adventures
he set out on his first attempt to get back to North America.
For this part of the voyage the manuscript of Saavedra's account
is defective, and Napoles becomes the primary authority. However, Saavedra's continuing narrative of the second attempt to get

[1] Krämer, A., *Ergebnisse der Südsee-Expedition 1908–1910. II. Ethnographie
B Mikronesien*, vol. xi (Hamburg, 1938), p. 1, gives much the same view.

back to North America the following year, which Napoles says followed the same course, corroborates and throws further light on Napoles's statements. The following summary therefore gives Napoles's account of the first attempt and Saavedra's account of the second attempt.

Saavedra set out from the Moluccas on 3 June 1528, on his first attempt to get back to North America. One of the survivors of Loiasa's expedition accompanied Saavedra as pilot.[1] There were thirty men in the ship's company, and a load of spices. Rounding Halmahera on the north, the *Florida* came down to 'an island of Papuas'. This was a big island, well peopled by black, frizzy-haired bare-skinned men who gave the Spaniards fowls, pigs, rice, beans, and other food. Because of adverse sailing conditions the *Florida* remained here 32 days. Saavedra then ran south for an unspecified distance, then east 14 leagues to an island along which they ran for an estimated distance of 100 leagues, passing a number of islands and so coming to an inhabited island where they remained for 3 days. Here some of the natives came out in canoes to attack them with arrows. Three of these men were captured by the Spaniards and were returned by Saavedra to the same island on his second attempt to return to North America the following year. The people of this island were black, bare-skinned, and ugly. Saavedra then left it and ran for more than 250 leagues, Napoles estimated, coming to some islands of which the latitude was taken as 7 degrees (north). These islands were peopled by light-coloured bearded people, who came out in canoes with slings and stones, threatened the Spaniards, and returned to their island. The ship then continued as far north as 14 degrees, and encountered such strong contrary winds that they were obliged to return. After leaving the island in 7 degrees they saw no more islands to the north before turning back. On the way back they came to an island identified as one of the Ladrones, but could not fetch it. They passed south of it and ran west to Mindanao in the Philippines, whence they got back to the Moluccas. On 3 May 1529 Saavedra set out again, taking with him his three prisoners from the previous year in order to return them to their home island. Napoles says that the *Florida* followed the same course as in the previous year, going by the same islands as far as the island where they had taken the prisoners. They arrived at 'the island of Paine' on 24 June, having taken 50 days to cover an estimated distance of 200 leagues because of calms, i.e. from the time of their leaving the Moluccas on 3 May. On 1 August they resumed their journey to the east, and on 15 August came to 'Urais la grande' (Big Urais), placed in 1⅔ degrees south, and anchored

1 *Colección . . . de Indias*, vol. v (Madrid, 1866), p. 31.

for the night. The distance from Paine was thought to have been about 140 leagues. Saavedra set sail from the anchorage the following day, covering 17 leagues that day, and the following day set sail again. Having spent 2 days trying to get to the east without success, the *Florida* came back to the western cape of the island, but could not round it because of the adverse wind. Returning to the east of the island Saavedra finally rounded it on the east side on 26 August 1529. After 3 days they struck to the north-east for North America. On 14 September 1529 they came near an island, the latitude of which was taken at 7 degrees north. This was 19 days after leaving Big Urais. Napoles says that there was one island 4 leagues in extent and four of 1 league, that the people were dark, bearded, and with cloaks made of palms, and that four or five people were in a canoe, one of whom threw a stone with so much force that it stove a plank in the *Florida*'s side. For 2 days they were becalmed in sight of this island, finally seeing the island 12 leagues to the west. They sailed for 5 days to the north-east, and on 21 September were near three low islands of which the latitude was about 9½ degrees. They continued on for 10 days, being beset by calms and unfavourable winds, and on 1 October came to three low islands which were estimated to be in 11½ degrees north. Here they anchored and remained for a week. Saavedra's account finishes with the arrival at these islands, and Napoles's account rounds out the story. The *Florida* continued on its way, and in 26 degrees north Saavedra, who had been sickening for some time, for which reason they stayed for so long at the islands in 11½ degrees, finally died. When the Spaniards reached 31 degrees north, they gave up and returned to the Moluccas, staying *en route* at 'an island of the Ladrones' to get supplies.

It is plain from these details that Saavedra came down to western New Guinea on both occasions and ran east to the Admiralty Islands, Big Urais being Manus, the main and north-easternmost of the Admiralty Islands. Manus extends east and west in 1⅔ degrees south for some 75 miles, being the only island large enough for the ship to sail back and forth along its south coast as described. Murai, an islet on Manus's south-west coast, may have been the place where the three prisoners were taken, the name Big Urais being perhaps a projection of this name to signify Manus as a whole. The only sequence of three lots of islands corresponding to those described on the second journey are Ponape and Ant for the bigger island and the four smaller islands in 7 degrees north, Ujelang for the islands seen in about 9½ degrees north, and Eniwetok for the islands seen in 11½ degrees. Ponape extends from 6¾ to 7 degrees north, and Ant is an atoll comprising several small islands some 5 miles south-west of Ponape. Ponape, with peaks of some 2,000 feet, is high enough to have acted as a landmark for a considerable distance while the ship was drifting as described, all the other islands in this area being low atolls. Ponape and Ant are in the eastern Carolines. Ujelang and Eniwetok are detached atolls, each comprising several islets, to the north-east of Ponape and in the vicinity of Saavedra's latitudes, in the Marshalls, with no other islands in positions to compete with them for the identifications. Since the islands seen in or about 7 degrees on the first attempted return were evidently not Ponape, they might have been Namoluk or the Nomoi Islands or Losap-Nama or Ngatik or Pingelap or Mokil, all of them being within range of the latitude and course, and in positions where no islands were likely to be seen before or after. These islands are all in the Caroline group and ranged round Ponape. The islands in the Ladrones referred to in the accounts both of the first and second of these journeys can be taken to be Guam or Rota, which would be known to the pilot from his participation in Loiasa's expedition, but these islands had been discovered (see section 2).

Napoles's account of the sojourn of the *Florida* at Eniwetok is worth giving in full:

'And we found some low islands, and at one of them we anchored; and being anchored we raised a flag, and saw some people, and calling them with the flag, six or seven canoes came to our ship, and anchored at the bow of our ship, and the captain went to the bow, and threw them a cloak and a comb, and they took them; and taking them, they came on board, and all entered to the number of twenty men, and among them a woman, who was thought to be a witch, whom they had brought to say what kind of people we were, since she touched each of them in the ship with her hands. The captain treated them very well, and gave them things we had on the ship, and we made friends with them, and so it was; and when he landed the head men of the place at once came to talk with the Spaniard, and took him with them to their houses, which are big and covered with palm. This people are light-coloured, and their arms and bodies are painted, and the women are pretty, and their hair black and long; they go with all the body covered with mats, which are very delicate and exquisite, and they walk bare-footed. They have for weapons charred lances, and for sustenance coconuts and fish; this isle would be one league; there the captain and all the company landed, and the men and women went to meet them, with drums and singing, and the captain sat in a thatched house with the chief, who, among his queries to the captain, asked him what a musket that he saw was; he said that they should fire it, and to please him the captain ordered it to be fired, and there was so big a panic that they all set off in a rush, and fell to the ground in a faint, and the chief was trembling, and all the people started to fly out of the houses, through the palm groves, and the chief and others stayed, though much frightened. And all the people, to the number of a thousand souls, ran away, got into their canoes, and fled to an island three leagues away; we ourselves were quiet, sustaining no harm. And since the captain was sick, we were eight days at this island, during which the inhabitants came back, and helped us to get eighteen casks of water, and gave us a thousand coconuts, and did every-thing we asked of them.'

The *Florida* during these intriguing happenings was no doubt anchored at the southern or lee end of the atoll, where there is an opening in the Eniwetok reef and a beach near by suitable to a landing on the main islet.

What became of Saavedra's two missing vessels? What islands they may have encountered in the Pacific after parting from the *Florida* we do not know, but since they were certainly well to the west of and leeward of the Hawaiian Islands, it can be taken that any islands that were seen must have been in the Marshalls, Carolines, and Marianas. The vessels were not parted from the *Florida* under circumstances suggesting that they were not capable of continuing on their way, for the accounts suggest that it was because of the high wind that they went on, which is credible, since small low-waisted sailing ships were vulnerable to cross-seas if they hove to or broached with little way on. Perhaps a clue to the mystery may be found in the following facts. In 1546 the survivors of the expedition of Villalobos (see section 7) were in Portuguese settlements in the East Indies. In 1548 Garcia de Escalante de Alvarado, the Emperor's Factor, reported that in Malacca on the way home he had met a Chinese pilot who told him that he had heard of two ships, one small and the other big, with people such as the Spanish, in an island beyond Japan, and that they were at war with the inhabitants of those islands. This made Escalante think that they were Spanish ships, but he does not make any suggested identification in his report. It will be remembered that one of Saavedra's missing two ships carried fifteen men and the other forty-five. It will be seen in due course that the *San Juan*, one of the ships of Villalobos's expedition, in an attempt to get back to North America from the Philippines, saw some of the islands not far south of Japan. Perhaps, therefore, Saavedra's two ships, having failed to find the *Florida*, had tried to get back to North America and had fetched up in Japanese waters. In that case it would appear possible that they made the first European contact with Japanese territory.

The discoveries of Alvaro de Saavedra in the Pacific Islands were as follows: On 29 December 1527 he discovered Utirik and Taka in the Marshall Islands. On 1 January 1528 he discovered Rongelap and Ailinginae in the Marshall Islands, landings being made. In the latter part of 1528 he discovered the Admiralty Islands off the north coast of eastern New Guinea, the precise islands in the Admiralty group and the groups near it on the west, apart from Manus, being uncertain; and also, in the Carolines, either Namoluk or the Nomoi Islands or Losap-Nama or Ngatik or Pingelap or Mokil. In August 1529 he was again in the Admiralty Islands area. On 14 September 1529 he discovered Ponape and Ant in the eastern Caroline Islands. On 21 September 1529 he discovered Ujelang in the Marshalls. On 1 October 1529 he discovered Eniwetok in the Marshalls, landings being made.

6. The Ship of Hernando de Grijalva

GARCIA DE ESCALANTE DE ALVARADO, in his account to the Spanish Emperor of the expedition of Villalobos[1] (see section 7), stated that on 16 May 1545 Villalobos sent the *San Juan* under Ortiz de Retes from the Moluccas on an attempt to reach New Spain. Escalante repeats Retes's account of how the *San Juan* came down to New Guinea, encountering on 15 June, on which the latitude was taken in 1 degree south, two islands, then two more islands to the east of these, and on the following day a number of islands from the biggest of which came some canoes of frizzy-haired negroes, there being eleven smaller islands near this latter one. It is evident from this detail, and from the subsequent course of the *San Juan* along the New Guinea coast, that these islands were the Schouten Eilanden lying across the mouth of Geelvink Bay in western New Guinea. In these islands, says Escalante, 'there was lost a ship of the Marquis del Valle (i.e. Cortes, the conqueror of Mexico), in which there came as captain Grijalva, whom the sailors murdered'. This information had presumably been secured by the Spaniards in the Moluccas.

Galvano, who was the Portuguese commander in the Moluccas at the time the survivors of Grijalva's ship arrived there, is the only authority of any consequence for its course. Some later historians, both Spanish and Portuguese, give accounts which purport to add to Galvano's and Escalante's references in certain particulars, but none of these has the authority of Galvano's gleanings, and none of them throws any further light on the discoveries themselves. It is not clear who was in command of the ship at the time of the discoveries.[2]

Galvano, writing in reference to the year 1537, says that the ship set out from Peru for the Moluccas 'all along near the line, as they were commanded'. The following is a literal translation of Galvano's account as preserved in the Portuguese by the British scholar Hakluyt:
'And it is said that they went more than 1000 leagues without sight of land on one side and the other of the line and in two degrees north, they discovered an island called o Acea, which appears to be from the Isle of Cloves 500 leagues more or less *a loeste*; but *onde hiaõ*, they had

[1] *Colección . . . de Indias*, vol. v (Madrid, 1866), pp. 153–8.

[2] Galvano, A., *Tratado* (London, 1862), pp. 202–5; Burney, J., *Discoveries in the South Sea*, vol. i (London, 1803), pp. 180–6.

sight of another to which they gave the name Dos Pescadores. Going thus in this course they saw an island called Haime, south of the equator, another which is called Apia, came to sight of Seri; having turned to the north to one degree, they anchored at another called Coroa. Thence they went to another under the line which is called Meōsū, and thence to Bufu in the same parallel. The people of all these islands are black, with fuzzy hair, whom the people of the Moluccas call Papuas. . . . From these islands they came to others called the Gelles standing in one degree north east and west with the island of Ternate in which there is a Portuguese fortress. These men have loose hair like those of the Moluccas, these islets are 124 or 125 leagues from the island of Moro.'

Hakluyt's defective English translation of this passage has given rise to confusion, making it appear that o Acea and Dos Pescadores were a great distance apart. Thus Hakluyt gives the words after Acea as 'which seemeth to be one of the Islands of Cloves: 500 leagues little more or lesse (to the west) as they sailed, they came in sight of another, which they named Isla de Pescadores'. Hakluyt's slip was pointed out by Burney in 1803. Galvano's real meaning, when the passage is taken literally, seems plain enough. A look at the map will show that a ship coming in the vicinity of the equator would find it hard to get past the Gilberts without seeing one or other of them, and would in due course be likely to encounter some of the islands near the north coast of western New Guinea. The latitude of Marakei in the northern Gilberts is 2 degrees north, which is the stated latitude in Galvano's account for the first island 'o Acea'. (The meaning of this name is obscure.) The natural interpretation to be put on the words *onde hiaō* is that Dos Pescadores, meaning 'The Fishermen', was an inhabited island seen as the ship sailed from 'o Acea'. Abaiang lies 18 miles west-south-west of Marakei. The situation of Marakei in relation to Peru on the one hand, and the Moluccas ('Isle of Cloves') on the other, is in proportion to the estimates of 1,000 leagues and 500 leagues in Galvano's account. The words *a loeste* pose the perennial perplexity in Portuguese and Spanish texts as to whether west or east is meant, the words for these, *oeste* and *este*, being a frequent source of confusion, but in the present instance east from the Moluccas is the only direction that makes sense. Haime, Apia, Seri, Coroa in 1 degree, Meōsū and Bufu south of the line were evidently islands or places in the western New Guinea area. Here it was that according to Escalante the ship was lost. The Gelles, to the east of Moro (Batochina do Moro, the Portuguese name for Halmahera), were the Asia Islands.

Of these islands the only ones which come into the purview of the Pacific Islands as defined for the present study are Marakei and Abaiang.

Can it therefore be concluded finally that 'o Acea' and Dos Pescadores were in fact Marakei and Abaiang? Perhaps the possibility that Dos Pescadores was Kapingamarangi, lying in 1 degree north several hundred miles west of the Gilberts, cannot be entirely ruled out, since the significance of *onde hiaō* is perhaps not entirely beyond doubt. When this is conceded, then the latitude alone cannot establish 'o Acea' as Marakei rather than another of the northern Gilberts in the vicinity of 2 degrees north, namely Makin, Marakei, Abaiang, or Tarawa.

The discoveries of the ship which left Peru under the command of Hernando de Grijalva and crossed the Pacific apparently in the year 1537 may therefore be summarized as being probably Marakei and Abaiang in the northern Gilberts, or alternatively either Makin, Marakei, Abaiang, or Tarawa for 'o Acea', and Kapingamarangi for Dos Pescadores.

7. The Expedition of Ruy Lopez de Villalobos

THE hazards to which the early Spanish expeditions were exposed, in unknown seas among strange and often hostile peoples, are evidenced by the casualties. Of Magellan's flotilla, only one ship survived; of Loiasa's and Saavedra's, none. Grijalva's ship was lost in New Guinea. The six ships of Villalobos's expedition in 1542–3 comprised the largest number of vessels to traverse the Pacific in the early centuries of exploration. None of Villalobos's ships got beyond the East Indies, and the survivors reached Europe eventually through the reluctant courtesy of the Portuguese.

The objects of Villalobos's crossing of the Pacific from Mexico were discovery, conquest, and colonization. A report for the Emperor was made by Garcia de Escalante de Alvarado, the Emperor's Factor, when the survivors reached Lisbon, Villalobos having died; and a report to the Viceroy of New Spain was written by the senior ecclesiastic of the expedition, Geronimo de Santisteban, in Cochin during the voyage home.[1] An account by Juan Gaetan, an Italian sailor who survived the expedition, was recorded by the Italian historian Ramusio.[2] Some light is thrown on the discoveries by references in the accounts of Legaspi's expedition which followed in Villalobos's track across the Pacific 22 years later (see section 8).

The fleet set out from Mexico on 1 November 1542. It comprised four larger ships, the *Santiago*, the *San Anton*, the *San Jorge*, and the *San Juan*, and two small vessels, the *San Cristobal* and the *San Martin*.

The expedition encountered three of the Revilla Gigedo Islands near the American coast, and two shoals. On 25 December 1542, which was the 55th day out from Mexico, the ships came to some low tree-covered islands. Santisteban says they were thought to be part of Los Reyes, which was no doubt a reference to the islands so named by Saavedra's expedition (see section 5). Escalante says that after much difficulty because of the depth of the water round the islands, they found port at an island which they called Santisteban because they landed on it on St. Stephen's Day, 26 December. This was an islet, the people of which fled in canoes to another part, leaving some women and children hiding in some dense vegetation. Escalante named the archipelago 'del Coral', and says that 35 leagues beyond, on 6 January 1543, they came on 'ten islands looking like the others' which they named Los Jardines (The Parks) because of their fresh appearance and trees, and that both these and the previous islands were in 9 to 10 degrees. Legaspi's fleet, following 22 years later in Villalobos's wake, were instructed to try to rediscover Los Reyes and Los Corales, stated to be in 9 degrees. Pablo de Carrion, one of the survivors of Villalobos's expedition, gave advice to Legaspi's expedition before its departure

---

[1] *Colección . . . de Indias*, vol. v (Madrid, 1866), pp. 117–209; vol. xiv (Madrid, 1870), pp. 151–65.
[2] Ramusio, G. B., *Delle Navigationi e Viaggi*, vol. i (Venice, 1588), pp. 375–7.

from Mexico.[1] According to Gaetan Los Reyes were in 9, 10, and 11 degrees, but Gaetan knew from Galvano's history that Saavedra's Los Reyes were in 11 degrees, and Santisteban's statement shows that the latter were thought to be part of the same group as Villalobos's discoveries, as indeed they were. Gaetan says that the Coralli, where they saw people like those of Los Reyes and took in wood and water, were 18 or 20 leagues past Los Reyes and the Giardini about 50 leagues farther west. Gaetan's estimation of the passage from Mexico to the Philippines was under-stated by the best part of 3,000 miles, showing that on balance the distances given by him were too low. From Los Jardines Villalobos continued west for a distance estimated by Gaetan at 280 leagues, when on 23 January 1543, according to Escalante, they passed a small well-populated island of very fine appearance in 10 degrees north. They could not find anchorage, but some of the islanders came out in canoes making the sign of the cross and saying 'Buenos dias, matelotes' (Good day, sailors), for which reason the name Matelotes was given to the island. In the same latitude—Santisteban says 3 days later, which would make it 26 January 1543—the expedition passed a much bigger island, where they could not get anchorage because of the reefs, for which reason they gave it the name Arrecifes (Reefs). Here, according to Santisteban, they were greeted by the same salutation as at Matelotes. Some days later they made the Philippines.

The details as summarized show that Villalobos passed through the sector of the Marshalls comprising Wotje, Erikub, Maloelap, Likiep, Kwajalein, Lae, Ujae, Wotho, and Ujelang, which extend from 8½ to 10 degrees north. Which of these islands were Los Reyes, Los Corales, and Los Jardines it is impossible to say with certainty, although Wotje, Kwajalein, and Ujelang may be the best contenders. Of the islands which were thus possibilities, only Ujelang had been previously discovered (see section 5). Continuing on to the west for a considerable distance in 9 to 10 degrees, the expedition missed the main mass of the Carolines apart from two of the north-western atolls, and at a shorter distance beyond them came to the Philippines. Matelotes is unmistakable as Fais, which is a small fertile island surrounded by a steep reef. Arrecifes was probably Yap, which would accord with the relative distances from Fais and the Philippines, but could have been Ulithi, both being reef-girt atolls. The position of these islands on the northern

[1] *Colección . . . de ultramar*, vol. ii (Madrid, 1886), pp. 223-5.

fringe of the western Carolines, with no islands to the west until the Philippines, and no islands for a considerable distance to the east until Ujelang, accords with the identifications. The signs of the teaching of Christianity have been examined in section 4, the implication being that the Portuguese may have preceded Villalobos in the discovery of one or more of the three islands.

Santisteban gives an interesting picture of the women and children in the Marshalls who were found in hiding. The Spaniards persuaded them to come out and treated them well, giving them small gifts. They wore fine mats less than a yard square round their middles. One old woman, when she saw a cup, appeared to indicate she had seen one before, but the others did not take any more notice of this than of the other things they were shown. In the island were fowls, coconut palms, and some trees which bore a fruit like pineapples, which, though big, had little that could be eaten.

Between the Marshalls and Fais the small vessel the *San Cristobal* was parted from the other vessels in a storm, rejoining them later in the Philippines. It seems unlikely it saw any islands, since according to Santisteban it struck the Philippines in a latitude to the north of the Carolines, and no discoveries are mentioned.

On 26 August 1543 the *San Juan* set out under the command of Bernardo de la Torre on an unsuccessful attempt to return to New Spain. Santisteban says that it struck off from one of the islands north of Mindanao, and that, having got as far as 29 or 30 degrees north, it met with such big seas that it returned. Escalante gives more details, saying that in a latitude of 26 degrees, as related by the people of the *San Juan*, they saw a small island, and 26 leagues later another two, which lay north and south with the Ladrones, and later again another three islands, one of which was a volcano. On 18 October, in about 30 degrees north, they met high winds and returned to the Philippines in 13 days. Gaetan gives further details again. He says they discovered an island in 16 degrees north, which they named Abriojos (Keep your eyes open), because it was almost on a level with the sea. Proceeding east by north for 26 leagues, they came to two large islands in 16 degrees and 17 degrees, which they named Las Dos Hermanas (The Two Sisters). Farther on to the east and north-east, in 25 degrees north, they saw three islands in 24 and 25 degrees, of which one was a volcano. On 2 October, having gone 30 leagues farther to the east by north, they saw another island. On 18 October, because of storms in 30 degrees north, they gave up. It will be noted that there is a discrepancy between Escalante and Gaetan in the latitude assigned to the first-discovered island, given as 26 degrees north by the former and 16 degrees north by the latter. Since Escalante mentions a distance of 26 leagues immediately thereafter, it is reasonable to think that the confusion in his account may have arisen from this figure. Gaetan's account specifies the latitude of the two islands discovered 26 leagues after the first as being in 16 and 17 degrees, which virtually confirms the latitude of 16 degrees for the former and not 26 degrees.

At the time of the year when the *San Juan* set out, the change from the south-west monsoonal season was due. This blows as far as somewhere near Guam. North of that the north-east trade wind is the prevailing wind throughout the year, and the North Equatorial Current flows from the east.[1] These facts, taken in conjunction with the latitudes, show that Abriojos and Las Dos Hermanas were three of the Marianas—probably Farallon de Medinilla, a low island in latitude 16 degrees north, and Anatahan and Sariguan, two high islands between the 16th and 17th parallels —and that the three islands in 24 and 25 degrees and the other beyond it were some of the Bonins, the *San Juan* having been set to the north-north-west in the latter part of her transit through these islands. Gonzalo de Vigo had probably seen the islands in the Marianas encountered by the *San Juan* (see section 2).

In 1545 the *San Juan* again set out for North America, this time working east along the New Guinea coast. The commander of the *San Juan* on this unsuccessful attempt to get back to North America was Yñigo Ortiz de Retes. According to Juan Pablo de Carrion,[2] a survivor of the expedition, they went along the coast of New Guinea as far as latitude 5 degrees south, which is approximately where the north coast of New Guinea terminates in some sixteenth-century maps. (See, for instance, the reproduction of Herrera's map of 1601. See Plate I.) It is plain, therefore, that Retes did not get as far east as New Britain. Escalante, retailing the information[3] given him later by Retes, states that after passing four coastal islands with five more to the east of them (i.e. the Schouten Islands area), at which time the latitude was taken at $2\frac{1}{2}$ degrees south, the ship was forced off-shore by south

---

[1] *Pacific Islands Pilot*, vol. i, pp. 46–48.
[2] *Colección . . . de ultramar*, vol. ii (Madrid, 1886), p. 206.
[3] *Colección . . . de Indias*, vol. v (Madrid, 1866), pp. 153–61.

PLATE I

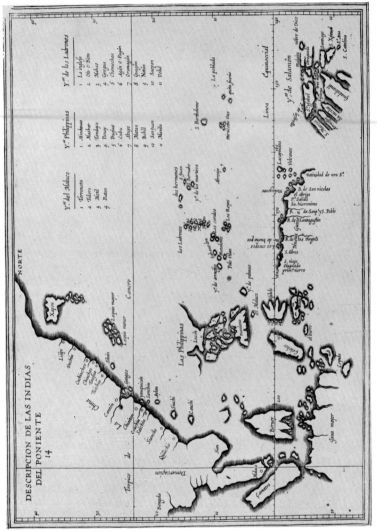

Herrera's *Las Indias del Poniente*

winds, that on 27 July three islands (La Barbada) were seen to the north-west running toward the north-east in $1\frac{1}{2}$ degrees, that on 28 July they sighted New Guinea again, that on 29 July these islands of La Barbada were seen again and while in sight of them four others were seen, three close and one a bit apart, which they called La Caimana, that on 1 August they were in sight of La Caimana and La Barbada, and that on 2 August they were to the east of La Caimana, which was surrounded by reefs, and from which came some negroes who flung by hand without bows arrows made of flint suitable for striking fire. On 4 August the *San Juan* regained the mainland, and on 16 August, having continued past more coastal islands, they went north. On 19 August, having gone an estimated distance of 35 leagues from the mainland, they came to two low islands, the latitude being taken as $1\frac{1}{4}$ degrees south. From one of these came some people in canoes, with whom a skirmish took place. The boats were particularly well made, the people were courageous and good-looking, and were light-skinned, for which reason the islands were called Hombres Blancos (The White Men). On 21 August the Spaniards, having lost sight of the Hombres Blancos, saw another island. They returned to the Moluccas via the western part of New Guinea.

It is evident that La Barbada, La Caimana, Los Hombres Blancos, and the island near the latter were all among the islands west of Manus, namely the Hermit Islands, Kaniet, Sae, Liot, the Ninigo group, Manu, Aua, and Wuvulu. A probable identification of La Caimana is the Hermit Islands, which from certain aspects show as if three islands close together with a larger one (Luf) slightly apart on the east side of them.[1] Luf, being a high island, would be a source of stone for arrow-heads, but these might of course have been transported round the islands in the vicinity. There are other possible groupings which could fit the details of La Caimana. If La Caimana was in fact the Hermit Islands, then La Barbada was presumably part of the Liot–Ninigo complex of islands, lying between 30 and 40 miles west of the Hermit group. Several possible guesses might be made in respect of Los Hombres Blancos and the island near by. All that can be said with certainty

[1] See profile sketch of Hermit Islands, *Pacific Islands Pilot*, vol. i, at p. 491. Nevermann, H., *Ergebnisse der Südsee-Expedition 1908–1910. II. Hydrographie B Melanesien*, vol. iii (Hamburg, 1934), p. 1, cites the previous opinion of Wichmann and Freiderici that La Caimana was the Hermit group, as against Graebner's view that it was the Admiralty Islands.

is that all the off-shore islands seen by Retes were in the groups west of the Admiralty Islands. Some of them may have been seen by Saavedra (see section 5).

The discoveries of the expedition of Ruy Lopez de Villalobos can be summarized as follows: From 25 December to 6 January 1542–3 Villalobos discovered some of the following islands in the Marshall group, landings being made—Wotje, Erikub, Maloelap, Likiep, Kwajalein, Lae, Ujae, Wotho—but which of these islands were in fact seen is uncertain. On 23 January 1543 Villalobos made the first certain contact with Fais, and on 26 January 1543 saw Yap or possibly Ulithi, in the.western Carolines, although these islands may possibly have been discovered by the Portuguese (see section 4). In the latter part of 1543, probably in September, Bernardo de la Torre, in the *San Juan*, saw three islands in the Marianas, probably Farallon de Medinilla, Anatahan, and Sariguan, although they had probably been discovered by Gonzalo de Vigo (see section 2). Yñigo Ortiz de Retes, in the *San Juan*, discovered, or rediscovered after Saavedra (see section 5), some of the islands to the west of Manus on 27 July, 29 July, 19 August, and 21 August 1545.

8. The Expedition of Miguel Lopez de Legaspi

IN 1564–5 Miguel Lopez de Legaspi crossed the Pacific from Mexico and succeeded in establishing a Spanish settlement in the Philippines. Andres de Urdaneta, formerly of the *Santa Maria de la Victoria* (see section 3), accompanied Legaspi.

The expedition of four vessels set out from Mexico on 20 November 1564. On 1 December the smallest vessel, the *San Lucas*, became separated from the other ships, eventually reaching the Philippines and returning to North America without being seen by the rest of the expedition again.

(a) THE VOYAGE OF THE *SAN LUCAS*

Alonso de Arellano was the commander of the *San Lucas*, and Lope Martin was the pilot. Arellano was later charged with having deliberately defected from the expedition, while Lope Martin in due course earned an evil reputation and a curious fate, as we shall see (see section 9). But this book is concerned with discovery, and the voyage of the *San Lucas* was one of the greatest in the history of Pacific exploration. Not only were a number of important Micronesian islands discovered, but the *San Lucas* was the first ship to cross the Pacific from west to east. These things were accomplished in a tiny vessel of 40 Spanish tons carrying about a score of men in all, half of them soldiers.

Arellano's account of the voyage,[1] signed both by himself and the pilot Lope Martin, gives copious nautical and topographical details, leaving no doubt of the identity of the discoveries.

Having separated from Legaspi on 1 December, 11 days out from Mexico, the *San Lucas*, which was a fast sailer, ran west in 9 degrees, thinking to pick up Villalobos's Los Reyes, until the pilot, assuming, as Legaspi was to do some days later, that they had missed Los Reyes, came up to 10 degrees with the thought of picking up Villalobos's Los Matelotes. On the night of 5 January 1565 they came to an island on which they narrowly escaped being wrecked. It proved to consist of thirty-six islets in the shape of a triangle running from the north-east to the south-west, surrounded by a reef. They went part of the way round it without being able to find bottom or get an entrance. It was uninhabited. The circuit of the islands within the reef was estimated to be 20 leagues. The pilot took the latitude at 10¼ degrees. At this point, states Arellano, thinking that they must have missed Villalobos's islands, they came down to the south in order to run west to the Philippines. On 7 January they discovered some other islands like the last, with a big reef, extending over 30 leagues, in latitude 9 degrees. Here they had contact with two families of visiting native fishermen. They remained overnight, and having no satisfactory anchorage departed the next morning. On the following day, 8 January, they came to a very small well-peopled island in 8½ degrees, which was covered with trees and yet was so low that the trees did not show up, and without bottom for an anchorage.

Even without the corroboration of the further course of the

[1] *Colección . . . de ultramar*, vol. iii (Madrid, 1887), pp. 1–76.

D

San Lucas, these three islands identify themselves on topography. The first island corresponds closely to the configuration of Likiep, in the eastern chain of the Marshalls, the second to Kwajalein, some 87 miles to the south-west of Likiep, and the third to Lib, an isolated small island some 20 miles south of Kwajalein. The *Pacific Islands Pilot* says that Lib is wooded, the reef is steep-to, and the inner parts of the island are lower than the sides.[1] The latitudes of Likiep, Kwajalein, and Lib correspond closely with those given in Arellano's account, and the sailing times with the distances. Of these islands, Lib was a new discovery. Likiep and Kwajalein might have been discovered by Villalobos (see section 7).

Arellano gives some comments on the inhabitants of Lib in 1565. He says that they would be fine for pulling an oar in a galley, being big and well made, and adds the interesting detail they they must be of the Devil because their island was a thousand leagues from firm land. A more valuable ethnological comment was that they were a warlike people, being expert at throwing stones with slings. This affords an interesting contrast with the data of Urdaneta's landing on Mejit a day later, as recounted in a later part of the present section.

From Lib the *San Lucas* resumed its voyage, taking a course to the west, being thus aimed for the heart of the Carolines. They ran for 8 days, and on the night of 15 January narrowly avoided a reef, extending north and south over more than 3 chains, the latitude of which was taken at 8 degrees. They saw a canoe proceeding east shortly before reaching it. They thought it must be near some island because of the large number of birds that were near it.

This must have been either one of the reefs of Oroluk Atoll, which consists of an extensive system of reefs with one small island in $7\frac{1}{2}$ to $7\frac{3}{4}$ degrees north, or Minto Reef, lying just north of 8 degrees.

On 17 January 1565, in the morning, the Spaniards saw a high island on the port side differing from the low islands that had hitherto been seen. They approached it thinking it was Mindanao in the Philippines. When they got near they found there were a number of islands, about fourteen or fifteen, some of them high islands encircled by reefs, others low keys. The high islands were about 2 leagues apart, each of them

[1] *Pacific Islands Pilot*, vol. ii, pp. 456, 463–4.

extending over 2 to 3 leagues, and giving good harbourage. The ship entered through a passage in the surrounding reef, and was met by a canoe, from which some people came aboard, gave them fish and something like mace, and invited them to come to their island called 'Huruasa'. They were entering a harbour in this island when a large number of canoes came from other islands with hostile intentions, whereupon the people of 'Huruasa' who had come on board fled. The ship drew off from the island because the pilot perceived that the wind was blowing into the harbour and would prevent their retreat. The ship was boarded by some of the people who had arrived from the other islands. They stole some things and then leapt overboard. After a hazardous passage through the island-studded lagoon, during which they had to repel an assault, the Spaniards hove to for the night inside the reef. In the morning, after another skirmish, they got out of the lagoon and continued on their way. The latitude of these islands was taken as $7\frac{1}{2}$ degrees north.

All this is a close description of Truk in the Caroline Islands. It comprises a large number of islands, both high and low, lying between 7 and $7\frac{3}{4}$ degrees. It is unique in those parts, consisting of a very large lagoon surrounded by reefs with low islands on them, while in the lagoon are a number of islands, some of them with peaks ranging from 1,000 to 1,500 feet.[1] The island 'Huruasa' was no doubt Toloas, which lies in the eastern part of the atoll, and has a good harbour facing the east.

From Truk the *San Lucas* bore north-west, shortening sail that night for fear of striking some island or reef. At dawn on the following day, 19 January 1565, three small islands disposed in a triangle, at a distance from Truk estimated at 25 leagues, were seen. These islands were in $7\frac{3}{4}$ degrees, some 2 leagues apart, about $\frac{1}{2}$ league each in extent. Again the *San Lucas* had trouble with the islanders who, like those of the preceding islands, were warlike, and armed with spears, slings, and clubs. Some of Arellano's men were killed by them.

Again these islands are identified from the topography. The three small islands of Pulap Atoll lie some 105 miles west-north-west of Truk, and there is no other triangle of islands anywhere in the vicinity.

From Pulap the ship sailed west-north-west, and on 22 January came to a small low island of an extent of about $\frac{1}{2}$ league, with two or three

[1] *Pacific Islands Pilot*, vol. i, pp. 520–3.

small islets close by, covered with coconut palms. They thought at first it was uninhabited, but some people came down to the beach, embarked in two canoes, and followed them to one of the islets brandishing their arms. The Spaniards repulsed them and continued on their way. This island was in 8 degrees. On the following night, 23 January, they passed another low island in the same latitude, and then bore up to 9 degrees. On 29 January they reached the Philippines.

The only two islands so placed in relation to Pulap, the Philippines, and each other as to satisfy these details are Sorol and Ngulu.

After various adventures in the Philippines, the *San Lucas* set out for North America on 22 April 1565 and ran up into high latitudes. In latitude 31 degrees north they encountered a small high crag rising sheer out of the sea, which was apparently one of the islands south of Japan. They went up to latitude 40 degrees and beyond, and having thus come into the zone of west winds and the east-flowing Japan Current made North America on 17 July 1565. They were thus the first to succeed in crossing the Pacific from west to east where the *Trinidad, Florida,* and *San Juan* had failed.

The discoveries of Arellano were as follows: He made the first discovery of Lib in the Marshall group on 8 January 1565; and gave the first firm report of Likiep and Kwajalein, on 3 and 5 January 1565, respectively, either or both of which may have been discovered by Villalobos (see section 7). He discovered either Oroluk or Minto Reef on 15 January 1565, Truk on 17 January 1565, Pulap on 19 January 1565, Sorol on 22 January 1565, and Ngulu on 23 January 1565, all these islands being in the Caroline group. He was the first European to cross the Pacific from west to east.

(b) LEGASPI AND THE MAIN EXPEDITION

The primary authority for the traverse of Legaspi from Mexico to the Philippines is the account of the chief pilot of the expedition, Esteban Rodriguez. This gives copious details permitting the certain identification of the islands that were encountered. A report sent back to Mexico from the Philippines after the arrival of the expedition there adds a few details.[1]

[1] *Colección . . . de ultramar,* vol. ii (Madrid, 1886), pp. 373–95, 217–52.

After the separation of the *San Lucas* there were three other ships—the flagship *San Pedro*, a large ship of 500 Spanish tons, on which were Legaspi, Urdaneta, and Rodriguez; the *San Pablo*, of 400 tons; and a smaller ship, the *San Juan*.

Having come down to a latitude of 9 degrees north, Legaspi ran west in this latitude until the 38th day out from Mexico. It was then concluded that they must have passed Villalobos's Los Reyes and Los Corales. The course was then changed to 10 degrees with the thought of picking up Villalobos's Los Matelotes. On 9 January 1565, after 50 days' sailing from Mexico, they came to a small island. Its circumference was 2½ to 3 leagues, and it was divided in the middle by a shallow channel which filled when the water came in and was waterless when it went out. The island was low, and was covered with trees. The expedition skirted it on the north, and could not find any satisfactory anchorage. Some of the Spaniards, including Urdaneta, went ashore, whereupon the people fled 'to the hill', but were persuaded to come out, and friendly relations were established. The latitude was taken at 10¼ degrees.

This island was obviously Mejit, the easternmost of the Marshalls, the latitude of which is 10⅓ degrees. It is a very small isolated island. *The Pacific Islands Pilot* says that it is fringed by a reef which is very steep-to, that it is divided into two parts by a shallow channel, that the northern half is flat but the southern half is undulating, and that the whole island is wooded.[1]

The Spanish accounts give a pleasing picture of this isolated spot in 1565. The houses were well made of timber, and covered with palm leaves. There were over a hundred inhabitants, good-looking, rather dark, with fine cloth made from palm leaves. They were bearded, so the island was named Los Barbudos (The Bearded Ones). The people caught many types of fish with hooks and lines. They also had little gardens where they grew 'potatoes' (patatas) and a grain like millet. They also had fowls. No weapons of any kind were seen. The islanders brought off much fish and many coconuts to the ships.

In the evening of the same day the fleet set off again. The next morning, 10 January 1565, they came to a very big island, which seemed about 15 leagues from the first. It extended north and south, and its

[1] *Pacific Islands Pilot*, vol. ii, p. 457.

length east and west was 9 or 10 leagues. They skirted it on the north side and could not find an anchorage. Its islands were low, and were joined together by banks, for which reason they called it Los Placeres (The Banks). Its latitude was 10 degrees. No sign of population was seen. In the evening of the same day they saw a small tree-covered island about 8 or 9 leagues from Los Placeres, to which they gave the name Los Pajaros (The Birds). It was low, about 2 leagues round, and was uninhabited. Its latitude was given as about 10 degrees.

As might be expected from the map in relation to a course to the west from Mejit, these descriptions conform closely with those of Ailuk and Jemo. Ailuk, a big island, is about 52 miles west of Mejit, and runs predominantly north and south, the latitude of the south part being $10\frac{1}{4}$ degrees. Jemo, some 20 miles west of the south of Ailuk, is a small tree-covered island.

As the sun set the fleet resumed its course, and 2 days later, on 12 January 1565, came to some islands and reefs joined up like those seen previously, for which reason they called them Las Hermanas (The Sisters); Rodriguez says they were also called Los Corales. Their circuit was more than 10 leagues, it was thought. They were low tree-covered islands. No anchorage could be found and the Spaniards went on without landing. The latitude was given as 10 degrees. The islands were considered to be uninhabited. Three days later, on 15 January 1565, they came to some low tree-covered islands in about 10 degrees, running east and west. No sign of habitation was seen. Urdaneta thought these were Villalobos's Los Jardines (see section 7).

A glance at the map will show that these islands could only have been Wotho and Ujelang, two comparatively detached atolls in the western part of the Marshall group. They are both close to latitude 10 degrees north, and the distances of 200 miles from Jemo to Wotho and 300 miles from Wotho to Ujelang conform with the relative sailing times. Wotho may have been discovered by Villalobos (see section 7). Ujelang had been discovered by Saavedra (see section 5) and possibly seen by Villalobos (see section 7).

Since the other pilots differed from Urdaneta, thinking they were not far from the Philippines, it was agreed a few days later that the fleet should go up to a latitude of 13 degrees, so that they

[1] *Pacific Islands Pilot*, vol. ii, pp. 456–7.

would pick up the Ladrones if Urdaneta were right. On 22 January they reached Guam.

The discoveries of Legaspi were as follows: On 9 January 1565 he discovered Mejit in the Marshalls, a landing being made. On 10 January 1565 he discovered Ailuk and Jemo in the Marshalls. On 12 January 1565 he discovered, or possibly rediscovered after Villalobos (see section 7), Wotho in the Marshalls.

(c) THE RETURN OF THE *SAN PEDRO*

On 1 June 1565 the flagship the *San Pedro* set out again to try to return to America. At this time the *San Lucas* was already half-way there. The *San Pedro*, under the command of Felipe de Salcedo, with Rodrigo de Espinosa as a pilot, and with Urdaneta and Rodriguez also on board, followed much the same course as the *San Lucas*. A detailed account by the pilot Espinosa is extant.[1] On 21 June they sighted a bank, looking like a ship, consisting of a small rock and a reef, within which was the sea, extending north-east and south-west over 2½ leagues, the latitude being about 20 degrees. This was no doubt Parece Vela, an isolated atoll consisting of a ring of rocks round a small lagoon, to the west of the Marianas.[2] No further land was sighted until 18 September, when they reached North America.

(d) THE TRACK OF THE GALLEONS

The *San Lucas* and the *San Pedro* established the practicability of return voyages between the Philippines and North America. On the other hand the Marshalls had proved a source of danger and no profit. For several centuries thereafter the Spanish ships came from North America to Guam and Manila in or about latitude 13 degrees north, and sailed back in the zone of westerlies in high latitudes to the north.[3]

---

[1] *Colección . . . de ultramar*, vol. ii (Madrid, 1886), pp. 427–56.
[2] *Pacific Islands Pilot*, vol. i, p. 548.
[3] For a résumé of these voyages, see Dahlgren, E. W., *The Discovery of the Hawaiian Islands* (Uppsala, 1917).

9. The *San Jeronimo*, 1566

FOLLOWING on the return of the *San Pedro* from the Philippines (see section 8), the authorities in New Spain sent a ship called the *San Jeronimo* to take help to Legaspi. The vessel set out from Acapulco in Mexico on 1 May 1566, the commander being one Pericon and the pilot Lope Martin, who had been pilot of the *San Lucas* on its voyage from Mexico to the Philippines and back the previous year. Lope Martin and some fellow conspirators murdered Pericon and later threw overboard the leader elected from their own ranks. Juan Martinez, one of a number who escaped with the ship later in the voyage, leaving Lope Martin and a number of the ship's company on an island, gave the story of this voyage after his arrival in the Philippines.[1]

On 22 June 1566 the ship made for Los Barbudos 'which are in 9 and 10 degrees'. On 29 June 1566, 60 days out from Mexico, low land was seen. It consisted of a chain of more than twenty small islets, the biggest about ½ league in circuit, joined together by reefs, tree-covered but uninhabited. Because of its uninviting character they did not land, preferring to continue on to other islands. Two days later, on 1 July 1566, they came to another chain of islands numbering more than 17, both bigger and smaller, from which a canoe came out. They made for this land, intending to anchor, but the wind was contrary and they passed onward, bringing to off the other part of the island because it was late and they were among islands. Next day, 2 July, some soldiers landed on the last of this chain of islands to get water, but could not find any. The following morning, 3 July, they came to another chain of similar islands, and anchored at the last of them. Here they were well received by the inhabitants, with whom they exchanged gifts, getting water and supplies. As night fell, the port being not very safe, the ship proceeded on its way, making for Guam. Four nights later, on 6 July, having gone not more than 40 minutes according to their estimation, and a distance judged to be 100 leagues, they suddenly found themselves in the midst of some islands, and were saved from disaster only by passing through a channel no wider than a stone's throw between two of the islands. They anchored, and in the morning found themselves in a lagoon, surrounded by many small islands and reefs. They found some deserted huts, and saw a canoe with some men,

[1] *Colección . . . de ultramar*, vol. iii (Madrid, 1887), pp. 371–475.

women, and children who had come across the lagoon from one of the other islands about 5 leagues away. The latitude was taken as 9⅔ degrees. On 21 July the ship sailed away through a good wide passage to the west of the first, leaving Lope Martin and a number of others behind. Fourteen days later the *San Jeronimo* reached the Marianas, staying at an island in 14 degrees near Guam, which was obviously Rota.

The only feasible identification of the atoll at which Lope Martin and his companions were left is Ujelang, the detached westernmost atoll of the Marshalls. Its latitude is 9⅔ degrees, there is a narrow and a wide passage in its south side, and it is the only island in such a position that a sailing time of 14 days to Guam and Rota and 4 days from a number of islands to the east in the neighbourhood of 9 degrees is of any significance. Legaspi's expedition had thought that Ujelang was deserted when they visited it in 1565, but only a few islanders were found by the *San Jeronimo*. Saavedra discovered Ujelang (see section 5). The previous island at which the landing was made and water and supplies procured in exchange for gifts, thought to be some 40 minutes to the south of Ujelang and 100 leagues distant, and described as a large atoll, must have been in the Ujae–Kwajalein–Namu sector of the Marshalls. When, 2 years later, Mendaña in 1568 came to an atoll which was undoubtedly Namu (see section 10), a landing party found a chisel made from a nail and some rope. Much the most feasible explanation of these is that they were some of the gifts made by the people of the *San Jeronimo* at the island at which the landing was made, but this cannot be assumed as certain, since Villalobos's expedition had possibly stayed at the near-by Kwajalein in 1542 (see section 7). The *Pacific Islands Pilot* says that a good landing can be made on the west side of Namu islet, the north-westernmost islet of Namu Atoll.[1] If Namu were the island in question, then the islands seen on 1 July, the last of which was landed upon on 2 July by the soldiers who searched for water, must have been those of Jabwot and Ailinglapalap, two closely contiguous atolls some 20 to 25 miles east and south-east of Namu, which do in fact comprise a number of larger and smaller islands. The islands seen on 29 June, described

[1] For descriptions of all these Marshalls atolls, see *Pacific Islands Pilot*, vol. i, pp. 454–6, 462–4.

as a chain of twenty small islands in 9 and 10 degrees, and uninviting, probably fit Erikub best, but could fit Maloelap to the south of it, or Wotje or Likiep to the north. It would not be an obstacle to these tentative identifications that Jabwot and Ailinglapalap are south of 9 to 10 degrees, because Lope Martin himself, when with Arellano in the *San Lucas* the previous year, had struck to the south-west from Likiep to Kwajalein and Lib, and therefore knew there were fertile islands in those latitudes. It is not, however, possible to identify precisely the islands in the Marshalls which were encountered by the *San Jeronimo*, apart from Ujelang. Since all the Marshalls atolls from 8 to 11 degrees had been already discovered with the possible exception of Maloelap, Erikub, Wotje, Lae, Ujae, Jabwot, Ailinglapalap, and Namu, the possibilities in reference to the *San Jeronimo* can be summed up by saying that any of these may have been discovered on this voyage, in the same way that it has already been said (see section 7) that any of the first five of them may have been previously discovered by Villalobos.

From Rota the *San Jeronimo* set out for Legaspi's camp in the Philippines. The ship struck very bad weather, being driven back several times. On one of these enforced retreats it came in sight of an island with high peaks which the pilot considered to be Guam, because it was in the right latitude. Some of the ship's company, says Martinez, thought it was too big for Guam and that it might be some island between Guam and the Philippines. Since no such island exists, and since the description and the latitude agree with Guam, the pilot's identification was no doubt correct.

10. The First Expedition of Alvaro de Mendaña

ON 19 November 1567 Alvaro de Mendaña set out from Callao in Peru in command of a Spanish expedition of two ships, the *Los Reyes* and the *Todos Santos*, to discover and settle the large continent which was reputed to exist in the South Pacific. Mendaña did not achieve this object, but made some remarkable discoveries before he sighted America again on 20 December 1568.

The course of the expedition is described in detail in the journal of the chief pilot Hernan Gallego. Some additional details are given in accounts by Mendaña himself, and by the purser Gomez Catoira.[1]

The ships sailed in a predominantly westerly direction for 58 days, and on 15 January 1568 discovered an island to which the name Isla de Jesus was given. It was low, small, and flat, with many reefs and a large beach, and there was a 'bay of the sea' in the middle of it. The latitude was taken as 6¾ degrees south. Some canoes came near the ship, the people being 'naked and mulattoes'. Mendaña says that the island was in barely 7 degrees, that on the west side it had a strand, with reefs in different parts, that towards the north it had a reef which entered the sea ¼ league and towards the south another smaller reef, that it had a shape like two galleys with a copse in the middle which appeared like a fleet of ships, and that it appeared to be about 6 leagues round. The vessels were unable to fetch the island, and proceeded west. From here on the winds were unfavourable. On 1 February 1568, 15 days after leaving the Isla de Jesus, a low line of shoals with several small islands lying in the midst of them was found. They lay north-east and south-west, and were about 15 leagues across as far as Gallego could judge. Mendaña and Catoira say that the ships coasted the reefs at about a league's distance, and called them Baxos de la Candellaria (Candlemas Banks). Their latitude was taken as about 6¼ degrees south. For 4 days they tried to keep in the vicinity of these reefs, but when Gallego took another latitude at the end of this period, he found it was slightly more than 7 degrees, which made him think he had drifted 15 leagues 'south-quarter-west'. He kept into the wind coming from the north. On 7 February high land was seen to the south at an estimated distance of about 15 leagues. They came down to it, and after some difficulty made port on the northern side of a large island, the latitude of the port being taken as 8 degrees less 10 minutes. To this island they gave the name Santa Ysabel.

This island was the modern Santa Isabel in the Solomons. It lies between 8½ and 7½ degrees south and is traversed by a range of mountains.

The 'Isle of Jesus', according to the sailing times, could only

[1] *The Discovery of the Solomon Islands*, ed. Lord Amherst and Thomson, B. (London, 1901).

have been one of the Ellice Islands. Nui is in 7¼ degrees, as compared with Gallego's figure of 6¾ degrees. In view of Gallego's tendency to a southerly error in his latitudes south of the line, the three northernmost islands of the Ellice group, Nanomana, Nanumea, and Niutao, no less than Nui, must all be considered to be possibilities. All these islands are small low atolls.

The Baxos de la Candellaria were probably Ontong Java, an atoll in latitude 5¼ degrees south, or possibly Roncador Reef, an atoll consisting of a lagoon fringed with reefs and rocks, in latitude 6¼ degrees south. The steady southerly error in Gallego's latitudes, coupled with the reference to the sight of islands rather than rocks among the reefs, points to Ontong Java rather than Roncador.

At Santa Ysabel the Spaniards built a small boat, known in the accounts as the brigantine, for the purpose of local exploration, and on 7 April a small company commanded by Pedro de Ortega, with Gallego as pilot, set out on a local voyage. From the south part of Santa Ysabel, on 11 April 1568, they saw a very high island lying east and west at a distance estimated as 14 leagues, called by the Spaniards Isla de Ramos. On rounding the south of Santa Ysabel on 16 April, they saw some islands to the south-east. They ran to the south-east with a fair wind. They came past a small island, named by them La Galera, to a larger one which they named Buena Vista, the latter being the easternmost of a chain of five islands lying east and west with one another. It was estimated to be about 12 leagues in circumference and ran east and west. Its native name was 'Pela'. There were a number of small inhabited islands round it. Here they made a landing, the latitude being taken as 9½ degrees south. They went to a near-by island and gathered some coconuts, after which Ortega made a landing on the large island, the ship returning to the small island for the night. They coasted next day along the southern shore of the large island, and from thence to another island about a league from it, to which they gave the name La Florida. It was in 9½ degrees, lay east and west with Buena Vista, and was about 25 leagues in circumference. They then went to other islands to the east, the first, of a circumference of about 25 leagues, being called San Dimas, and two other islands, to which they did not go, being named San German and Guadalupe. (Mendaña and Catoira, who were not on the brigantine, say that the island where events described by Gallego as happening on La Florida occurred was San Dimas, and that the largest island was called Pascua Florida. They do not mention the names San German and Guadalupe.) The brigantine came down to a large island lying to the south, the latitude of which was taken as 10½ degrees, passing on the way to it a high, round island with a volcano in the middle, in 9¾ degrees, lying 5 leagues south-east of Buena Vista, and named by Gallego Sesarga, after the Spanish island of that name. They made a landing on the large island on 19 April, at a point estimated to be 9 leagues north and south of the highest point of Buena Vista. This large island they named Guadalcanal. From here they returned to Santa Ysabel. When one-third of the way along its western side, they saw at an estimated distance from Santa Ysabel of 6 leagues two large islands, called San Nicolas and Isla de Arrecifes, thought to be in latitude 9½ degrees, lying east and west of each other, and with much land ahead. From the north of Santa Ysabel they saw a large island estimated to be about 6 leagues away, which they named San Marcos. They thus completed the circuit of Santa Ysabel and returned to the ships.

A comparison of these details with the modern charts and topographical details shows that Ortega and Gallego, on 11 April 1568, discovered Malaita, called by them Isla de Ramos. On 16 April 1568 they sighted the Florida group to the south-east of Santa Ysabel. They came south-east to the eastern part of Florida Island and the small islands on the reefs on its north side, one of which they called La Galera. They then coasted the group on its south side. Since Florida Island, the chief of the group, which actually consists of two segments divided by a narrow channel, looks from the south like three islands, Buena Vista may be identified as the eastern segment of Florida Island, and La Florida and San Dimas as the western segment seen as two apparent islands, San German and Guadalupe being evidently Oveluga and Vatilau, lying close to the western end of Florida. Guadalcanal was the large island to the south of the Florida group known today by the same name Guadalcanal. Actually it lies between 9¼ and 10 degrees south. The volcano seen between the Florida group and Guadalcanal was Savo. The two islands and other land seen to the west of Santa Ysabel were the eastern islands of the New Georgia group, namely Gatukai, Vangunu, and New Georgia. San Marcos was the southern part of Choiseul. The precise dates of the discoveries of Guadalcanal, Savo, the New Georgia islands, and Choiseul are not given.

After the return of the brigantine from this first local voyage, the expedition came down to Guadalcanal, bringing the brigantine. The latter set out again on 19 May, under the command of Hernando Henriquez, again with Gallego as pilot, to explore further. They came along the northern side of Guadalcanal to its eastern point, and passed over to the previously discovered Malaita, seeing to the south-east a large island estimated to be 7 leagues off. They came down the south-west side of Malaita and saw from its end another island some 8 leagues away to the east, on which they made a landing, giving the name La Treguada to the island, the native name of which was 'Uraba'. It was thought to be in latitude 10½ degrees south and about 25 leagues in size. From 'Uraba' they sailed past some low islands at a distance of about 3 leagues, naming them Las Tres Marias. On 1 June 1568 they came to a low island about 3 leagues from Las Tres Marias, thought to be 6 leagues round, and in 10⅔ degrees. They named this San Juan. Thence they went to a large island, north and south 2 leagues with San Juan, which they called Santiago. It was estimated to be about 40 leagues long on the north side, the latitude 10¾ degrees, and 12 leagues south-west from La Treguada. A high wind from the north-east took them to the head of Santiago, from which they saw an island thought to be south-west 18 leagues, 4 leagues from Guadalcanal, and in 10½ degrees south, to which they gave the name San Urban. They did not investigate this, but returned to the main expedition at Guadalcanal.

From this detail the island seen while passing to Malaita was the modern San Cristobal, which was, as will be seen, the same island as was later christened Santiago, and later again rediscovered by the main expedition and named San Christoval, from which it gets its present name San Cristobal. It is the southernmost of the main Solomon Islands. 'Uraba' or La Treguada was Ulawa, Las Tres Marias were the three islands of Olu Malau, San Juan was Ugi, and Santiago the modern San Cristobal seen from the north. No island corresponding to San Urban exists, the presumption being that this was one of the cases in Pacific exploration where cloud banks seen from a distance without investigation were thought to be land.

From Guadalcanal the full expedition set out to find Santiago or San Juan. They had strong head winds and Gallego decided to pass to the south of Santiago. They came to an island 'which had not been seen by the brigantine' and named it San Christoval. They found a port estimated to be in 11 degrees south, 'very close to the island of

Santiago, on the south-east'. The brigantine set out on its third local voyage on 4 July under the command of Francisco Muñoz Rico with Gallego as pilot. As far as the middle of the island the coast ran predominantly from north-west to south-east, and thereafter east and west. At the extremity of the island, estimated to be in 11½ degrees south, they discovered two small islands to the south-east and east, 2 and 3 leagues, to which they gave the names Santa Catalina and Santa Ana. Landings were made on each. The brigantine then returned along the coast to the main expedition.

It is evident from these details that the Spaniards had come on the southern shore of the modern San Cristobal without realizing it was the same as Santiago. Santa Catalina and Santa Ana were the two small islands at the southern extremity of San Cristobal known today by the same names.

After the return of the brigantine, it was decided to make for America. The two ships rounded San Cristobal on the south side on 17 August 1568, and then struck up on a predominantly north-east course. They crossed the equator, and on 17 September 1568 came upon some shoals and islets in latitude 8 degrees north which Gallego identified with Salazar's San Bartolomeo, i.e. Taongi (see section 3), although the latter was a long way to the north. Mendaña says they called them the San Mateo Shoals. These islands ran north-west and south-east for a distance judged to be about 15 leagues, and had two lines of reefs running close to each other, at the north-west end of each being two little islands a league apart. The islands numbered more than twenty. There were many houses. A landing party found a chisel made of a nail, and pieces of rope. From these islands the expedition continued on, and in a latitude estimated as 19½ degrees north, on 20 October 1568, discovered a low barren island judged to be 8 leagues in circumference, to which they gave the name San Francisco.

The latitude and description of the first islands show that they were Namu Atoll in the Marshalls. The nail and rope were presumably some of the gifts left by the San Jeronimo on 1 July 1566 (see section 9), or possibly relics of Villalobos's expedition brought from the near-by Kwajalein. San Francisco was the isolated and barren Wake Island, in latitude 19⅓ degrees north.

The Spanish accounts of Mendaña's first voyage contain a number of sidelights on the people, crafts and plant life of the southern Solomons in the sixteenth century. The people were in

a state of constant warfare with other communities in their neigh-
bourhoods. The native weapons were bows and arrows, lances,
clubs, and stones. Canoes were extensively used for transport and
warfare. Pigs, fowls, yams, coconuts, fish, and fruits were in
copious supply. The islands were for the most part densely
populated.

The discoveries made by the first expedition of Alvaro de
Mendaña were as follows: On 15 January 1568 Mendaña dis-
covered either Nanomana, Nanumea, Niutao, or Nui in the Ellice
Islands. On 1 February 1568 Mendaña discovered either Ontong
Java or Roncador Reef in the Solomons—more probably Ontong
Java. On 7 February 1568 Mendaña discovered Santa Isabel in the
Solomons. On 11 April 1568 Pedro de Ortega, on a local voyage
of exploration, discovered Malaita, on 16 April 1568 the Florida
group, and between then and 28 April 1568 Guadalcanal, Savo,
the eastern islands of the New Georgia group (Gatukai, Vangunu,
New Georgia), and Choiseul, all in the Solomons. In the last few
days of May and the first few days of June 1568 Hernando Henriquez, on a local voyage of exploration, discovered San Cristobal,
Ulawa, Olu Malau, and Ugi in the Solomons. On 17 September
1568 Mendaña encountered Namu in the Marshall group. On 20
October 1568 Mendaña discovered the isolated North Pacific
island, Wake Island. Landings were made on Santa Isabel, Florida,
Guadalcanal, Malaita, Ulawa, Olu Malau, Ugi, San Cristobal, and
Namu.

11. Francis Drake

IN the years 1577–8 Francis Drake came from England into the
Pacific and up the west coast of the Americas. On 25 July 1578 he
left the San Francisco area of the modern California for the
Moluccas.

Two accounts of Drake's traverse of the Pacific in the *Golden
Hind* are extant. The longer of these accounts was prepared by
Drake's nephew from the notes of Drake's chaplain Francis
Fletcher and others of Drake's company. A comparison of this

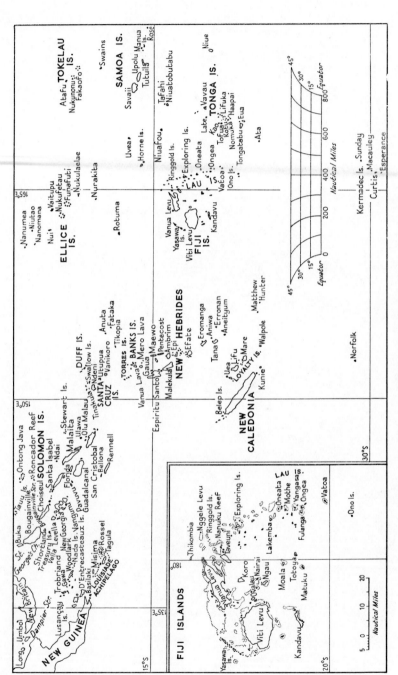

MAP 3. Southern Melanesian Groups and Western Polynesia

with an extant manuscript of Fletcher's account which does not include the traverse of the Pacific shows that it is for the most part an edited version of Fletcher. The shorter account of Drake's crossing, which is anonymous, is plainly a summary of the same material as the longer, recapitulating the same phraseology. Hondius, a Dutchman living in London, drew a map, published in 1595, to illustrate Drake's voyage.[1]

The fuller account states that on 30 September 1578 Drake's ship came to 'certain islands, lying about eight degrees to the northward of the line', where great numbers of canoes supported by outriggers on both sides came out, with high prows and sterns, and decorated with shells. In the canoes were 'coquos, fish, potatoes, and certaine fruits to small purpose'. The people hung 'things of a reasonable weight' in the lobes of their ears, the nails on the fingers of some of them were at least an inch long, and their teeth as black as pitch from the eating of a herb with a kind of powder. They showed a treacherous and thieving disposition, attacking the ship with stones. These islands were called the Islands of Thieves. The ship was becalmed in sight of these islands, left them on or about 3 October, and continued within sight of land till 16 October, when they 'fell with four islands in 7 deg. 5 min. to the northward of the line', coasted these islands till 21 October, and then anchored and watered at the biggest of them, called Mindanao. The shorter account says that on the morning of 13 October they 'fell with certaine islands 8 degrees to the northward of the line', where the same contacts with the islanders as in the longer account are related, that 'leaving this island the night after we fell with it, the 18 of October, we lighted upon divers others, some whereof made a great show of inhabitants'. From the anchoring place at Mindanao Drake came via Sarangani and the Talaud Islands to the Moluccas. Hondius's map shows Drake's course direct to the Moluccas without indicating any encounters with islands in the Pacific itself.

The natural interpretation of these data would be that the ship spent all the time, from its first landfall until anchoring, at no great distance from the east coast of Mindanao, which extends from well north of 8 degrees to well south of 7 degrees 5 minutes. The references conform with the view that Drake came to the east coast of Mindanao in latitude 8 degrees north, where there are some islets on the coastal reefs, that he drifted in calms as described and stood off making slowly south, without recognizing he was

[1] *The World Encompassed by Sir Francis Drake* (London, 1854).

near a continuous coast, that he came in to the main coast again
in the vicinity of latitude 7 degrees north near the peninsula making the east side of Davao Gulf, came round it into Davao Gulf,
and anchored on the west side of Davao Gulf near the two islands
in Davao Gulf, Samal and Kud, dominating the view to the north,
the 'four islands in 7 deg. 5 min.' being thus the east side of Davao
Gulf, Samal, Kud, and the west side of Davao Gulf, where the
travellers at their anchorage would be told that they were at
Mindanao. Coming out of Davao Gulf they would come to
Sarangani at no great distance to the south, and thence go on to
the Moluccas.

The view made conventional by a number of writers that
Drake's islands in 8 degrees were the Palaus or Ngulu or Sorol in
the western Carolines is therefore a dubious one. Furthermore,
while it cannot be said that double outrigger canoes were not used
in the western Carolines, the mention of great numbers of such
canoes, and the lack of mention of single outrigger *praus*, is much
more typical in later times of the native Mindanao craft than of
the Carolines vessels. However, in view of the discrepancies in
the documentation, it would perhaps be questionable to reject
this view out of hand. Ngulu and Sorol had been discovered by
Arellano (see section 8), and the Palaus may have been discovered
by the Portuguese (see section 4), so that the view referred to is
comparatively academic so far as discovery is concerned, being
confined to the possibility—if possibility it is—that Drake discovered the Palaus.

12. The Second Expedition of Alvaro de Mendaña

IN 1595 Alvaro de Mendaña set out from Peru on a second
expedition. The chief authority for the course is a report by the
chief pilot Pedro Fernandez de Quiros.[1] Two other narratives

---

[1] *The Voyages of Pedro Fernandez de Quiros*, ed. Markham, C. (London, 1904),
pp. 149–57.

broadly recapitulating each other, and purporting to be derived from Quiros, are extant in compilations by the Spanish historians Figueroa and Zaragoza.[1] Quiros's account is followed here except where otherwise specified.

The expedition, according to Figueroa, set out from Payta for the 'Isles of Solomon' on 16 June 1595, with 400 people including women and soldiers, with the intention of conquest and settlement. There were two larger vessels, the flagship San Jeronimo and the Santa Ysabel; and two smaller vessels, the San Felipe and the Santa Catalina.

On 21 July, in 'fully 10 degrees of latitude', they sighted an island to which they gave the name Magdalena, inhabited by a fine-looking people. It appeared to be about 6 leagues round, and the south side, as they passed it, was high, precipitous towards the sea, with rocky ravines. They discovered three other islands. The first, named San Pedro, some 10 leagues north and north-west of Magdalena, appeared to be 3 leagues round. To the south-east of it (Zaragoza says north-west), about 5 leagues off, was a fine-looking thickly inhabited island named Dominica, appearing to be about 15 leagues in circumference. To the south of it, a little more than a league distant, another island, perhaps 8 leagues round, was named Santa Christina. They sailed through the channel between Dominica and Santa Christina and found a good port on the west side of the latter. According to Figueroa the four islands were named Las Marquesas de Mendoça and the port on Santa Christina was named Madre de Dios.

These details are a close description of the four southernmost islands of the Marquesas group, Fatu Hiva, Motane, Hiva Oa, and Tahuata. The modern name for the whole group commemorates Mendaña's discovery.

According to the Spanish accounts the Marquesans of Tahuata had fowls, fish, sugar cane, plantains, nuts, and fruits. Their town was built on two sides of a rectangular space, the houses being of timber and intertwined canes. A building which the Europeans supposed to be a religious one stood outside the town, in a space enclosed with palisades, and containing some ill-carved images before which were offerings of provisions. The people had large

[1] Zaragoza, J., Historia (Madrid, 1876), vol. i; Figueroa, C. S. de, Hechos de D. Garcia, Marques de Cañete (Madrid, 1613), vol. vi.

and well-constructed sailing canoes. Their tools were made of shells and fish-bones. They used slings, stones, and lances as weapons.

On 5 August the expedition set sail again, and on 20 August saw four low islands, with sandy beaches, full of palms and woods, and on the south-east side, towards the north, a great sand-bank. The four islands together appeared to be about 12 leagues in circuit. Figueroa says that the eastern side was covered with continuous sand-banks and reefs which were seen to extend one way to the north of the group and the other way to the south-west, and that at the south-west part there appeared to be a termination of the reef. The latitude was taken as $10\frac{1}{4}$ degrees south, and the estimated distance from Santa Christina was 400 leagues. To these islands they gave the name San Bernardo. The fleet continued on between 10 and 11 degrees with south-east winds, and on 29 August came to a round low islet which appeared to be about a league in circumference, surrounded by reefs. They could not land on it. It was taken as being in $10\frac{2}{3}$ degrees. To this island they gave the name La Solitaria (Lonely). The ships continued on a westerly course, and on 7 September came to a large island with a volcano to the north of it. They gave the name Santa Cruz to this large island, and stayed there for several weeks in various locations, their main port, according to Figueroa, being called by them Graciosa. Santa Cruz was a fine-looking, well-wooded island in 10 degrees south, its circumference being thought to be very considerable, and it had some inhabited islands near it. The volcano to the north of the island was judged to be about 7 leagues distant, and was lofty, with a well-shaped peak, its circumference being thought to be about 3 leagues. North-east of the volcano, at a distance of some 7 or 8 leagues, were some small inhabited islets and many shoals, and also islets to the north-west of the volcano, while to the south-east of Santa Cruz was another island of moderate size. Figueroa's and Zaragoza's accounts make it plain that the islands beyond the volcano to the north, and the island of moderate size to the south-east of Santa Cruz, were discovered by Lorenzo Barreto while in command of one of the smaller vessels on a local voyage round Santa Cruz.

Santa Cruz was the modern Ndeni, the largest island of the Santa Cruz group north of the New Hebrides and Banks Islands. The name Santa Cruz commemorates Mendaña's discovery. The volcano to the north was Tinekula, a round lofty island, and the islands beyond it were the modern Swallow Islands. The island to the south-east was Utupua, an island 1,240 feet high 37 miles south-east of Ndeni. Since Vanikoro, an island over 3,000 feet high, lies 20 miles beyond Utupua in the same direction from Ndeni, it is probable that Barreto saw Vanikoro at the same time without realizing there were two islands.

For the identification of San Bernardo and La Solitaria, we must look for two islands between the Marquesas and Santa Cruz groups, in the vicinity of 10 to 11 degrees, answering to the topo-graphical descriptions in the Spanish accounts. The only islands which conform with these data are Pukapuka in the northern Cooks, which consists of three main islands and a detached islet to the west, the surrounding reef having numbers of banks on it on the eastern side and being invisible on the south-west side; and Nurakita, the southernmost of the Ellice Islands, a small round islet surrounded by extensive reefs.[1] Swains Island in the Tokelau group could answer to the stated latitude and description of La Solitaria, but is much too far from the Santa Cruz group for a sailing time of 9 days, and too near to Pukapuka for another 9 days to have been spent in the passage with favourable north-east winds.

The Spanish accounts give a vivid picture of the people of Ndeni in the sixteenth century. Some were dark and some were tawny, with frizzled hair and teeth dyed red from chewing betel, wearing woven stuff, necklaces, and other ornaments of bone, fish teeth and mother-of-pearl. They had bows and arrows, clubs, stones, and spears. At night they made music and danced, striking wooden drums and tambourines. They used small looms for weaving. They had both small and large canoes. Their villages consisted of round houses made of overlapping boards, with roofs of inter-laced palms, and lofts to which they ascended by ladders. They practised fruit culture, grew some crops, and had pigs, fowls, plantains of many sorts, coconuts, sweet canes, nuts, and fish. There were profuse plantings of 'sweet basil', and several kinds of beautiful red flowers, which were much prized.

During the stay of the expedition at Ndeni, Mendaña died, bequeathing the command of the expedition to his wife Ysabel Barreto. Eventually the *San Jeronimo* reached Manila, having been

[1] *Pacific Islands Pilot*, vol. ii, p. 425.

separated from the *San Felipe* and the *Santa Catalina* on the way. The *San Felipe* eventually reached the Philippines, but no record of any discoveries it might have made has been found. The *Santa Ysabel*, which disappeared the night that Santa Cruz was sighted, and the *Santa Catalina*, similarly left no records.

The *San Jeronimo*, while making for Manila in a wretched condition, on 21 December 1595 came on an island in 'full 6 degrees north latitude', appearing to have a circumference of some 25 leagues, thickly wooded, well inhabited from the number of canoes which were seen, and with large reefs. On its western side, about 4 leagues off, there were some low islets. Zaragoza says that the island was round and not excessively high, that at 3 leagues to the west there were four low islands and many others near them, surrounded by reefs, that they rounded the reefs of the large island at 3 o'clock in the afternoon, and that in the evening they found themselves surrounded by two small islands and many rocks as in a yard. It is not entirely certain from Zaragoza's description whether he meant that there were two lots of islands to the west. It is, however, plain that the *San Jeronimo* skirted the large island on the north side, because it is stated that the wind was north-easterly and they could not tack, and only got round the reefs by a narrow margin. The *San Jeronimo* reached Guam on 1 January 1596, taking a north-west course from the islands that had been encountered.

The only island in the vicinity of 6 degrees north, of sufficient size to merit an estimate of being 25 leagues in circuit, with some low islets some 3 or 4 leagues to the west of it, and at such a distance to the south-east of Guam that 11 days sailing is feasible, is Ponape, the main island in the eastern Carolines. The *San Jeronimo*, having rounded Ponape on the north side, at 3 o'clock in the afternoon, evidently came on the islets of Pakin, some 18 miles to the west, that evening. If Zaragoza's references are to two separate lots of islands near Ponape, the other would be those of Ant, some 8 miles south-west of Ponape. In reference to Zaragoza's statement that the island was not very high, Ponape in fact has peaks of 2,600 feet, but the *Pacific Islands Pilot* states that these are often obscured by cloud.[1] No other identification is compatible with the data. Ponape and Ant had been discovered by Saavedra (see section 5), so that the only discovery by Ysabel Barreto was that of Pakin.

[1] *Pacific Islands Pilot*, vol. i, pp. 527–8.

The discoveries of the second expedition of Alvaro de Mendaña were as follows: On 21 July 1595 Mendaña discovered Fatu Hiva, and the next day Motane, Hiva Oa, and Tahuata, in the Marquesas group. A landing was made on Tahuata. On 20 August 1595 Mendaña discovered Pukapuka in the northern Cooks, and on 29 August 1595 Nurakita in the Ellice Islands. On 7 September 1595 Mendaña discovered Tinakula and Ndeni in the Santa Cruz group, a number of landings being subsequently made on Ndeni. Some days later Lorenzo Barreto discovered the Swallow Islands, Utupua, and probably Vanikoro, in the same group. On 21 December 1595 Ysabel Barreto discovered Pakin in the eastern Carolines.

13. The Remnant of Mahu's Expedition

THE first Dutch ships to cross the Pacific were the remnant of an expedition which set out from Rotterdam under the command of Jacob Mahu in 1598. Mahu died in the Atlantic, and various other disasters befell the expedition. Two ships of this expedition separately completed the traverse of the Pacific.

One of these ships, under the command of Balthasar de Cordes, crossed from Peru to the Moluccas, where it was captured by the Portuguese. No account of any discoveries which Cordes may have made in that passage was apparently preserved.[1]

The voyage of the other ship was subsequently described by the chief pilot, William Adams, in two letters sent by him from Japan.[2] He says that the commander was one 'Hudcopee', no doubt Huydecoper, and that the name of the vessel was the *Hope*. On 27 November 1599 this vessel, in company with another called the *Charity*, together with a pinnace, sailed from the island of Santa Maria, south of Valparaiso in Chile, for Japan, thinking to do some trade there. The ships took their course direct for Japan, passing the equator with a fair wind which continued for several months. They 'fell in with certain islands in

[1] *De reis van Mahu en de Cordes*, ed. Wieder, F. C., vol. i (The Hague, 1923), pp. 275–85.
[2] Purchas, S., *Purchas his Pilgrimes*, vol. i (London, 1625), book 3, pp. 125–32.

16 degrees north, the inhabitants of which were man-eaters'. The pinnace, containing eight men, deserted to these islands. Between the latitudes of 27 and 28 degrees north, they met variable winds. On 23 February 1600 the *Charity* was separated from the *Hope* and was not heard of again. On 24 March they saw an island, and on 19 April reached Japan in 32½ degrees north.

It is barely possible that the islands in 16 degrees were the islets of Johnston Island, in 16¾ degrees, which were uninhabited in later times, but may have been intermittently inhabited. It is much more likely, however, that they were some of the Marianas, reached relatively quickly with the favourable winds, and that later the vessel, encountering variable winds, made heavy weather of its passage, passing one of the Bonins before arriving at Japan.

14. The Discoveries of Pedro Fernandez de Quiros, Diego de Prado, and Luis Vaez de Torres in 1606

PEDRO FERNANDEZ DE QUIROS, Mendaña's chief pilot on the latter's second voyage (see section 12), led a further expedition across the Pacific in 1605–6. This consisted of two larger ships, the *Pedro y San Pablo* and the *San Pedrico*, and a small shallow-draught vessel known as a *zabra*, called the *Los Tres Reyes*. The *San Pedrico* and the *zabra* became separated from Quiros in the flagship in the latter part of the voyage, eventually reaching Manila via Torres Strait between New Guinea and Australia, while Quiros returned directly to North America.

The authorities for the course of the combined expedition until the time of separation are the journal of Gonzalez de Leza, who started as second pilot of the flagship and later became chief pilot, a detailed narrative by Quiros recorded by his secretary Belmonte Bermudez, and accounts by Diego de Prado, (one of the senior officers), and Luis Vaez de Torres, the captain of the

San Pedrico.[1] The course of the *San Pedrico* and the *zabra* after the separation is described in the accounts of Prado and Torres and in maps sent to Spain from Manila by Prado. The following details are taken from Leza except where otherwise specified. The Spanish place-names given are those which became classical through use by later geographers, the accounts themselves giving a variety of Spanish names for the islands which were encountered.

From Callao in Peru the expedition set off on 21 December 1605, and continued on a predominantly south-west course to latitude 26 degrees south. On 22 January the course was changed to west-north-west. On 26 January 1606 the expedition came to a very low, wooded, uninhabited island (Encarnación), almost level with the sea, running north-west and south-east, at which they could not find anchorage. According to Prado a reef and sand-banks ran far into the sea. The latitude was taken as just under 25 degrees south. On the 29th a second uninhabited island (San Juan Bautista) was discovered. It is described as being in 24¾ degrees south, flat with a hill to the south, full of trees and open spaces, and with clean rock all round the coast. A landing party landed on a small bit of beach on the south side but went no farther. The ships went almost round the island without finding anchorage, but judged that landings would be easier on the north side. Leaving this island on 30 January, the expedition took a west-north-west course, and on 3 February 1606 came to a very low, long, narrow island (Santelmo). No anchorage could be found along its coast. Leaving this island on a west-north-west course, at dawn on 4 February 1606, they sighted another island 5 leagues to the south-west, and ran along its north-east side. This was the first of four islands seen that day, and named Las Cuatro Coronadas. They were 3 or 4 leagues from each other, in latitudes taken as between 20 and 21 degrees south, all uninhabited and without anchorage being found. From this group the expedition struck off again to the north-west on 5 February, and 3½ days later, on two of which the sailing was well below average, they saw a small island (San Miguel) about 3 leagues to the north-east, in a latitude of about 19 degrees south, but could not make it because it was to windward, and continued on their course. This island was seen in the morning of 9 February 1606. The next day, 10 February 1606, at dawn, they came to a large island (Conversión de San Pablo), the coast of which ran, from the south end, east and west, and from the north, north-west to south-east. The latitude of the east end was

[1] *The Voyages of Pedro Fernandez de Quiros*, ed. Markham, C. (London, 1904), pp. 161–403, 455–66; *New Light on the Discovery of Australia*, ed. Stevens, H. N. (London, 1930), pp. 86–205 and maps.

considered to be a shade over 18 degrees south, and of the north, according to Torres, $17\frac{2}{3}$ degrees south. The interior was under water and the atoll, according to Torres, was completely overflowed in parts, a comment made by him in describing the passage of the ships past the west side. Landings were made on this island. On 12 February the expedition sailed along the south and west sides of this island and then left it, seeing at an estimated distance of 5 leagues another island to the north (La Deçena). Torres refers to it as if it were near San Pablo, and Leza says later that the next island to be seen (La Sagitaria) was 20 leagues from 'the others'. This next island was seen bearing north at noon on 13 February, according to Leza, but 14 February according to Quiros. They could not make sufficient easting to fetch it because of the wind. Quiros says they continued to hold the wind. At dawn they sighted a large island (La Fugitiva) estimated to be about 5 leagues to the east, the latitude of which was estimated to be 15 degrees south. The ship then fell off to the west because they had little sail on. Leza comments that in their passage through these islands the direction was not steadily maintained because the ships were on occasion yawing from north-west to north-east. They saw no more islands for 7 days.

Of these islands Santelmo and Las Cuatro Coronadas correspond only to Marutea and the Actaeon Islands in the Tuamotu Archipelago, Marutea being a low long narrow atoll east-south-east of the Actaeon group, which consists of four small islands lying close together between 21 and 22 degrees south as described by Leza. Encarnación and San Juan Bautista must have been Ducie and Henderson, lying close to latitudes 25 and 24 degrees south to the south-east of the Tuamotus, for the following reasons. Ducie, Henderson, Pitcairn, and Oeno are the only islands in that vicinity. Pitcairn bears no resemblance to the descriptions, being a high uneven island. Encarnación must therefore have been either Ducie or Henderson, and San Juan Bautista must have been either Henderson or Oeno. Henderson is an uplifted atoll 100 feet high, of plateau-like character with coral cliffs except on the north, whereas Encarnación is described as little higher than the sea, with reefs and sand-banks, which is true of Ducie.[1] That San Juan Bautista was Henderson is supported by the sailing times, since $2\frac{1}{2}$ days for the 190 miles from Ducie to Henderson and $4\frac{1}{2}$ days for the 380 miles from Henderson to Marutea, during which time

[1] *Pacific Islands Pilot*, vol. iii, p. 67.

the sailing weather from Leza's data was apparently steady, is realistic as compared with the distance of 320 miles from Ducie to Oeno and much the same from Oeno to Marutea. For San Pablo we must look for a large atoll in the vicinity of latitude 18 degrees south, the southern portion of which runs east and west, and the northern portion north-west and south-east, preferably with the west side overflowed in parts, and with an island close to it on the north, so placed that a sailing time of 4½ days from the Actaeon group, on two of which days, according to Leza, the distance traversed was below average, is feasible. These details agree only with Hao. This is a large atoll, the south part of which extends east and west and the northern part from north-west to south-east, with the reef so low here and there on the western side that the sea washes into the lagoon.[1] The northern coast of Hao is in latitude 18 degrees south. Another atoll, Amanu, lies about 9 miles north-east of it. San Pablo could not have been Anaa, an atoll some 250 miles east of Hao in much the same latitude, although without an extended part running east and west. The distance from the Actaeon group to Anaa is some 500 miles, which, as compared with the other sailing times, is much too far to have been accomplished in 4½ days, on two of which the distances covered were below average. The average sailing rate from Ducie to Marutea works out at about 80 miles a day, and from the Actaeon group to Hao (about 260 miles) at about 60 miles a day, which accords with Leza's relative estimates. If San Pablo were Anaa, the average daily distance would have been about 110 miles, and higher again on the better sailing days, with nothing to account for the discrepancy with the sailing rate from Ducie to Marutea, and in contradiction with Leza's own estimates, which are relatively the other way round. Furthermore there is no satisfactory identification of La Deçena if San Pablo is thought to be Anaa, for the nearest island, Faaite, lies 35 miles to the north-east of Anaa. With San Pablo identified as Hao, La Deçena, the large island seen to the north of San Pablo, fits in with Amanu. San Miguel, the island seen the day before reaching San Pablo, must have been Vairaatea, 85 miles south-east of Hao, the sailing

---

[1] *Pacific Islands Pilot*, vol. iii, p. 100.

distance between them from the time when they were each seen being somewhat less, and therefore again according with an average daily sailing rate of somewhere round 80 miles a day. That La Sagitaria, the island in the vicinity of $15\frac{3}{4}$ degrees, was seen on 14 February, $2\frac{1}{2}$ days after leaving Hao, as stated by Quiros, and not on 13 February as stated by Leza, is evident from the latitudes, since a change of latitude from over 18 degrees to somewhere round $15\frac{3}{4}$ degrees could not have been achieved so soon. For La Sagitaria and La Fugitiva we must look for two islands so placed that the first was passed on the west and the second was seen to the east at dawn after holding the east wind during the night, with no great change in the estimated latitude between them. Raroia lies on either side of the 16th parallel some 160 miles from the south side of Hao, and Takume is a large atoll, close to Raroia on the north-east side, and extending up to $15\frac{1}{2}$ degrees. North-west of Takume is open sea. Raroia and Takume are the only satisfactory identifications for La Sagitaria and La Fugitiva. Two very small atolls, Tauere and Rekareka, lie slightly east of the direct line from Hao to Raroia, but, as so often happened with such low islands, must have been passed at night, or in low visibility, or when the ships were yawing off course.

The only view, therefore, which conforms with the Spanish accounts is that on 26 and 29 January 1606, respectively, Quiros discovered Ducie and Henderson to the south-east of the Tuamotu Archipelago, a landing being made on Henderson; and that on 3, 4, 9, 10, 12, 14, and 15 February 1606, respectively, he discovered Marutea, the Actaeon Islands, Vairaatea, Hao, Amanu, Raroia, and Takume in the Tuamotu Archipelago, landings being made on Hao.

The contacts with the people of Hao were friendly, and they exchanged presents with the Spaniards, including a turban of feathers. Half of a cedar pole of Nicaraguan or Peruvian style was found on the island, and an old woman wore a gold ring with an emerald—relics, perhaps, of a vessel from Peru, not necessarily European, and not necessarily on a two-way voyage. Numbers of crosses of local wood were put up by the Spanish sailors on the island, but the thought that they survived for more than a few years is an unlikely one.

The expedition continued to the north-north-west until 18 February and then turned west. On 21 February 1606, it came to an island called by Leza the Island of Fish, running north-north-west and south-south-east, on the west side of which they found a large sheltered harbour. A landing party found coconuts but no water. The island, which was overflowed, was thought to be in latitude 10½ degrees south and about 12 leagues round. Prado says that the landing party found it consisted of about twenty-two islets. From this island they continued on their westerly course in 10 degrees latitude for another 8 days, and on 2 March sighted a small low island (Gente Hermosa) estimated to be 3 or 4 leagues in circuit, and in latitude 10½ degrees south. It was inundated inland, and apart from this lagoon and some cultivated patches was all one palm grove. During the 15 days from the Tuamotus to Gente Hermosa the expedition had steady sailing weather with normal average daily sailings, the distance being estimated by Leza at 343 leagues in all. There were many people on the shore. The *zabra* anchored and the natives ran out a rope to it from the shore. The island, according to Quiros, was in latitude 10½ degrees and was very flat, the anchorage was on the north side of the island, and a landing party found some drinking water of comparatively negligible quantity at a distance from the ships, being apparently seepage of rain water through the beach sand. Torres says he subdued the hostility of the natives throughout the island. After leaving Gente Hermosa on 4 March, the sailing was less steady, with calms and squalls. On 7 April 1606 they came to a number of small islands, at one of which, called Taumaco by the inhabitants, they anchored. The islanders of Taumaco said that Santa Cruz with its adjacent volcano, as identified by them from the Spaniards' signs, was several days' sailing towards the west. Leza estimated the distance from Gente Hermosa to Taumaco as 427 leagues in all.

These latter small islands were the Duff Islands, of which Taumako is the chief. Gente Hermosa was a low, small, flat island in the vicinity of 10½ to 10⅓ degrees south with an internal lagoon, not so diffuse or broken that it could not be covered for the most part in a few hours on foot, and shallow near the reef on the north side. Gente Hermosa could not have been the modern Swains Island, south of the main islands of the Tokelaus. The relative sailing times of 15 days from the Tuamotus to Gente Hermosa, in which 343 leagues were estimated to have been traversed in steady sailing weather, and a further 34 days to the Duffs over a distance estimated to be 427 leagues, rule this out, since Swains Island is in fact much farther from the Tuamotus than from the Duffs. Furthermore, Swains Island was uninhabited when discovered in the early nineteenth century, whereas the Spanish descriptions of Gente Hermosa give every impression of viable continuing settlement. For Gente Hermosa we must look for another island in the vicinity of the stated latitude and conforming to the descriptions, nearer to the Tuamotus, and preferably inhabited at the time of later European contact. The island could not have been Pukapuka, which had been described by Quiros himself in 1595 (see section 12) in very different terms from his description of Gente Hermosa. Manihiki is a large diffuse atoll, and according to the *Pacific Islands Pilot* does not have an anchorage.[1] Rakahanga, on the other hand, is a small low fertile island, in latitude 10 degrees south, with an internal lagoon. As compared with the Spanish statements that anchorage was found by the *zabra* on the north side of Gente Hermosa and that the natives ran a rope to it from the shore, the *Pacific Islands Pilot* says that anchorage can be obtained off the north-western point of Rakahanga at one cable from the edge of the reef.[2] The distance from Takume to Rakahanga on a north-westerly and then westerly course is about 1,240 miles, which works out at a daily average of about 83 miles in 15 days.

The 'Island of Fish', which was seen in the vicinity of $10\frac{1}{2}$ degrees south 7 days after leaving La Fugitiva, and which consisted of some twenty-two small islets, with a large bay on the west side, must have been Caroline Island, for Vostok, the only other possibility from the course and sailing time, is a small compact island.

A course from the Tuamotus first to the north-west and then west to Caroline Island supports the view that Conversión de San Pablo was Hao and La Sagitaria and La Fugitiva were Raroia and Takume, the expedition having skirted the main concentration of the Tuamotu atolls on the east and not the west side, since in the latter case they would have been too far west for such a course to have been realistic.

---

[1] *Pacific Islands Pilot*, vol. iii, pp. 209–10.
[2] Ibid., p. 210.

The people of Rakahanga are described in the Spanish accounts as a fine-looking spirited people, growing a root crop for food, with fine mats, and armed with lances and clubs. They had some small dogs. They used large and beautiful pearl shells for making fish-hooks and other instruments. They also had double canoes in which they went on off-shore voyages. The people of Rakahanga and Manihiki were found at the time of later European contact to be voyaging in double canoes over the 25 miles between these islands.[1] When Bellingshausen came on Rakahanga in 1820 (see section 87), the islanders assailed him with stones and spears from their canoes in much the same way that Quiros's *zabra* was assailed.

The people of Taumako gave Quiros a lot of information about the local geography. On 18 April the ships set sail again and came down to the south-east, discovering an inhabited island (Tucopia) with a high rounded peak on 21 April 1606, the latitude being taken as 12 degrees south. They proceeded on a south and south-west course, and on 25 April 1606 came in sight of a very high island (San Marcos), on which they saw inhabitants and crops. The latitude was taken as $14\frac{2}{3}$ degrees. The same day they saw to the south a great land, and north-west of San Marcos, at an estimated distance of 8 leagues, another island (Virgen Maria), with a rock in mid-channel between the two. On the 26th, as they steered for Virgen Maria, they saw another island to the north-west with very high mountains. Virgen Maria was estimated to be about 30 leagues in circumference, and the island to the north of it 50 leagues. Friendly contacts were made with some of the inhabitants of Virgen Maria who came out in boats. On the 27th they saw a 'great land with high mountains', and since they could not get to the north-west on account of calms and adverse winds, they decided to go to this great land, which bore south of Virgen Maria. While off the west of Virgen Maria on the 29th, they saw an island to the north-west of the island which they had seen on the 26th to the north-west of Virgen Maria, this new island being smaller and very high. On 1 May they arrived in a large bay (St. Philip and St. James) in the great land, which they called Austrialia del Espiritu Santo.

The island to the south-east of the Duffs was the modern Tikopia, an isolated island with a 1,200-foot peak, the latitude of which is a shade over 12 degrees south. San Marcos, the very high

[1] Gill, W., *Gems from the Coral Islands*, vol. ii (London, 1856), pp. 273-4.

island south and south-west of Tikopia, was Mero Lava in the
Banks group, which rises to a peak of 2,900 feet. The great land
seen to the south of Mero Lava on 25 April was one or more of
the north-eastern islands of the New Hebrides group, of which
Maewo (sometimes called Aurora) is the nearest to Mero Lava.
Virgen Maria was Gaua—still sometimes called Santa Maria—in
the Banks group, the rock seen between it and Mero Lava being
Merig. The two islands seen north-west of Gaua were Vanua
Lava, and Ureparapara, which rises to 2,400 feet on the western
side. The great land of Austrialia del Espiritu Santo was the northernmost island of the New Hebrides, the modern Espiritu Santo.

After various adventures at Espiritu Santo, the flagship, with
Quiros and Leza, became separated from the other two ships and
eventually returned by the North Pacific route to New Spain. While
on a north and then north-east course from Espiritu Santo, they
sighted, on 8 July 1606, at a distance of 4 to 5 leagues, a small island
(Buen Viage) which was not high, in $3\frac{3}{4}$ degrees north.

This island must have been Makin Meang, the northernmost of
the Gilberts.

After Quiros's departure, Prado and Torres, with the *San Pedro*
and the *zabra*, made some discoveries of their own. Their own
accounts and maps are the authorities for these.

Prado and Torres first went far enough around Espiritu Santo to
think that it was an island and not an extensive continent. They may
have seen Malekula to the south. They then went south-west to $20\frac{1}{2}$
degrees south, and having found no more land, struck north-west. On
a date in July 1606, given by Prado as the 14th, they came to very
high land running east and west, which they identified with New
Guinea. Being unable to go to the east on account of adverse winds,
they ran west. Torres says that the land which was first encountered
was in latitude $11\frac{1}{2}$ degrees south, Prado says 12 degrees. Prado states
that they ran along shoals extending out from the coast without finding
an opening, that on the sixth day they found some lofty islets shaped
like sugar loaves, and that subsequently they went in among numbers
of islands, on some of which they made landings, and found an extensive bay on one of them which they called San Millan. One of the
maps sent by Prado to Spain shows the Baya de San Millan and islands
round it. This map contains legend saying that the area in it was discovered by Torres in $10\frac{2}{3}$ degrees south on 18 July 1606 (see Plate II).

PLATE II

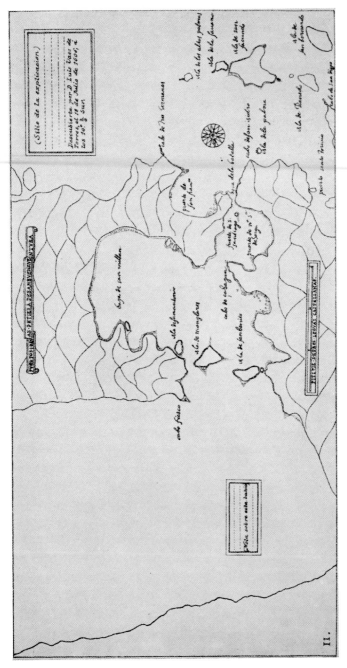

Prado's Chart of Basilaki and Environs

The map sent by Prado shows that the Bay of San Millan was Jenkins Bay on the west coast of Sideia, which with Basilaki and other islands lies east of the south-eastern extremity of New Guinea, from which they are divided by China Strait. The latitude of Jenkins Bay is 10½ degrees south. These facts, coupled with the details in the accounts, show that the high land which was first encountered was Tagula, the south-easternmost island of the Louisiade Archipelago, the southern portion of which is in 11½ degrees, with a barrier reef on the south. The ships then ran west along the barrier reefs of the Louisiade Archipelago and so came to the high islands to the east of New Guinea, of which Sideia is one. The dates of these discoveries are not entirely clear, apart from their being in mid-July 1606.

Prado says that the people they saw in Sideia and adjacent islands were light-coloured, and were naked apart from coconut matting round their middles. They ate fruit, yams, and coconuts, and kept pigs, dogs, and turtles. The Spaniards saw well made fishing-nets, pearl-shell, and stone tools with wooden handles. The arms of the islanders were wooden clubs, small darts, and shields. There were many varicoloured parrots on these islands, as well as magpies.

The discoveries of Pedro Fernandez de Quiros in 1606 may be summarized as follows: On 26 and 29 January 1606 he discovered Ducie and Henderson respectively, to the south-east of the Tuamotu Archipelago, a landing being made on Henderson. On 3, 4, 9, 10, 12, 14, and 15 February 1606, respectively, he discovered Marutea, the Actaeon group, Vairaatea, Hao, Amanu, Raroia, and Takume in the Tuamotu Archipelago, landings being made on Hao. On 21 February 1606 he discovered, or rediscovered after Magellan (see section 2), Caroline Island, a landing being made. On 2 March 1606 he discovered Rakahanga in the northern Cooks, a landing being made. On 7 April 1606 he discovered the Duff Islands, landings being made. On 21 April 1606 he discovered Tikopia. On 25 April 1606 he discovered Mero Lava, Gaua, and Merig in the Banks Islands, and Maewo and possibly other north-eastern islands of the New Hebrides. On 27 April 1606 he discovered Espiritu Santo in the New Hebrides, landings being subsequently made. On 26 and 29 April 1606 he discovered Vanua Lava and Ureparapara in the Banks Islands. On 8 July 1606 he discovered Makin Meang in the Gilbert Islands.

The contributions of Diego de Prado and Luis Vaez de Torres were as follows: In June 1606 they may have discovered Malekula in the New Hebrides. On a date given by Prado as 14 July 1606 they discovered Tagula, the south-easternmost island of the Louisiade Archipelago. In the following few days they skirted the southern barrier reefs of that archipelago to the west of Tagula, and discovered the islands east of the south-eastern extremity of New Guinea of which Sideia is one, staying for a time at the latter island.

15. Some Suppositious Early Discoveries

(a) NAMES IN OLD MAPS

IN 1786 the French explorer La Pérouse (see section 40) concluded that Juan Gaetan, the chronicler of Villalobos's expedition (see section 7), discovered the Hawaiian Islands in 1542. He reached this view because certain islands called by the Spaniards 'la Mesa', 'los Majos', and 'la Disgraciada' were in his opinion identical with the Hawaiian Islands, La Mesa, meaning The Table, being supposed by La Pérouse to be a reference to the mountain of Maunoloa in the island of Hawaii.[1] A variant of the same suggestion was given in the Spanish archives, where a chart showing the Hawaiian Islands under Cook's name Sandwich Islands, and containing a note saying that Juan Gaetan discovered these islands in 1555, calling them Islas de Mesa, was found.[2]

In the year 1542 Villalobos's expedition crossed the Pacific from Mexico, encountering three of the Revilla Gigedo Islands relatively near the American coastline. In the latter part of 1543 Villalobos sent the *San Juan* on an attempt to return to North America,

[1] *Voyage of La Pérouse*, ed. Milet-Mureau, M. L. A. (London, 1798), vol. i, pp. 85–95. Cf. Burney, J., *Discoveries*, vol. v (London, 1817), p. 161.

[2] Fornander, A., *An Account of the Polynesian Race*, vol. ii (London, 1880), pp. 361–3.

during which it encountered some of the Marianas and Bonins. Gaetan, an Italian, attained notice because the Italian historian Ramusio published Gaetan's account of Villalobos's expedition in his well-known collection. There is no known record, and no good reason to believe, that Gaetan made another voyage in the Pacific in 1555. Nor is there any record of an off-shore voyage into the Pacific between Villalobos and Legaspi in the detailed archives of New Spain as published in the eighteenth century. The late charac- ter of the chart and note referring to Gaetan's supposed discovery is shown by the use of Cook's name Sandwich Islands, which was not current until the last two decades of the eighteenth century.

In a chart found by the Englishman Anson in a Spanish vessel captured by him near Manila in 1743,[1] three islands 'La Mesa', 'Los Mojos', and 'La Disgraciada' are shown in or about latitudes 16 to 18 degrees north, and relatively near the American coast. It is plain that this, or a similar chart or record, was the basis for La Pérouse's reference to the islands called by the Spaniards 'la Mesa', 'los Majos', and 'la Disgraciada', and for later references of the same character. In a number of other Spanish navigation charts of the North Pacific current in the eighteenth century,[2] the name La Mira, but not La Mesa, appears close to others of the names in Anson's captured chart, giving the strong impression that La Mesa in the latter chart was a variant for or mistake for the name La Mira. The name or description *Mira como vas*, meaning 'Watch how you go', occurs in several early Spanish navigation charts. Anson's chart has a number of obvious misspellings. The descrip- tion of Maunaloa as a table is fanciful, since it is a typical rugged volcanic mountain. La Pérouse himself did not see Maunaloa.

In a map by the Dutch geographer Ortelius, dated 1570,[3] three islands Los Mauges, La Vezina, and La Desgraciada are shown relatively near China and Japan somewhere round 19 and 18 de- grees north. Perhaps they relate to the islands seen by the *Trinidad* of Magellan's expedition in the Marianas including the Maug

---

[1] Walter, R., *Voyage* (London, 1748).
[2] Burney, J., *Discoveries in the South Sea*, vol. v (London, 1817), pp. 157–62.
[3] Reproduced in Dahlgren, E. W., *The Discovery of the Hawaiian Islands* (Uppsala, 1917).

Islands (see section 2). In another map in Ortelius's Atlas dated 1592,[1] the names 'Vezina' and 'Desgraciada' are repeated, but 'Mauges' has become 'Monges'. The three islands of the Revilla Gigedo group named by Villalobos S. Thomé, Annublada, and Roca Partida are shown by Ortelius relatively near the American coastline. In Anson's captured chart Roca Partida is shown relatively near the American coastline, Annublada and S. Thomé have disappeared, Los Mojos and La Disgraciada, which are obvious variants of the Mauges or Monges and the Desgraciada of the earlier cartographers, have been shifted across to the Eastern Pacific, and La Mesa is shown near Roca Partida.

These examples show that map-makers, being unable to relate previous maps and charts to the realities of Pacific geography, particularly in reference to longitude, made arbitrary selections from and alterations in them.

It is manifest that the suggestions that either Gaetan or anyone else discovered the Hawaiian Islands before Cook were purely speculative and have no evidence to support them.

In Anson's captured chart (see above) there is shown a sequence of islands in latitudes of about 8 to 11 degrees north, to the south of an island in 14 degrees which appears to be Taongi, discovered by Salazar (see section 3). Some of the islands in this sequence are unnamed, others having the names Barbudos, Picadores, La Perfanes, Casbobos, and Islas Arecites appear. Burney, an English historian of Pacific exploration in the early nineteenth century at a time when the geography of Micronesia was still obscure, thought these names were evidence of some otherwise unknown Spanish discoveries.[2] The disposition of these islands as a whole, however, bears no discernible resemblance to any actual sequence of islands, but again gives the impression of being derived at second or third hand from old charts and maps by arbitrary selection. Barbudos was no doubt a reminiscence of Legaspi's name for Mejit (see section 8), while Islas Arecites presumably represents Villalobos's

---

[1] Reproduced in *The Discovery of the Solomon Islands*, ed. Lord Amherst and Thomson, B., vol. i (London, 1901).

[2] Burney, J., *Discoveries in the South Sea*, vol. ii (London, 1806), pp. 195–6; vol. v (London, 1817), pp. 157–62.

Arrecifes (see section 7). Barbudos became a vague geographical term for the northern Marshall atolls, as Arrecifes did for the western Carolines. Another name in early maps which suggested to Burney an otherwise unknown discovery was Gaspar Rico. The pilot of the *San Juan*, one of the vessels of Villalobos's expedition, was named Gaspar Rico. An island named Gaspar Rico appears in early maps of the north coast of New Guinea in association with other names showing that it was one of the coastal islands seen by the *San Juan* during the exploration of that coast by Retes, although it does not appear in the extant accounts.

There is abundant evidence that varying names were frequently given in the accounts of the early Pacific voyages by one or other of the participants to the islands that were encountered. There is also evidence that navigation charts of the early Spanish voyages containing differing place-names from those in the extant accounts were known to the early geographers and cartographers.

That a chart (or charts) of the exploration of the north coast of New Guinea by Retes was in fact known to some sixteenth-century cartographers appears plain from a consideration of the maps of the aforesaid cartographers. Thus Plancius's well-known world map, published in Amsterdam under date 1594, contains a quite realistic representation of the north coast of New Guinea as far east as Astrolabe Bay with names partly recapitulating those of the extant accounts of Retes's exploration and partly varying from or adding to them. This is not surprising, since a chart intended as a guide to navigators had a different purpose from that of a written report or official account. The map of Herrera published in 1601 gives somewhat the same representation as Plancius, and Herrera, who had access to the Spanish royal archives, says in his text that the area marked Natividad de Nuestra Señora was the farthest point of New Guinea that had been attained up to that time. This area is in latitude 5 degrees south, according with the statement of Juan Pablo de Carrion, a survivor of Villalobos's expedition, that this was as far as the *San Juan* went. This is the Astrolabe Bay area, and accords with the location of the name 'Natividad de Nuestra Señora', as in Herrera's map (see section 7 and reproduction of map, Plate I). When Tasman thought he had reached the east of

New Guinea when in fact he was still in the Bismarck Archipelago, he referred to a 'Cabo Santa Maria' as shown on a chart. This was no doubt a variant for 'Natividad de Nuestra Señora', both referring to the Virgin Mary (see section 18 and cited analysis by Reche).

A chart of New Guinea, published in 1700 in the collection of French marine charts entitled *Suite du Neptune françois*,[1] showed what purported to be the north, west, and south coasts of New Guinea with Spanish place-names. A map of New Guinea by Robert de Vaugondy, reproduced in Charles de Brosses's *Histoire des Navigations aux Terres Australes* (Paris, 1756), also gives a similar representation, with both Spanish and Dutch place-names. De Brosses's reproduction of the latter caused Cook on his first voyage (see section 33) to surmise that New Guinea had been circumnavigated by the Spanish and Dutch. The supposed east coast of New Guinea, however, in both these maps is palpably an arbitrary joining up of the eastern terminal point of Retes's exploration, i.e. the Natividad de Nuestra Señora or Astrolabe Bay area, with the commencement of Prado's and Torres's exploration from Basilaki west (see section 14). The fairly realistic representations of the south coast of New Guinea in these maps, with Spanish place-names partly recapitulating, partly varying, and partly adding to those in the extant accounts, can, on the same lines as the north coast detail in the early maps of New Guinea in relation to Retes's exploration, be satisfactorily explained as being derived from a chart or charts of Prado's and Torres's exploration, eked out in Vaugondy's case with Dutch material from their later explorations.

The inability of the sixteenth-, seventeenth-, and early eighteenth-century navigators and cartographers to fix locations accurately by longitude, coupled with the varying place-names given in the early records and the probability that charts with other varying names were known in earlier times, makes it unlikely that any real evidence of voyages in the Pacific Islands which are not otherwise known can be deduced from early maps.

A discussion of 'Iave la Grande' in the 'Dieppe' maps of 1542

---

[1] Reproduced in Beaglehole, J. C. (ed.), Introduction, in *The Journals of Captain James Cook*, vol. i (Cambridge, 1955), p. clviii.

and after, and of Terra Australis in the world maps of Mercator, Ortelius, Hondius, Plancius, and Wytfliet, is more relevant to the discovery of Australia and Torres Strait than to that of the Pacific Islands, unless and until there is some evidence that any hypo-thetical voyagers through Torres Strait in the sixteenth century also encountered some of the islands east of New Guinea.

(b) A NOTE BY HAKLUYT

The following note, under the heading 'A note of Australia del Espiritu Santo, written by Master Hakluyt', appears in Purchas's work on exploration:[1]

'Simon Fernandez, a pilot of Lisbon, told me Richard Hakluyt, before other Portugals in London, the 18th of March, 1604; that he having been in the city of Lima in Peru, did perfectly under-stand that four ships and barks departed from the said city of Lima about the year 1600, in the month of February, towards the Philippinas. Their General was a mestizo, that is to say, the son of a Spaniard and an Indian woman. And that seeking to make way toward the Philippinas, they were driven with strong Northern winds to the south of the equinoctial line, and fell in with divers rich countries and islands as it seemeth, not far from the Isles of Salomon. . . . They report that this place is two months sailing from Lima, and as much back again.

'Concerning this voyage also, the Licentiate, Luis de Tribaldo, a gentleman of quality in the Conde de Villa Mediana, the Spanish Ambassador's house, told me Richard Hakluyt, that two years past he saw at Madrid, a Captain of quality suing for licence to conquer this place, and that he obtained the same. And that divers religious men and fathers were to go to convert them to Christianity. They arrived at their return from this voyage at Peru, in the month of August.'

The circumstances set out in the first paragraph bear a resem-blance to those of Mendaña's second expedition, comprising as it did four vessels of different types which discovered islands reputed to be near the Isles of Solomon, the survivors reaching the Philip-pines. The second reference no less strongly suggests Quiros's

[1] Purchas, S., *Purchas his Pilgrimes*, vol. iv (London, 1625), p. 1432.

expedition of 1606, this 'captain of quality' having in fact pleaded his case at the Spanish court. The reports appear to have had the garbled character which is usual in accounts at third or fourth hand, and the references have no claim to be derived from otherwise unknown discoveries. They are, however, evidence of the way reports of voyages were passed round the ports and capitals of the world.

(c) A RESERVATION CONCERNING POSSIBLE UNKNOWN DISCOVERIES

Of necessity nothing can be said of any encounters with undiscovered islands which may have been made by the lost ships which were recorded as having entered the Pacific but were not heard of again. It is a reasonable surmise that most of these foundered or were wrecked, for survivors that might have reached established ports might be expected to have borne witness in some way or other to their experiences. It is indeed remarkable how, through the freemasonry of the sea, knowledge of the traverses of the Pacific in the exploration period became disseminated, being indeed rare and wonderful events. In any case 'discovery' implies that the fact was demonstrable through records.

There remains a small residue of early European voyages across the Pacific which have been recorded as successfully accomplished in the days when numbers of islands still remained undiscovered, but for which adequate documentation of islands that may have been encountered is not extant. The voyages of Diogo da Rocha and Francisco de Castro (see section 4), and of Balthasar de Cordes (see section 13) are cases in point. Another instance is the voyage of Maarten Gerritszoon Vries referred to in section 19 hereafter, and that of Oliver of Edwards's expedition (see section 47).

Perhaps some unknown ships encountered islands in the Pacific without leaving any substantial record, either direct or oblique. It may well be considered that, for the reasons given in the present section, there is no real evidence of any. Nevertheless, it is desirable to keep in mind that the word discovery, both in the Pacific and elsewhere, means the first European or American discovery so far as this can be ascertained from known records.

16. Jacob Le Maire

IN the year 1616 a Dutch ship named the *Eendracht* crossed the Pacific from the east on an exploratory expedition for commercial purposes. The President was Jacob Le Maire and the sailing master was Willem Cornelisz. Schouten. An account attributed to Schouten and associates, which is obviously that of an experienced nautical observer in possession of authoritative data, was published in 1618. Virtually the same account with minor variations and additions, attributed to Le Maire, was published in 1622.[1] The nautical data cited hereafter are taken from the first published account. It is usual to speak of this voyage as that of Le Maire and Schouten, but Le Maire was the undoubted head of the expedition.

Leaving Juan Fernandez on 3 March 1616 the ship proceeded towards the north-west until 24 March. When in latitude 15 degrees south the course was changed to west. On 10 April 1616 they came to a small low tree-covered island with an internal lagoon, on which a landing was made. Three dogs but no inhabitants were seen, the island being called Honden (Dogs). Its latitude was taken as 15 degrees 12 minutes. On 14 April 1616 they came in the evening to a low large inhabited island extending north-east and south-west. They approached the north side, and then ran during the night an estimated distance of 10 leagues to the south-west end of the island, where a landing was made. The distances in the account confirm that the Dutch or German league or mile of about 4 geographical miles was meant. The latitude at the north end of this island was taken as 15 degrees south and at the south end as 15¼ degrees. The island, which was only a border surrounding a saltwater lagoon, was narrow although long. They called this island Sonder grondt (Bottomless). Leaving this island the same day that they reached its southern end, namely 15 April 1616, they continued to the west, and on 16 April 1616, at dawn, discovered another island to the north of them, at an estimated distance of 15 leagues from the previous one. The latitude of the ship on this day was taken as 14¾ degrees south. A landing party got some fresh water from a pit, the island being therefore called Waterlandt (Water Land). It was not inhabited. Leaving Waterlandt the same evening, 16 April 1616, the expedition resumed its westerly course, and on 18 April 1616, in the morning, discovered another low inhabited island to the

[1] Both are given in *De ontdekkingsreis van Jacob Le Maire en Willem Cornelisz. Schouten*, ed. Engelbrecht, W. A., and Herwerden, P. J. van (The Hague, 1945).

south-west, extending west-north-west and east-south-east as far as could be seen, distant from Waterlandt an estimated 20 leagues. The latitude near its northern coast was taken as 15 degrees 20 minutes south. The border of this island was covered with trees but the interior was a saltwater lagoon. A swarm of flies from this island infested the ship, from which the island was called Vlieghen (Flies). No further land was seen until 10 May.

A comparison of these data with charts and descriptions of the Tuamotu Archipelago will show that on 10 April 1616 Le Maire came to Pukapuka (Honden), a small detached atoll in latitude 14 degrees 50 minutes south; that on 14 April 1616 he came in the evening to Takaroa-Takapoto (Sonder grondt), two closely contiguous atolls extending over some 23 miles from north-east to south-west, between latitudes $14\frac{1}{3}$ and $14\frac{2}{3}$ degrees south, and sailed down the coasts of these atolls during the night without realizing that they were separated by a narrow channel (the actual sighting of Takapoto being, therefore, on 15 April 1616); that the following morning, 16 April 1616, they saw either Manihi or Ahe (Waterlandt) lying some 40 to 55 miles from Takapoto in about latitude $14\frac{1}{2}$ degrees south, and that a day and a half later, on 18 April 1616, they saw from the north Rangiroa (Vlieghen), the northern coast of which is around 15 degrees south. It is possible that Magellan discovered Pukapuka (see section 2). The other islands were new discoveries.

The only close contact made by the Netherlanders in this part of their voyage was with the islanders of Takapoto. They were of good stature and build. Their ears were pierced and they hung in them nails and other gifts they received. They were tattooed. They wore a small piece of matting or cloth round the middle. Their weapons were slings, clubs, and spears.

Leaving the Tuamotus on 18 April 1616, the expedition continued on a westerly course, sailing slowly or lying to at night, until 9 May, when at noon they came upon a double sailing canoe. On 10 May 1616 they came to a very high island, with another island, longer and flatter, 1 league to the south of it. They anchored at the northern island, called by them Cocos (Coconut Trees), the latitude being taken as a little more than 16 degrees south. They had both friendly and hostile contacts with the people of these two islands. As the result of an attack they called the southern island Verraders (Traitors). Leaving these islands on 13 May 1616 the expedition the next day, 14 May 1616, came to a small hilly island at an estimated distance from Cocos and Verraders of 30 leagues, the latitude being taken as 16 degrees south. This island, which was inhabited, was called Goede Hope (Good Hope).

These islands are unmistakable as the northern detached Tongan islands, Tafahi (Cocos), in a little under 16 degrees south, rising to 2,000 feet, Niuatobutabu (Verraders), a larger, more level island 350 feet high 4 miles south of Tafahi, and Niuafou (Goede Hope), a craggy volcanic island some 120 miles west of Tafahi. The canoe that was seen, from the accompanying drawing of it in the accounts, was of Tongan type, presumably making for the Samoa group, which lay about 100 miles north of the expedition's course.

The islanders of Tafahi and Niuatobutabu had large and small sailing canoes. They were big and well-proportioned, and had slit ears which were stretched almost to their shoulders. They traded coconuts, bananas, yams, fowls, and pigs.

Continuing on their way, the Netherlanders decided a few days later to go north-north-west in order to get to the north of New Guinea. On 19 May 1616 they discovered two high islands. They anchored in a bay at one of them, with a stream coming down from the mountains and through a valley at the head of the bay. The latitude of this bay was taken as just under 15 degrees south. The accompanying charts show the islands as being west-north-west and east-south-east of each other. These were called the Hoornse Eylanden (Hoorn Islands).

These islands were the modern Horne Islands, Futuna and Alofi. Futuna rises to 2,500 feet, Alofi to 1,300 feet. They are separated by a narrow channel about 1 mile wide, Alofi being south-east of Futuna. There is a cascade beyond the head of Sigave Bay in Futuna.[1]

Here the expedition stayed for almost a fortnight. The Dutch and the islanders, after some initial skirmishes, became friendly, and entertained one another with dancing, music, and ceremonial, and with the drinking of kava and feasting on pigs, yams, bananas, and coconuts. The colour of the people was between yellow and brown, and they were courageous, strong, and intelligent. No sign

[1] *Pacific Islands Pilot*, vol. ii, pp. 352-3.

of cultivation was seen. The houses were small, conical in shape, with thatched leaves on the outside.

Eighteen days after leaving the Horne Islands, the expedition, on 20 June 1616, saw land to the south-west. It proved to be a cluster of small, low islands with reefs and banks extending to the north and north-west. From these islands came two canoes, the men in them being tattooed and resembling the inhabitants of the Horne Islands. They were armed with bows and arrows. The latitude was taken as being 4 degrees 47 minutes south. On 22 June 1616 the ships came to a compact group of twelve or thirteen low, small islands named Marquen after the Dutch island of that name, the estimated distance from the previously seen islands being 32 leagues, the latitude 4 degrees 45 minutes south. On 24 June 1616 they came to three low islands, green and full of trees, two of them being thought to be 2 leagues in length, the third small. They named these Groene Eylanden (Green Islands). Passing north of these, the same afternoon they saw a high island to the north-west, called by them S. Jans (St. John's), on which were seven or eight hillocks. Beyond this island they came, on 25 June 1616, to high land which was thought to be New Guinea.

The first lot of islands were evidently Nukumanu, an atoll with many islets in $4\frac{1}{4}$ degrees south. The persistent southerly error in the latitudes of Le Maire's voyage south of the line can be taken to rule out Ontong Java 30 miles south of Nukumanu. When Tasman, following Le Maire's course, encountered Ontong Java (see section 18), he thought it was Le Maire's discovery, but did not know there were two atolls. The only islands which conform with the data for Marquen, the Groene Eylanden, S. Jans, and 'New Guinea' are the Tauu Islands, the Green Islands, the Feni Islands, and New Ireland. The Tauu Islands are a small cluster comprising some twenty low islets 130 miles west-north-west of Ontong Java. Tasman later commented on the resemblance of one conspicuous islet to the Dutch island of Marquen. The Green Islands, about 130 miles from the Tauu Islands, actually consist of five islands, but since three of them lie close together west of the largest, Nissan, their precise configuration would be obscured from the north-east. The Feni Islands consist of two islands close together, stated by the *Pacific Islands Pilot* to look like five rounded hummocks from a distance.[1] They lie 29 miles north-west of the

[1] *Pacific Islands Pilot*, vol. i, p. 431.

Green Islands. At a short distance beyond them is the east coast of New Ireland in the Bismarck Archipelago.

Landings were made on the coast of New Ireland, where black people, with some tattooing, chewing betel, and with holes in their noses in which they wore rings, were seen.

Le Maire now came north along the east coast of New Ireland. From some near-by islands came people with flat noses, thick lips, and wide mouths, in canoes of good workmanship. On 2 July 1616 they were abreast a large bay with high land beyond it. On 3 July 1616 the coast declined towards the south, and the expedition continued towards the west. In the afternoon they saw high land to the west, which the next day, 4 July 1616, proved to be part of a large number of islands, the latitude being taken as about 2½ degrees south. An accompanying chart describes them as '25 islands' and shows high land to the north-west of them. Beyond these islands the expedition came to a coast which proved to be the north coast of New Guinea.

These details show that Le Maire, in coming along the north-east coast of New Ireland, reached the strait dividing it from New Hanover on 2 July 1616, seeing the latter island as high land to the north-west, but did not realize they were separated, thinking he was crossing the mouth of a bay. Which of the off-shore islands in this area were seen by the expedition is doubtful. Those from which the canoes are specifically mentioned as coming appear to have been the Tabar Islands, which are the nearest of the off-shore islands immediately before the expedition would reach the 'bay' dividing New Ireland and New Hanover. It seems possible, however, that they saw the Tanga or Lihir Islands, each of which lies close to the New Ireland coast between the Feni Islands (S. Jans) and the Tabar Islands. There is no reason to think, on the other hand, that Le Maire's expedition had any sight of Mussau, a high island north-north-west of New Hanover, since no land which might correspond to it is mentioned either in the accounts or apparently shown in the accompanying chart. Tasman's very detailed data of his own passage in Le Maire's wake round the north of New Hanover similarly contain nothing which might correspond to Mussau. On 3 and 4 July 1616 Le Maire encountered the Admiralty Islands, the high land in the chart being Manus, and the '25 islands' to the south-east and south of it being the various islands of the Admiralty group to the south-east and south of Manus. Manus and others of the Admiralty Islands had already been discovered by Saavedra (see section 5), but since the precise details of Saavedra's discoveries apart from Manus are not known, some of the twenty-five islands referred to as having been seen by Le Maire's expedition may have been new discoveries, particularly those to the south-east of Manus, to which it is unlikely that Saavedra penetrated.

The discoveries of Jacob Le Maire were as follows: On 10 April 1616 he discovered, or rediscovered after Magellan (see section 2), Pukapuka in the Tuamotu Archipelago, a landing being made. On 14, 15, 16, and 18 April 1616, respectively, he discovered Takaroa, Takapoto, Manihi or Ahe, and Rangiroa, all in the Tuamotu Archipelago, landings being made on the second and third of these. On 10 May 1616 he discovered Tafahi and Niuatobutabu, and on 14 May 1616 Niuafou, all in the Tonga group. On 19 May 1616 he discovered the Horne Islands (Futuna and Alofi), landings being made. On 20 June 1616 he discovered Nukumanu. On 24 June 1616 he discovered the Green Islands and the Feni Islands in the Bismarck Archipelago. On 25 June 1616 he discovered New Ireland in the Bismarck Archipelago, landings being made. In the following few days one or more of the Tanga Islands, the Lihir Islands, and the Tabar Islands near the north-east coast of New Ireland were discovered. On 2 July 1616 Le Maire discovered New Hanover in the Bismarck Archipelago without realizing it was a separate island. On 3 and 4 July 1616 he discovered a number of islands in the Admiralty group to the south-east of Manus, subject to the unlikely possibility that he had been anticipated by Saavedra (see section 5). Le Maire also proved that New Guinea was not part of a great continent extending indefinitely to the east in tropical latitudes.

17. Gheen Hugo Schapenham (The Nassau Fleet)

IN 1623 a number of Dutch vessels sailed from Holland and attacked some of the Spanish possessions on the west coast of the Americas. The ships then crossed from New Spain to Guam, passing a low island surrounded by reefs some 10 days before reaching Guam. This island was no doubt Taongi, the detached northernmost atoll of the Marshalls, which had been discovered by Salazar (see section 3).

On 11 February 1625 the fleet sailed from Guam for the Moluccas. At this time the commander was Gheen Hugo Schapenham, sailing in the flagship *Eendracht*. The authority for the course is a journal written by an unknown but obviously knowledgeable member of the *Eendracht*'s crew.[1]

At noon on 14 February 1625, 3 days after leaving Guam, when the reading of latitude was 10½ degrees north, an island was seen at a distance to the west-south-west. The next morning, 15 February 1626, at 9 o'clock, they saw another island to the south-east, which was high land like Guam. Its latitude was taken as 9¾ degrees north. Its width from the north-east to the north-west points was estimated to be about 4 miles, the Dutch or German mile being about 4 geographical miles; and the breadth was considered to be about the same. A large reef ran into the sea from its north-eastern extremity. The island was inhabited and appeared to be well cultivated, some canoes putting off from the shore with people having long black hair and resembling the people of Guam in size and appearance.

The only sequence of two islands south of Guam in the vicinity of latitude 10 degrees north, the second of which is high, is Fais or Ulithi for the first, and Yap for the second. Fais had already been discovered, and Ulithi may have been (see sections 4 and 7). The account of the second island conforms with Yap, which has a ridge of hills in the western part rising to 600 feet, a projection of its reef to the north–north–east at its northern extremity, and extends from 9½ to 9¾ degrees north over some 15 miles.

[1] *Journael vande Nassausche Vloot* (Amsterdam, 1626), p. 93.

The encounter with Yap by the Nassau Fleet under Gheen Hugo Schapenham on 15 February 1626 is the first clearly established European contact with that atoll, although it is probable that it was discovered by Diogo da Rocha and may have been seen again by Francisco de Castro (see section 4), and was probably seen yet again by Villalobos (see section 7).

18. Abel Janszoon Tasman

ON 14 August 1642 an exploratory expedition consisting of two ships, the *Heemskerk* and the *Zeehaen*, set out from Batavia under the command of Abel Janszoon Tasman, with Frans Jacobszoon Visscher as chief pilot. The authority for the course of this expedition is the journal of Tasman, which is extant in two main copies with accompanying charts, illustrations, and minutes, including charts by or based on the nautical data of Visscher.[1]

Tasman passed south of Australia, discovering the modern Tasmania. On 5 December the expedition set off east from Australian waters, and on 13 December 1642, on which day the observed latitude was 42 degrees 10 minutes south, saw a large high land. The expedition breasted a point to the north-east, and anchored in a bay where some people came off in canoes and made a hostile attack on the *Zeehaen's* boat, killing four of its seven occupants. The ships bore east without finding a passage to the east, and then bore north, skirting coastline as far north as an observed latitude of 34 degrees 25 minutes. More people were seen on some islands off the northern cape. No landings were made. Charts of the coastline commencing at about latitude 43 degrees 10 minutes south, and some profile drawings of it were made. This land was called Staten Landt because it was conjectured that it might possibly be connected with Le Maire's Staten Land at the south of South America.

These details show that Tasman, on 13 December 1642, discovered New Zealand at a point slightly south of the north-western extremity of the South Island, that he came some way

[1] *Abel Janszoon Tasman's Journal*, ed. Heeres, J. E. (Amsterdam, 1898); *De reizen van Abel Janszoon Tasman . . .*, ed. Meyjes, R. P. (The Hague, 1919).

into Cook Strait without discovering that there was a passage to the east, and that he then skirted the west coast of the North Island. Cape Maria van Diemen and the Three Kings Islands, at the northern extremity, are the modern English names corresponding to those given by Tasman's expedition. The names Nova-Zeelandia or Nieuw Zeeland, from which New Zealand gets its modern name, were given by later Dutch geographers, no doubt because Hendrik Brouwer in 1643 showed that Le Maire's and Schouten's Staten Land was not a continent.

Tasman describes the Maoris of New Zealand who came out to his ships as being of ordinary height, their colour between brown and yellow, with black hair tied on top of their heads with a large white feather in the tuft. An accompanying illustration shows a double canoe.

Quitting New Zealand on 6 January 1643, Tasman went on a mainly northerly course for 13 days, and on 19 January 1643 came on a small, high, barren island looking like a woman's breasts. The latitude was taken as 22½ degrees south. It was christened Hooge Pijlstaerts Eylandt (High Tropic-bird Island). The next day the expedition came to two islands north-east of the former, lying nearly south-east and north-west of each other, with a passage between them, the one to the south-east being the higher, the northernmost, which was the larger, being a low-lying one. The latitude, at a point on the north-west coast of the northern island at which they anchored, was taken as 21⅓ degrees south. They called these islands Middelburch and Amsterdam. At Amsterdam they had many friendly contacts with the inhabitants. An accompanying illustration at the place of anchorage shows a narrow spit or isthmus. Setting out to the north-east on 24 January, they passed two high small islands and on the same day came to a group of islands consisting of one larger low-lying island with five smaller low-lying islands to the east and south-east of it, and seven more small islets to the north and north-east by north of it. To the north-west was a large, high island, close to the east of which was a round and much higher island. They anchored at the aforesaid large low-lying island with the smaller islets round it, in latitude 20½ degrees south, naming this island Rotterdam. Some accompanying illustrations show it as 'Anamocka', and depict other islands 'Namocaki', 'Amo', 'Amoa', 'Amango', Kaybaij', 'Amatafoa'. On 2 February 1643 they continued their voyage, passing west of the two high islands north-west of Rotterdam or 'Anamocka', and in the afternoon saw another high island north-east by east. They turned west when north of 17 degrees and did not see any more islands for 3 days.

These details record Tasman's discovery of the southern islands of the Tonga group. Hooge Pijlstaerts Island was Ata or Pylstart Island, in latitude 22 degrees 20 minutes, described by the *Pacific Islands Pilot* as having two peaks.[1] Middelburgh (Middelburch) and Amsterdam were Eua and Tongatabu, some 75 and 85 miles north-east of Ata, conforming in relative location and appearance with Tasman's description. The latitude of the north-western extremity of Tongatabu, which forms an elongated spit as depicted in the illustration of the anchorage, is 21 degrees. From Tongatabu Tasman's ships came up past Honga Hapai and Honga Tonga to Nomuka ('Anamocka'), about 55 miles to the north-east, seeing Nomuka Iki ('Namocaki') close by, and other islands of the Nomuka group, including Mango ('Amango'), to the east, and the nearer islands of the Kotu group to the north and north-east, and Tofua and Kao ('Amatafoa' and 'Kaybaij') to the north-west, the latter being 1,660 and 3,380 feet high respectively, and conforming to the drawing in Tasman's journal in shape and relative location. The island seen to the north-east of Tofua was Late, which is 1,700 feet high. Two charts of Tasman's passage in this area of the Pacific give very fair representations of these islands.

Tasman gives a number of details of the Tongans of Tongatabu and Nomuka in the seventeenth century. The contacts in both places were friendly, and the Dutchmen were given large supplies of pigs, fish, fowls, yams, and bananas in exchange for nails, knives, and clothes. At Tongatabu, in addition to small canoes, a large double one resembling that figured in Le Maire's journal was seen and drawn. Tasman visited a chief of Tongatabu and a village in Nomuka, where he saw gardens and fruit trees which were a pleasure to look at.

Continuing to the west for 3 days in or about 17 degrees latitude south, on 5 February 1643, at night, the expedition came on some more islands. The next morning they saw there were three small islets surrounded on all sides by shoals and reefs. They tacked to the south and

[1] *Pacific Islands Pilot*, vol. ii, p. 362.

found themselves confronted by a very large reef, with another to the north of them, but managed to get through it. All about them were reefs, and eighteen or nineteen islands. Their estimation was that they were in 17½ degrees south, although they could not get a sight. They made to the west-south-west till noon, then turned north, where they found themselves again confronted by reefs, but managed to get through them. In the evening they saw three hills which they thought to be islands. After plying back and forth during the night, they saw the island which on the previous evening had been north by west. Sailing to the north, the next day, 8 February, they saw another island, estimated to be in latitude 16 degrees south. Tasman comments that the weather and visibility were bad during their encounter with these reefs and islands. The two charts describe the reefs which were crossed as the Heemskerck's Shoals, and the islands beyond them as Prince William's Islands.

These details show that on 5 February 1643 Tasman came upon the chain of reefs and islets south of Nggele Levu in the Ringgold Islands sector of the Fiji group, this being the first European contact with that group. On 6 February 1643 he passed through that part of the Ringgold Islands known as the Nanuku Reef, came down towards Taveuni and the small islands immediately east of it, then turned north, and from 6 to 8 February 1643 passed between Vanua Levu and the Ringgold Islands, finally seeing Thikombia, the northernmost island of the Fiji group.

From Fiji Tasman's ships pursued a predominantly north-westerly course, and on 22 March 1643, at noon, sighted some very small islands, numbering close upon thirty, surrounded by a reef, from which another reef ran off to the north-west, the latitude being a shade over 5 degrees south. These islands were named Onthong Java. An illustration of them as seen from the south-west accompanies Tasman's description. Tasman identified them with the unnamed islands discovered by Le Maire after leaving the Hoorn Islands (see section 16). Continuing their westerly course, on 24 March 1643, the expedition came on more land showing as two islands south-east and north-west of each other, which they identified with Le Maire's Marcken. There were fifteen or sixteen islets, with one detached islet to the north-west. An accompanying illustration shows a large number of small islands as seen from the west. The latitude was taken as just under 5 degrees south. Here a canoe came off, the people looking rough and savage, with blacker skins than in the previous islands, and armed with bows and arrows. From these islands Tasman continued on for another

3 days, and on 28 March came on some islands which he identified with Le Maire's Groene Eylanden. They were green and beautiful, in latitude 4½ degrees south, and comprised two large islands and three smaller ones, the latter three being on the west side. From these islands Tasman could see a high island with two or three very small ones to the north-west, which he identified with Le Maire's S. Jans. Beyond it he came to the coast of what he thought was New Guinea.

The first lot of islands were those of the large atoll still known as Ontong Java (Luaniua), which runs from latitude 5½ to 5 degrees south, and conforms with the topography in Tasman's description. It was probably discovered by Mendaña (see section 10), but Tasman gave the first firm record of it. The other three lots of islands were the Tauu Islands, the Green Islands, and the Feni Islands, and the coast beyond, which Tasman thought was New Guinea, was the eastern coast of New Ireland. All these islands had been discovered by Le Maire.

Having reached New Ireland, Tasman skirted it to the north-west, passing three lots of off-shore islands which he called Anthony Caens Eylandt, Gerrit de Nijs Eylandt, and Visschers Eylandt, between 2 and 5 April 1643.

These were evidently the modern Tanga, Lihir, and Tabar Islands, which may have been seen by Le Maire and Schouten's expedition, although Tasman was the first to refer to them specifically.

On 7 April 1643, at a point called by Tasman Salmon Sweers Cape, he found the coast trended to the south, and therefore came south, thereby departing from Le Maire's westerly track. On 12 April 1643 Tasman saw a low, small island at a distance south by west. On 13 April 1643, high land was seen from south-west by west to east-south-east. On 15 April a tolerably high island was seen due north-west. Tasman then ran west along what he thought was the continuous north coast of New Guinea, making the specific comment that he did not find a through passage to the south to Cape Keerweer (on the north coast of Australia).

These details show that Tasman came along the north-east coast of New Ireland, past the northern extremity of New Hanover (Salmon Sweers Cape), and then south, passing between the Vitu Islands and Willaumez Peninsula on the north coast of New

Britain.[1] He did not realize that New Ireland, New Hanover, New Britain, New Guinea, and Australia were separated by straits, and thought that New Britain, Umboi, and Long Island formed a continuous coast with New Guinea.[2] He was the discoverer of the southern Vitu Islands and New Britain, since there is no reason to believe that any previous Europeans had reached this area.

Abel Janszoon Tasman's contributions to the discovery of the Pacific Islands were as follows: He discovered New Zealand on 13 December 1642, skirting the north-west coast of the South Island and the west coast of the North Island between that date and 5 January 1643. In the Tonga group he discovered Ata on 19 January 1643, Eua and Tongatabu on 20 January 1643, the Nomuka group, the Kotu group, Tofua, and Kao on 24 January 1643, and Late on 2 February 1643, making landings on Tongatabu and Nomuka. From 5 to 8 February 1643 he discovered most of the Ringgold Islands, Taveuni, the eastern side of Vanua Levu, and Thikombia, which together form the north-eastern sector of the Fiji Islands. On 22 March 1643 he gave the first firm report of Ontong Java, although it is probable that it was discovered by Mendaña (see section 10). Between 1 and 5 April 1643 he discovered, or rediscovered after Le Maire, the Tanga, Lihir, and Tabar Islands in the Bismarck Archipelago. From 12 to 15 April he discovered the southern Vitu Islands and New Britain in the Bismarck Archipelago. Tasman also proved that Australia did not extend indefinitely into the south-eastern areas of the Pacific Ocean.

[1] Tasman's course from New Hanover to New Britain and thence to New Guinea is plotted, with adjustments of Tasman's longitudes for his demonstrated persistent small error, by O. Reche in *Ergebnisse der Südsee-Expedition 1908–1910. II. Ethnographie B Melanesien*, vol. ii, part 1 (Hamburg, 1954), pp. 1–19.

[2] This is shown graphically in a chart containing data from Tasman's voyage now in the Mitchell Library, Sydney, Australia.

19. Maarten Gerritszoon Vries

SOMEWHERE around 1645 Maarten Gerritszoon Vries, one of the captains of the Dutch East India Company, made a voyage from Batavia along the north coast of New Guinea and as far as the western extremity of New Hanover, and thence to the Marianas.[1] No further details of this voyage are known. Vries may have encountered some of the previously undiscovered islands to the west of the Admiralty Islands, and possibly Mussau, Emirau, or Tench, lying north of and close to New Hanover.

20. The Spanish Penetration of the Marianas

IT has been seen that Magellan discovered Guam and Rota (see section 2), that Gonzalo Gomez de Espinosa discovered the Maug Islands and another island to the south of them which was presumably Agrigan or possibly Asuncion (see section 2), that Gonzalo de Vigo traversed the Marianas from the Maug Islands to Guam (see sections 2 and 3), that Bernardo de la Torre either discovered, or rediscovered after Vigo, three of the middle islands of the Marianas chain which were probably Farallon de Medinilla, Anatahan, and Sariguan (see section 7), that Rota was visited by the *San Jeronimo* in 1566 (see section 9), and that Huydecoper and William Adams probably rediscovered some of the Marianas in the vicinity of 16 degrees north (see section 13). By 1600, therefore, it is probable that all the Marianas from the Maug Islands to Guam had been seen at least once by one or other of these early voyagers. Nevertheless, the only islands which can be precisely identified in these earlier accounts are Guam, Rota, and the Maug Islands.

[1] Heeres, J. E., 'Abel Janszoon Tasman: His Life and Labours', in *Abel Janszoon Tasman's Journal*, ed. Heeres, J. E. (The Hague, 1898), ch. xiii, pp. 110–11.

In 1600 the Spanish vessel *Santa Margarita* was wrecked on Saipan, some of the survivors being rescued in 1601 by the *Santo Tomas* and in 1602 by the *Jesus Maria*, the latter vessel being 40 days in getting clear of the Marianas. In 1638 the *Nuestra Señora de la Concepción* was wrecked on Saipan, some of the ship's company went from Saipan to Guam, and a few survivors got to Manila in two boats. The northern islands of the Marianas were seen on occasion by Spanish ships returning from Manila to North America.[1]

In 1688 and the years following, Spanish missionaries, of whom Luis de Morales was the foremost as far as exploration was concerned, established the geography of the Marianas, comprising Guam, Rota, Agiguan, Tinian, Saipan, Farallon de Medinilla, Anatahan, Sariguan, Guguan, Alamagan, Pagan, Agrigan, Asuncion, the Maug Islands, and Farallon de Pajaros (Urac). It was then that the name Marianas was adopted.[2]

21. The Spaniards Learn of the Western Carolines

IN 1686 a Spanish vessel fell in with a large inhabited island which was named La Carolina in honour of Charles II of Spain. The accounts of this encounter[3] vary somewhat, but agree in placing the island in question at no great distance to the south or southwest of Guam.

The most likely view of the identity of this island was that it was Ulithi, the north-westernmost island of the Carolines, which is a very large atoll, and the nearest of the Caroline Islands to Guam.

[1] Dahlgren, E. W., *The Discovery of the Hawaiian Islands* (Uppsala, 1917), pp. 53–56, 85, 93; Burney, J., *Discoveries in the South Sea*, vol. v (London, 1817), pp. 159–60.

[2] Gobien, C. le, *Histoire des Isles Marianes* (Paris, 1700).

[3] Cited in Dahlgren, E. W., *The Discovery of the Hawaiian Islands* (Uppsala, 1917), pp. 96–97.

The details given are not, however, enough to establish it beyond doubt as Ulithi rather than Yap or Fais, which also lie south-west of Guam on the northern fringe of the Carolines. Yap and Fais, and possibly Ulithi, had been discovered (see sections 4, 7, and 17).

The name given to this island, La Carolina, in due course became the genesis of the name for the whole group of the Caroline Islands.[1]

It was in 1696 established to the Spaniards that there were a large number of islands in this area, for in that year some Caroline Islanders who were blown to the Philippines gave some Spanish missionaries the names of most of the western Carolines.[2]

22. Edward Davis

FROM 1680 to 1690 various companies of buccaneers preyed on the Spanish settlements on the west coast of the Americas. One of the most celebrated was Edward Davis, with whom the even more celebrated William Dampier sailed for a time. Lionel Wafer, a surgeon in Davis's company, has left an account of a discovery by Davis in the *Batchelor's Delight* in 1687,[3] and Dampier, although not a member of Davis's company at the time, has given a note of what Davis himself said to him later about it.[4]

Wafer says that, from the Galapagos Islands (off the coast of the modern Ecuador), at a date in 1687 which Wafer does not specify, Davis went south intending to touch nowhere until he came to the island of Juan Fernandez (off the coast of Chile). From a point in 12½ degrees south and 'about 150 leagues from the main of America', they 'steered S by E ½ Easterly' until they came to the latitude of 27 degrees 20 minutes south, when they fell in with a low, sandy, flat island, 'without any guard of rocks'. They stood in within ¼ mile of the shore, and could see it plainly, for it was a clear morning. To the westward,

---

[1] Gobien, C. le, *Histoire des Isles Marianes* (Paris, 1700), p. 377.
[2] Clain, P., in letter of 10 June 1697, quoted in Gobien, C. le, *Histoire des Isles Marianes* (Paris, 1700), pp. 395–410.
[3] Wafer, L., *A New Voyage* (London, 1934), pp. 125–6.
[4] Dampier, W., *A Collection of Voyages* (London, 1729), vol. i, p. 352.

about 12 leagues by judgment, they saw a range of high land, which they took to be islands, 'for there were several partitions in the prospect'. It seemed to extend for about 14 or 16 leagues, and great flocks of birds came from it. Some of the crew wanted to go to this land but the captain would not agree. The small island 'bore from Copiapo almost due east 500 leagues', and 'from the Galapagos under the line was distant 600 leagues'. Copiapo was in Chile. They resumed the voyage and in due course at the end of the year they reached Juan Fernandez.

Dampier says that Captain Davis told him that while standing to the south from the Galapagos Islands for wind to bring him about the Tierra del Fuego, they saw, in the latitude of 27 degrees south, at about 500 leagues from Copayapo on the coast of Chile, a small sandy island, and to the westward of it a long tract of high land, trending to the north-west out of sight.

There are some puzzling features about these accounts. From the description of the course it is hard to see how the ship could have been borne as far west as the estimated position of the land that was seen. Easter Island, which is high in itself, lies well to the west of the estimated position of the low, sandy island, and has no low sandy island near it on the east. Sala y Gomez, some 200 miles east of Easter Island, might well be described as a low, sandy island, but has no high land near it on the west. San Felix and San Ambrosio, two islands with high ground lying close together between the Galapagos Islands and Juan Fernandez, are relatively near the American coast. On the other hand, the report of the sighting cannot be dismissed as imagination, being seen at close quarters and described with circumstantial detail, by two separate witnesses, so far at least as the low, flat, sandy island is concerned. There is, however, abundant evidence that supposed high land seen at a distance in unknown waters without being investigated has often proved later not to exist, being presumably a sight of cloud banks, while large flocks of birds frequent all desert islands. If notice were taken of the statements both by Wafer and Dampier that the low island was a great distance west of Chile, it could possibly be argued that it was Sala y Gomez, and that the supposed land to the west was a cloud bank. When Wallis was in the vicinity (see section 30), he saw 'a large flock of brown birds, flying to the westward, and something which had the appearance of high land in the same quarter', toward which he ran till two in the morning without coming to any land. If, on the other hand, these distances are discounted, then Carrington's view[1] that Davis came on San Felix and San Ambrosio, which are on a course from the Galapagos Islands to Juan Fernandez and in the stated latitude, and agree reasonably well with the descriptions given by Wafer and Dampier, would fit all the details.

The important point, so far as the present study is concerned, is that Davis's Land was plainly not Easter Island.

23. Juan Rodriguez and Bernard de Egui

IN 1696 a ship of which one Juan Rodriguez was pilot discovered an island named 'Farroilep', with two smaller islands near it. The latitude was thought to be between the 10th and 11th degree of latitude, and the distance from Guam under 45 leagues. The Spanish missionary in Guam who recorded this discovery, Juan Cantova, later made a chart setting out with reasonable accuracy the positions of most of the western Carolines from information given him by some people from 'Farroilep' who had been driven to Guam in a storm in 1721. Cantova shows 'Farroilep' in a position south-east of Guam.[2]

Faraulep, an atoll immediately south of Guam, consists of three islands, of which Faraulep, from which the atoll takes its name, is the chief, with two small islands near it, Pigue and Eate. The latitude of Faraulep is 8½ degrees. One of the islets of Ulithi is Falalap, and its latitude is 10½ degrees, but Ulithi consists of a large number of islets, which does not agree with the description of 'Farroilep' as consisting of an island with two smaller islands near it. Furthermore, Cantova himself knew of both Faraulep and Falalap, for in his chart he shows the Falalap of Ulithi, under the name 'Falalep', as one of the islands visited by a ship under the command of one Bernard de Egui in 1712, and shows Faraulep, with its two near-by islands, as the island from which the islanders

---

[1] Carrington, H., *The Discovery of Tahiti* (London, 1948), pp. 274–6.

[2] Cantova, J., in *Choix de lettres ... des missions étrangères* (Paris, 1770), pp. 188–247.

driven in the storm had come and as the island discovered by Juan Rodriguez. Cantova therefore had no doubt, from the descriptions of Faraulep given by the islanders, as compared with the accounts of 'Farroilep' given by Rodriguez, that they were identical.

Cantova's evidence, and in particular the description of 'Farroilep' as an island with two smaller islands near it, establishes Juan Rodriguez as the discoverer of Faraulep in 1696.

Bernard de Egui must be credited with the first firm report of Ulithi, although it is probable that it had already been discovered (see sections 4, 17, and 21). Egui made this contact on 6 February 1712, in a vessel named the *Santo Domingo*, while coming from Guam.[1]

24. William Dampier

THE ex-buccaneer William Dampier, whose writings about his earlier voyages had attracted much attention, was sent in the year 1699 by the British Admiralty as commander of the *Roebuck* on a voyage of exploration of the unknown east coast of New Guinea and New Holland (Australia). Dampier's own account is the authority for this voyage.[2]

Dampier came round the Cape of Good Hope to the western coast of Australia, and thence via Timor to the north coast of New Guinea. After standing off the coast while coming east, he decided to come south again. On 25 February 1700 he came to an island appearing to be about 9 or 10 leagues long, and mountainous, which he named Matthias. He stood to overnight, and next morning saw a fairly low island to the east of the other, about 2 to 3 leagues long, with a small, low, island at the south-west point joined to it by a reef. He came along the south side, intending to look more closely at the island, but was blown to the east by a gale, for which reason he called the island Squally.

[1] Krämer, A., *Ergebnisse der Südsee-Expedition 1908–1910. II. Ethnographie B Mikronesien*, vol. iii, part 1 (Hamburg, 1917), p. 75.

[2] Dampier, W., 'A Voyage to New Holland', in *A Collection of Voyages* (London, 1729), vol. iii.

These two islands were the modern Mussau and Emirau, to the north of New Hanover, in the Bismarck Archipelago. Mussau is a large, high island, and Emirau a relatively low island 13 miles south-east of Mussau, with an islet and reef at the south-west extremity as described by Dampier. These islands may have been seen by Vries (see section 19).

Dampier then skirted the east coast of New Ireland and after passing the Feni Islands came to the unknown southern coast of New Ireland and New Britain, thinking it was the mainland coast of New Guinea. He came past a large 'bay' which he called St. George's Bay, not realizing it was in fact the strait separating New Ireland and New Britain. A landing was made on the south coast of New Britain. Dampier thus came to the western end of New Britain. In the last days of March 1700 he passed through the strait separating New Britain from New Guinea, proving that they were not continuous. He called the strait Dampier's Passage. It is usually called Dampier Strait today. He gave the name Nova-Britannia, translated in his preface as New-Britain, to the land east of the strait, thinking the modern New Britain, New Ireland, and New Hanover were continuous land.

Dampier was again in the Pacific in 1705, this time on a privateering expedition against the Spanish settlements. He came across the Pacific in a small Spanish vessel which he had captured, and stayed for a time at Rota, the island in the Marianas immediately north of Guam. The authority for this voyage is the account by William Funnell, a member of Dampier's crew.[1]

From Rota Dampier came south-west. The date of departure is not given by Funnell. On 17 April 1705 Funnell says they 'saw the Island of Arracife, bearing E. by N., distant ten leagues. It seemed to be a very high island.' He did not know whether it was inhabited.

The thought that this was 'Arracife' no doubt arose from the occurrence of that name in the crude charts of the period, the origin being Villalobos's discovery of Los Arrecifes, namely Yap or Ulithi, the latter being low (see section 7). The only islands in the Carolines which could have been seen at a distance by Dampier and described as high islands are Fais and Yap, and of these the more probable identification is Yap because of the course to the

[1] Funnell, W., Narrative in *A Collection of Voyages* (London, 1729), vol. iv.

south-west of the Marianas and Yap's relatively greater height (600 feet). But both of these islands had been previously discovered (see sections 4, 7, and 17), so that Dampier's contribution to the discovery of the Pacific Islands was confined to that given in the following paragraph.

William Dampier was the discoverer of Mussau and Emirau, subject to the reservation that Vries is known to have been somewhere in this area when striking north from somewhere near New Hanover (see section 19). Dampier, in the last days of March 1700, discovered Dampier Strait, separating New Guinea from New Britain. He also proved that New Britain, New Ireland, and New Hanover were separate from Australia.

25. Woodes Rogers

In the years 1708–10 an English privateering expedition under the command of Woodes Rogers came into the Pacific from the east, and, after various conflicts with Spanish ships and settlements, sailed from California to Guam, and thence to the Moluccas. The expedition at this time consisted of the two original ships, the *Duke* and the *Dutchess*, and two captured ships. William Dampier was the chief pilot of the *Duke*, Rogers's ship. The authorities for the course are Rogers's own account, and an account by Edward Cooke, who had been put in command of one of the prizes.[1]

Leaving Guam on 21 March 1710, the expedition sailed for the Moluccas, going carefully on account of the possibility of encountering some of the islands which were known to lie between. On 10 April 1710 they passed a pleasant, low island, small, green, and full of trees, at a distance of about 4 or 5 leagues, the latitude being taken as 2 degrees 54 or 55 minutes north. They saw the trees long before the land. Three days later they reached Morotai.

The only islands in the vicinity of 3 degrees latitude north and 3 days' sailing distance to the northward from Morotai are Tobi

[1] Rogers, W., *A Cruising Voyage* (London, 1712); Cooke, E., *A Voyage to the South Sea* (London, 1712).

and Helen Reef, the southernmost islands of the western Carolines, some 150 miles from Morotai and 35 miles west and east of each other. Tobi, according to the *Pacific Islands Pilot*, is covered with coconut palms which attain a height of 118 feet, and Helen Reef, while consisting for the most part of reefs, has a low, thickly wooded islet at the northern end.[1]

The details given in the accounts are not enough to establish whether the island encountered by Woodes Rogers on 10 April 1710 was Tobi or Helen Reef. These islands may have been discovered by the Portuguese (see section 4).

26. Francisco Padilla

IN 1710 a Spanish ship named the *San Trinidad*, under the command of Francisco Padilla, with Josef Somera as pilot, went with some Spanish missionaries from Manila to find the islands which were known to exist to the east of the Philippines (see section 21). An account of this voyage was left by Somera.[2]

The Spaniards found, in latitude $5\frac{1}{4}$ degrees north, the two islands of Sonsorol, so named to them by the islanders themselves; and heard from the latter that the principal island 'Panloq' lay to the north-north-east, at a distance which the Spaniards judged to be probably about 50 leagues from Sonsorol. Sonsorol itself had already been discovered by Gonzalo Gomez de Espinosa (see section 2). Padilla decided to try to discover 'Panloq'. Leaving Sonsorol on 9 December 1710, he duly found 'Panloq' on 11 December 1710, the latitude being taken as 7 degrees 14 minutes north. Six canoes came off when the ship was a league off shore, and a skirmish took place. The ship passed between two islands, through a channel barely a league wide. On 13 December, without further contact, the ship returned to Sonsorol.

This is the first clearly established European contact with the Palau Islands, lying between latitudes 6 degrees 40 minutes and 8

[1] *Pacific Islands Pilot*, vol. i, pp. 507–8.
[2] Somera, J., cited in English by Burney, J., *Discoveries in the South Sea*, vol. v (London, 1817), pp. 12–16, from *Lettres . . . des missions étrangères* (Paris, 1781), vol. xi.

degrees 20 minutes north, some 150 miles north-east of Sonsorol. They may have been discovered by the Portuguese (see section 4). See also the discussion of Drake (section 11).

27. Jacob Roggeveen

IN 1722 Jacob Roggeveen crossed the Pacific from the east as the head of a Dutch exploratory expedition with commercial objects. Three ships entered the Pacific, namely the *Arend*, the *Thienhoven*, and the *Africaansche Galey*, but the *Africaansche Galey* was wrecked in the Tuamotus. The authorities for this voyage are the journals of Roggeveen himself, and of Cornelis Bouman, the captain of the *Thienhoven*.[1] Roggeveen's account is followed, with cited details from Bouman.

Roggeveen's first aim was to find the land reported by Davis (see section 22), supposed to be 500 leagues west of Copiapo in Chile. The expedition left Juan Fernandez on 17 March 1722. On 5 April 1722 a well-peopled hilly island, named by Roggeveen Paasch Eyland (Easter Island), was discovered, the latitude as they approached it being taken as 27 degrees 4 minutes south. The ships remained here until 13 April, during which time a landing was made on the island, and the presence of some large statues was noted.

This was the detached island known, from Roggeveen's name, as Easter Island, the latitude of which is 27 degrees south. It is not credible that this island was seen by Davis, for the reasons given in section 22.

The Dutchmen landed on Easter Island in force, headed by Roggeveen himself, with Bouman also in attendance. The following combines details from both their accounts. The people of Easter Island were well-proportioned, with big strong muscles. Their colour was not black, but pale-yellow or grey-brown, as could be seen from looking at the young men, who did not paint their bodies dark blue or were of higher rank and accordingly not obliged to do agricultural work. Their teeth were snow-white and

[1] *De reis van Mr. Jacob Roggeveen*, ed. Mulert, F. E. Baron (The Hague, 1911).

exceptionally strong, as shown by the fact that even the old people could crack hard nuts by biting them. The hair and beard of most of them was short, but some had their hair long and hanging over their backs or plaited and rolled together on the top of the head. Their clothing consisted of material which looked like a kind of cotton but was not woven or twined. It appeared to be dyed with red or yellow earth. The islanders had no utensils but calabashes. They cooked fowls by wrapping them in grass and putting them on glowing stones with leaves on top. Their huts consisted of a framework covered with rushes or long grass, with a low entrance, and with mats for floor coverings. Outside the huts were large, wide-polished stones, apparently used as seats. Ornaments seen were a mother-of-pearl necklace, a shell on a chief's chest, and ear-drops which seemed to be of vegetable matter, to accommodate which there were big slits in the wearers' ears. Their canoes were made of many small pieces of timber tied together with cord, were about 10 feet in length apart from the very high sharp prows, and were leaky because there was no efficient caulking of the seams. The people had fowls, bananas, a few coconut-trees, yams, sugar cane, sweet potatoes, and an unknown variety of swede or turnip. Their cultivations on gently sloping hills were neatly divided by furrows into square patches, in which the sweet potatoes and aforesaid variety of swede or turnip were grown. The islanders cut their bananas with a sharp piece of black stone, and then twisted them off. The statues, says Roggeveen, were up to 30 feet high and more, these being made of clay or sticky earth into which small, smooth pebbles had been put very neatly and closely together so that the impression of a human body was created, the conclusion about the method of construction of the big statues being reached after pulling a piece off. All the statues were covered with a long cloth hanging from the neck to the soles of the feet, under which a slight protuberance gave the indication of arms. On the head was a basket containing stones painted white and piled together. The islanders lighted fires in front of some of these and subsequently squatted on their heels with their heads bent, bringing the palms of their hands together and moving them up and down.

Leaving Easter Island on 13 April 1722, Roggeveen came west, decreasing his latitude with the intention of following Le Maire's track (see section 16). On 18 May 1722 a small island was seen, the latitude being considered to be 15 degrees 12 minutes south. It was thought at first to be Le Maire's Honden Island (Pukapuka, in the Tuamotu Archipelago), but when this did not appear to fit in with the expedition's further contacts Roggeveen called it Bedrieglyke (Doubtful or Deceptive). Shortly after leaving this island the *Africaansche Galey* was wrecked on a large, low island comprising several islets, the latitudes near which were taken as about 14¾ degrees south. The crew of the galley were rescued and divided among the other ships. While at this island five sailors deserted. This island was named Schadelijk (Disastrous). The expedition left this island on 24 May, and the following morning, 25 May 1722, another large, low island considered to be west of the south of Schadelijk was encountered, the latitude near it being taken as 14 degrees 33 minutes south. This island was named Dagenraad (Dawn). Some alarm was caused by these encounters with dangerous islands. They decided to come south. On 27 May 1722, in the evening, another low island was seen. This was named Avondstond (Evening). At midday on this day the latitude had been taken as about 15½ degrees south. On 28 May 1722 another low island, close to the west side of Avondstond, was found. It was called Meerder Zorg (More Trouble). On this day the latitude was taken as 15 degrees 10 minutes south. On 29 May, according to Bouman, the expedition passed between Avondstond and Meerder Zorg to the south, skirting the latter on its south side, and on 30 May 1722 they had the western part of Avondstond south-east of them at 3 Dutch miles (about 12 geographical miles), and Meerder Zorg north-east of them. They soon saw another low island to the north-west by west, which they named Goede Verwaghting. This extended east and west. At noon on this day the latitude was taken as 15 degrees 17 minutes south. On 2 June 1722, or 1 June according to Bouman, they encountered a moderately high craggy island. The latitude near it was taken as 15 degrees 43 minutes south. A landing party collected some greenstuff, in consequence of which the island was called Verkwikking (Refreshment). The islanders first welcomed them but later threw stones at them. No more land was seen for several days after leaving Verkwikking.

A comparison of these data with a detailed map of the north-western sector of the Tuamotu Archipelago will show that they correspond with the following sequence of islands. The small island that was first seen was Tikei. Schadelijk, where the *Africaansche Galey* was wrecked, was Takapoto. When John Byron visited an island which was undoubtedly Takapoto in 1765 (see section 29), a landing party found relics of a Dutch longboat. Takapoto had, however, been discovered by Le Maire. The island to the west of Schadelijk, namely Dagenraad, was either Manihi or Ahe. It may have been discovered by Le Maire. Coming south, the expedition then saw Apataki (Avondstond), and then Arutua (Meerder Zorg), which lies 9 miles west of Apataki. The ships passed south of Arutua, and then saw Rangiroa to the north-west by west. Rangiroa had been discovered from the north by Le Maire. Then the expedition came to Makatea (Verkwikking), which is unique in those parts in being of moderate height and hilly. All these islands fit in with Roggeveen's relative locations, topographical descriptions, sailing times, and broad latitudes. The new discoveries among them were Tikei, Apataki, Arutua, and Makatea, and possibly Manihi or Ahe according to which of these was seen by Roggeveen and which before him by Le Maire.

On 6 June 1722, 3 days after leaving Makatea, two more islands were seen to the south. Bouman of the *Thienhoven*, which was nearer these islands, said that when seen at daylight, at a distance of 8 to 9 Dutch miles (about 32 to 36 geographical miles), one of these, a very high island, was to the south-east of the ship, and the other, a lower island, was to the south-west by south. According to Roggeveen, the latitude on this day was taken as 15 degrees 37 minutes south, and the two islands were 2 Dutch miles apart. He identified them with Le Maire's Cocos and Verraders (Tafahi and Niuatobutabu).

These two islands were the northern islands of the Society Islands, Borabora and Maupiti. The sailing time of 3 days from Makatea is realistic in relation to these islands. Their latitudes are about 16½ degrees south. Borabora has peaks of over 2,000 feet. Maupiti is a good deal lower, its highest point being 698 feet.[1] Tubai, also known as Motu Iti, a low atoll, lies between Borabora and Maupiti at a distance of 7 miles from Borabora and 24 miles from Maupiti. While Borabora and Tubai might appear to agree with Roggeveen's figure of 2 Dutch miles between the two islands, this does not accord with Bouman's bearings, nor with the fact that Tubai at a long distance would not be visible, nor with the

[1] *Pacific Islands Pilot*, vol. iii, pp. 180-1.

further fact that, if Tubai had been visible, Maupiti would have been more so. Roggeveen was thus the discoverer of Borabora and Maupiti.[1]

On 13 June 1722 a low island estimated to be about 1 Dutch mile in circumference was seen, and was called Vuyle Eyland (Bird Island). The latitude on this day was taken as 14½ degrees south. Very soon thereafter high land was seen to the north-west, first from the *Thienhoven*. The next day the two ships stopped off this high land on its south side, the latitude near it being taken as 14 degrees 9 minutes south. It was found to consist of four islands. The easternmost was the largest; to the west of it were two islands divided by a narrow channel; and west of these was a small island. These islands were called Boumans Eylanden.

Bird Island was the modern Rose Island, a small atoll in latitude 14 degrees 33 minutes south, the easternmost of the Samoa Islands. The Bouman Islands to the north-west of Vuyle Island were the Manua Islands of the Samoa group. Of these, Tau, the easternmost, is 3,056 feet high, Olosenga, 5½ miles north-west of Tau, is 2,095 feet high, Ofu, ¼ mile west of Olosenga, is 1,589 feet high, and two islets lie close together near the west side of Ofu.

While the Dutch ships were at Tau three canoes came out to them. They were not made out of a log, but constructed of framework and planks in a workmanlike way. A ship's boat went in to the shore, where large numbers of people were gathered. There were numbers of canoes there to meet them, one of which was very large. In this sat a man who was obviously a person of authority, and with him a girl who wore a blue coral necklace. The men had spears, bows, and arrows. The people resembled the Easter Islanders in having good physiques: also in painting themselves, but not so abundantly, as the painted adornments began at the thighs and went down to the legs. Nothing else was seen that the islanders used for clothing their nakedness except a belt round their waists, to which a great number of long and wide leaves or rushes or some other plant was attached.

Early the next day, 15 June 1722, a high island was seen, first from the *Thienhoven*, being named Thienhoven accordingly. Bouman says

[1] These identifications accord with those of Mulert, in *De reis van Mr. Jacob Roggeveen* (The Hague, 1911), p. 165 n.

they sailed on a west-north-west course along it at a distance of 7 to 8 Dutch miles, and later in the day saw another high island to the west-south-west, the previous island being still in sight. They could not get much idea of the extent of the second island to the west. The second island was named Groeningen.

The first of these islands, Thienhoven, was Tutuila, which rises to 2,141 feet, and the second, Groeningen, was Upolu, which has a number of peaks of which the highest is 3,607 feet[1]—both in the Samoa group. Tutuila is about 50 miles west of the Manua Islands, and Upolu is about 38 miles west-north-west of Tutuila. It is plain that the expedition did not proceed far enough before dark to appreciate the full extent of Upolu, or to see Savaii to the west of it.

No more islands were seen until Roggeveen reached New Ireland on 17 July 1722.

The contributions of Jacob Roggeveen to the discovery of the Pacific Islands were as follows: On 5 April 1722 he encountered Easter Island, a landing being made. This was a new discovery because it is not credible that Davis had seen it (see section 22). On 18 May 1722 Roggeveen discovered Tikei; on 25 May 1722 he discovered, or rediscovered after Le Maire (see section 16), either Manihi or Ahe; on 27 May 1722 he discovered Apataki; on 28 May 1722 he discovered Arutua; and on either 1 or 2 June 1722 he discovered Makatea, a landing being made; all these islands being in the Tuamotu Archipelago. On 6 June 1722 Roggeveen discovered Borabora and Maupiti in the Society Islands. On 13 June 1722 Roggeveen discovered Rose Island and the Manua Islands, and on 15 June 1722, Tutuila and Upolu, in the Samoa group, these discoveries being first seen from his second ship the *Thienhoven*.

[1] *Pacific Islands Pilot*, vol. ii, pp. 405–6, 410–11.

28. Norton Hutchinson, James Dewar, and Thomas Baddison

On 5 March 1761 three British ships, the *Carnarvon* (Captain Norton Hutchinson), the *Warwick* (Captain James Dewar), and the *Princess Augusta* (Captain Thomas Baddison) passed Mapia, south of the western Carolines, on the way to China, and some months later came back over the same course, being on occasion separated from one another. A chart embodying the information of one Scott of the *Warwick* shows that the expedition on the way to China, after leaving Mapia, encountered an island in the western Carolines, the position shown for it being that of Pulo Anna. It would appear that another island to the south-east of this position and corresponding to that of Merir was seen by the *Carnarvon* on the way back.[1]

These would appear to be the first reasonably well-established European sightings of Pulo Anna and Merir. Either or both of these islands may have been seen by the Portuguese (see section 4).

29. John Byron

In 1765 John Byron came through Magellan Strait into the Pacific as commander of a British expedition of two ships, the *Dolphin* and the *Tamar*, sent by the British Government on a voyage of exploration. The authority for this voyage is Byron's journal as edited by Hawkesworth.[2]

By Byron's time the improvement in navigation had reached a stage where figures for latitude were fairly precise, although not yet for longitude. The modern abbreviations for degrees, minutes, and seconds were becoming generally adopted, being a token of the improvement. These latter are therefore used in the present and ensuing sections.

[1] Eilers, A., in *Ergebnisse der Südsee-Expedition 1908–1910. II. Ethnographie B Mikronesien*, vol. ix, part 1 (Hamburg, 1935), p. 164—citing Dalrymple, A., *A Collection of Charts* (London, 1781–94).

[2] Hawkesworth, J., *Voyages* (London, 1773), vol. i, pp. 1–139.

Leaving Masafuera near the South American coast on 30 April 1765, Byron took a predominantly north-west course. On 7 June 1765 he came to two low inhabited islands, the position given being close to latitude 14° S., lying close to each other north-west and south-east, the south-east one, which consisted of a cluster of islands, most of them joined by a narrow neck of land, being the larger, the other being judged to be about 5 miles in circumference. Being unable to anchor, or to land on account of the hostility of the inhabitants, Byron called them the Islands of Disappointment. Leaving these islands on the morning of the 8th, the expedition came the next afternoon, 9 June 1765, to a long low inhabited island with a lagoon, the latitude given being 14° 29′ S., with another island south-west by west, these two islands being separated by about 4 leagues. A landing party found on the first of these islands, in one of the huts, an old worm-eaten rudder from a Dutch longboat, with some metal items. The latitude here was taken as 14½° S. These islands were named King George's Islands.

These data show that the first two islands were Napuka and Tepoto, and the second two were Takaroa and Takapoto, on the northern fringe of the Tuamotu Archipelago, corresponding closely in latitude and description with Byron's details. The latter two were not a new discovery, having been visited previously by Le Maire (see section 16), and Takapoto again by Roggeveen (see section 27). Napuka and Tepoto were, however, discovered by Byron. The remains of the Dutch longboat were no doubt relics from the wreck of Roggeveen's *Africaansche Galey*, which was wrecked on Takapoto 43 years previously. Apparently no survivors of the five deserters from Roggeveen's expedition remained on Takapoto to welcome Byron's men, or to tell the world what other islands they might have seen in the meantime.

Byron describes the people of Napuka and Tepoto as of a deep copper colour, well made and active, and armed with very long spears. The people of Takaroa and Takapoto were armed in the same manner, and had large, double sailing canoes as well as small ones, very well constructed. Their economy was largely based on the coconut tree. They had dogs and pearl oysters. Close by their huts were funeral places, near which were boxes full of human bones.

The next day the expedition came to a long, narrow, inhabited island lying east and west, to which they gave the name Prince of Wales's Island. This appears to have been Manihi, which may have been discovered by either Le Maire or Roggeveen or both (see sections 14 and 27).

On 21 June 1765 Byron came to land having the appearance of three islands from the north-east, lying north-east by north and south-west by south, with rocks and broken ground between them and reefs at either end, the latitude being taken as 10° 15′ S. Byron called them the Islands of Danger. The next island was discovered on 24 June 1765, and called Duke of York's Island. It was a low, tree-covered island with a lagoon, in latitude somewhere near 8° S., as judged by the fact that after leaving the island and proceeding west for several days, Byron says that this was the latitude at that time. A landing party found no sign of habitation. On 2 July 1765, while making in the direction of the Ladrones, they saw to the north a low flat island, of delightful appearance with trees, but with much foul ground on which the sea broke. They skirted the south-west side, which they judged to be about 4 leagues long, seeing great numbers of islanders on the beach, from which more than sixty canoes, 'or rather proas' (this being the current term for Micronesian outrigger canoes as known from contacts with the Marianas), put off. This island was named Byron's Island. The latitude was taken as 1° 18′ S. The expedition reached the Ladrones on 28 July 1765, having seen no more islands.

The 'Islands of Danger' were no doubt Pukapuka in the northern Cooks, consisting of three main islets and some rocks and sand-banks. These are still occasionally called the Danger Islands. They had been discovered by Mendaña on his second voyage (see section 12). Byron's Duke of York's Island must have been Atafu, the northernmost island of the Tokelau group, in 8½° S. When visited by Captain Hudson of the U.S. Exploring Expedition in 1841, who was looking specifically for Byron's Duke of York's Island and who subsequently saw both Nukunonu and Fakaofo to the south, some people on Atafu told the Americans that they were subject to Fakaofo and mentioned Nukunonu, which lies between. Later contacts with the people of these three islands indicate that Fakaofo and Nukunonu had been inhabited since long before Byron's time.[1] In reference to Byron's Island, when Wilkes of the U.S. Exploring Expedition of 1838–42 visited

[1] Macgregor, G., *Ethnology of Tokelau Islands* (Honolulu, 1937).

Tabiteuea, the largest of the southern Gilbert Islands, he was told
that there were other islands in the vicinity including Nukunau,
and identified the latter with Byron's Island, although he did not
visit Nukunau.[1] Nukunau is, however, a small island, and if it had
been Byron's Island it would have been hard for Byron to miss
the main Gilbert chain on his north-west course after leaving it.
Tabiteuea itself answers much better to Byron's description, being
a large island with much foul ground on the south side, and
densely populated in historical times, which conforms with the
launching of sixty canoes from one part of the island in question.
It is also the most likely island in the vicinity of the stated latitude
to be seen from the south-west and south without sight of any
other island before or after. On the other hand, Byron's longitudes
of other islands in the South Pacific are all several degrees to the
west of their true position, whereas his longitude for Byron's
Island is one degree only to the west of Tabiteuea. There are not
sufficient grounds for an identification of Byron's Island beyond
concluding that it was either Tabiteuea or Beru or Nukunau, all
of which are in or near the stated latitude.

Byron gives a lively picture of the Gilbertese he saw in the
canoes and on the ship at the time of this first European contact.
Their canoes contained between three and six people. Some of
the men came aboard, and showed an intrepid and cheerful disposition. They were tall, well-proportioned, and clean-limbed,
their skin a bright copper colour, their features extremely good.
One of them captivated the Englishmen by his lively antics and
clowning. They wore attractive shell ornaments round their necks,
wrists, and waists, and their ears were bored and elongated. Some
of them had a kind of spear stuck full of shark teeth, sharp as a
lancet, for about 3 feet of its length.

John Byron, on 7 June 1765, discovered Napuka and Tepoto in
the Tuamotu Archipelago; on 24 June 1765 Atafu, the northernmost of the Tokelau Islands, a landing being made; and on 2 July
1765 either Tabiteuea or Beru or Nukunau in the southern Gilbert
Islands.

---

[1] Wilkes, C., *Narrative of the United States Exploring Expedition* (Philadelphia,
1845), vol. v, pp. 5–17, 80.

30. Samuel Wallis

AFTER Byron's return to England (see section 29) the *Dolphin*, in command of Captain Samuel Wallis, was sent on another voyage of exploration, in company with the *Swallow*, commanded by Philip Carteret. Carteret's ship became separated from the *Dolphin* as they were entering the Pacific, and its voyage across the Pacific, being virtually an independent one, is covered in the next section. The authorities for Wallis's exploration are his own journal as edited by Hawkesworth,[1] and the log or diary of the master, George Robertson.[2] The first of these is followed except where Robertson is specifically named.

Having come out of Magellan Strait on 12 April 1767, Wallis decreased his latitude slowly, and on 6 June 1767 discovered a low island about 4 miles long and 3 miles wide, with a large internal basin, the latitude given being 19° 26′ S. To this island he gave the name Whitsun Island. Here, according to Robertson, some of the men swam ashore to visit the island. Another island lay to the north-west distant about 4 leagues, some 6 miles in length and a mile wide according to Wallis's estimation. At this latter island, to which the name Queen Charlotte's Island was given, the Englishmen made contact with the inhabitants, who sailed off to the west-south-west in some large double canoes. A landing was made on Queen Charlotte's Island. The expedition proceeded in the direction the canoes had taken, and saw an island south-west of Queen Charlotte's Island while the latter was still in sight. This new island, which they called Egmont Island, had the appearance of two islands joined by a reef, the whole enclosing a lagoon, the latitude given being 19° 20′ S. They saw some inhabitants. The date of the finding of Egmont Island was 10 June 1767. Leaving in the evening, the next day they saw another inhabited island surrounded by rocks, of much the same appearance as Egmont Island, but narrower, to which they gave the name Gloucester Island, the latitude given being 19° 11′ S. This was on 11 June 1767. At five the next morning, 12 June 1767, they set off again, and soon saw another island to which they gave the name Cumberland Island. At dawn the next morning, 13 June 1767, they saw another small island which had the appearance of small keys, to which they gave the name Prince William

---

[1] Hawkesworth, J., *Voyages* (London, 1773), vol. i, pp. 362–522.
[2] In *The Discovery of Tahiti*, ed. Carrington, H. (London, 1948).

Henry's Island, the latitude given being 19° S. They did not see more land for 4 days.

The six islands, all conforming closely in latitude, relative location, and topography to Wallis's details, were Pinaki (Whitsun), Nukutavake (Queen Charlotte), Vairaatea (Egmont), Paraoa (Gloucester), Manuhangi (Cumberland), and Nengonengo (Prince William Henry), all in the Tuamotu Archipelago. Vairaatea was the island called San Miguel, seen by Quiros the day before reaching San Pablo (Hao). The other five islands were new discoveries.

At Nukutavake Robertson went round the island making observations of the islanders and their arts and crafts. They were armed with spears up to 14 feet in length pointed with bone. They had double canoes about 30 feet long, 4 feet broad, and 3½ feet deep, fastened together with transverse beams, the mast being stepped in the middle of the midship beam. Even bigger vessels were in process of being built on stocks, but they did not give the impression of being used for long voyages. Many turtle-backs, as well as fine tortoise-shell, were found, as well as much pearl-shell. Graves with canopies near by were found, the canopies consisting of four pillars of stone with coconut-leaf roofs and sides made of twigs.

Four days after Nengonengo, on 17 June 1767, the ship came to a very high well-peopled island, nearly circular, about 2 miles across, to which Wallis gave the name Osnaburgh Island, the latitude given being 17° 51′ S. The next day, 18 June 1767, shortly after leaving Osnaburgh, they came to a very high, large island of delightful and romantic appearance, the native name of which later proved to be 'Otaheite'. Here they stayed 5 weeks. This island Wallis named King George the Third's Island. On 27 July 1767 they set sail and passed another high island, called the Duke of York's Island, 2 miles west of King George the Third's Island. The references to it indicate that it had been seen previously from Tahiti. On 28 July 1767 they passed another inhabited island about 6 miles long, with a mountain in the middle, the latitude given being 17° 28′ S., which Wallis called Sir Charles Saunders's Island. Next day, 29 July 1767, they passed another island thought to be about 10 miles long and 4 miles broad, the latitude given being 16° 46′ S., which Wallis called Lord How's Island. In the afternoon they saw some low islands and breakers, the latitude given being 16° 28' S., naming them the Scilly Islands. No more land was seen till 13 August.

These islands were Mehetia (Osnaburgh), Tahiti (King George the Third's Island), Moorea (Duke of York's Island), Mopihaa (Lord How's Island), and Motu One (Scilly Islands), all in the Society Islands, and all new discoveries. The latitudes, relative location and sailing times, and topographical descriptions all conform with these identifications.

Wallis's account of the stay of the *Dolphin* at Tahiti is, together with Robertson's observations, outstanding in the annals of discovery. The Englishmen had to fight their way to an anchorage against hundreds of canoes, but they became so friendly with the inhabitants and their chieftainess Purea that when they left 'our Indian friends, and particularly the Queen, once more bade us farewell, with such tenderness of affection and grief, as filled both my heart and my eyes'. The people were well made, active, the women handsome, and some of them very beautiful, with ideas of virtue which did not accord with European convention. They used cloth made of the beaten inner bark of a tree. Their ornaments were flowers, feathers, shells, and pearls. Both men and women practised breech tattooing. They had in profusion pork, poultry, dog flesh, fish of many sorts, bread-fruit, bananas and plantains, yams, apples, and a sour fruit. They used huge nets for catching fish, as well as hooks. They cooked their pork, bread-fruit, and yams in pits with hot stones, leaves, and embers. Their weapons, scars, and surgical skill indicated their practice of warfare. Their canoes comprised single sailing canoes with outriggers, dug-out canoes made from the trunk of the bread-fruit tree, two-masted double canoes, and ceremonial canoes with awnings, all of them well made. Their principal weapons were slings, bludgeons, and spears, their bows and arrows being only fit to knock down a bird. The climate appeared to be good and no disease was seen. To these details Robertson adds the following. There was a large place of worship with three stone walls within one another. Images were cut in the trunks of trees one above the other, five such in one trunk being seen on one occasion. The chieftainess's house was very large, being 320 feet long and 36 feet broad, supported by fourteen large wooden pillars in the middle of the house, each about 15 to 16 inches in diameter and about 24 feet high.

Taking a westerly course from Motu One, Wallis, on 13 August 1767, came to two inhabited islands close together, one like a sugar loaf and the other in a peak, the latitude being given as 16° S. These were plainly Niuatobutabu and Tafahi, discovered by Le Maire (see section 16).

Continuing on from Niuatobutabu and Tafahi, the voyagers 2 days later, on 16 August 1767, came to an island which was low at the coast but appeared to be high inland, surrounded by reefs. The ship's boats, while examining the coast, found a passage through the reef, and had a contact with some canoes. The latitude given was 13° 18′ S. The island was named Wallis's Island.

This was Uvea, sometimes called Wallis Islands, consisting of a main island and several islets within a barrier reef with several channels through it, in latitude 13° 20′ S. The main island has a hill 470 feet high near its middle.[1] This was a new discovery.

At Uvea Robertson went with the boats near the shore, but after contact with some of the islanders there he withdrew. He got two wooden clubs from the islanders, who had shark-bone and shell necklaces and shell ear pendants.

On 3 September 1767 land was seen bearing east-north-east distant 5 miles; half an hour later more land was seen in the north-west, and half an hour again a 'proa' was seen sailing at a distance. Two hours later the two islands were distant about 3 leagues on either hand, and many others, much farther off, were in sight. The latitude of one of the two islands was given as 11° N., the latitude of the other as 11° 20′ N. No more land was seen before they reached the Ladrones.

These data show that Wallis saw first Rongerik and then Rongelap in the western chain of the Marshalls, and passed between them. They are the only islands in the vicinity of the stated latitudes far enough apart and yet near enough to each other to be seen at a fair distance on either hand. Rongelap had been discovered by Saavedra (see section 5). Wallis was the discoverer of Rongerik.

[1] *Pacific Islands Pilot*, vol. ii, p. 355.

Samuel Wallis, on 6 June 1767, discovered Pinaki and Nuku-tavake, landings being made. On 11 June 1767 he discovered Paraoa, on 12 June 1767 Manuhangi, and on 13 June 1767 Nen-gonengo. These five islands are all in the Tuamotu Archipelago. On 17 June 1767 he discovered Mehetia; on 18 June 1767 he discovered Tahiti, numbers of landings being subsequently made; some days later he discovered Moorea; on 28 July 1767 he dis-covered Tubuai Manu; and on 29 July 1767 he discovered Mopihaa and Motu One; all six of these islands being in the Society Islands. On 16 August 1767 he discovered the mid-Pacific atoll Uvea. On 3 September 1767 he discovered Rongerik, in the Marshall Islands.

31. Philip Carteret

PHILIP CARTERET, commanding the *Swallow*, was separated from Samuel Wallis in the *Dolphin* (see section 30) as they came out of Magellan Strait, and made an independent voyage across the Pacific. The authority for this voyage is Carteret's journal as edited by Hawkesworth, which contains reproductions of charts and sketches of the islands that were seen.[1]

Carteret left Masafuera, near the South American coast, on 24 May 1767, and on 2 July 1767 came to an island like a great rock rising out of the sea, appearing to be about 5 miles in circumference and to be uninhabited, a profile sketch of it being given. On 11 July 1767 he discovered a small, low, flat island appearing to be almost level with the water's edge, but as it was to windward south of them they could not fetch it. Its latitude was given as 22° S. They called it Bishop of Osna-burgh's Island. The next day, 12 July 1767, they fell in with two small wooded islands which appeared to be uninhabited. The southernmost, on which a landing was made from the ship's boat, was a slip of land in the form of a half-moon, low, flat, and sandy, and from the south end a reef ran out for about ½ mile. The other of these two islands, distant from it some 4 or 5 leagues to the west-north-west, very much resembled it. Their latitudes were given as 20° 38′ S. and 20° 34′ S. respectively. To these Carteret gave the name Duke of Gloucester's Islands.

[1] Hawkesworth, J., *Voyages* (London, 1773), vol. i, pp. 523–676.

The only sequence of four islands which conforms with these data is Pitcairn (Pitcairn's Island), Tematangi (Bishop of Osnaburgh's Island), and two of the three islands of the Duke of Gloucester group (Nukutipipi, Anuanurunga, Anuanuraro). Pitcairn is south of the Tuamotu Archipelago, Tematangi and the Duke of Gloucester Islands are in it. A profile sketch of Pitcairn's Island confirms its identification. (The latitude of Pitcairn is actually 25° S. as compared with 20° 2′ S. in the published journal. The other latitudes in relation to the stated course to the north show that this latter figure is erroneous.) The descriptions of the Duke of Gloucester's Islands and their relative positions in relation to Carteret's course are compatible only with two of the modern Duke of Gloucester Islands. For the Bishop of Osnaburgh's Island we must look for a small, low, flat island close enough to the Duke of Gloucester Islands to conform with a sailing time of a day as compared with 9 days from Pitcairn, and a latitude of about 22° S. Only Tematangi does this. This identification is further supported by the fact that a number of Carteret's longitudes of known points in his traverse of the South Pacific are several degrees east of the true position, and this applies to Carteret's position for the Bishop of Osnaburgh's Island in relation to Tematangi (see also section 108).

From the Tuamotus Carteret came across the Pacific looking for Mendaña's Solomon Islands (see section 10), and like Mendaña on his second voyage (see section 12) came to the northern sector of the Santa Cruz Islands, some 230 miles east of the Solomons. Carteret identified Ndeni with Mendaña's Santa Cruz from the descriptions of the latter. He saw Utupua and Vanikoro to the south as he approached the east side of Ndeni, calling them Edgecomb's Island and Ourry's Island. He thought that Vanikoro was immediately east of Utupua and smaller, whereas it is 19 miles beyond it and some 3,000 feet high as compared with Utupua's 1,240 feet, but this is accounted for by seeing them at a distance.

Utupua had been discovered by Barreto on Mendaña's second expedition (see section 12), and since Vanikoro is much higher than Utupua and in the same direction from Ndeni, it is probable that Barreto saw both these islands. Carteret, however, gave the first firm report of Vanikoro.

Sailing from Ndeni on 18 August 1767, Carteret came up with a favourable east wind towards the west-north-west. On 20 August 1767 he discovered a small, low, flat island, the latitude given being 7° 56' S. He named this Gower's Island. During the night the ship drifted south and next morning they saw two more islands nearly east and west of each other, the nearer one, which was 'lofty, and has a stately appearance', being named Carteret's Island, the other, which was smaller, being called Simpson's Island. Carteret's Island, the east end of which bore about south from Gower's Island, was about 6 leagues long, they estimated, from east to west. Its latitude was given as about latitude 8° 26' S. These islands being to windward, they came back to Gower's Island, which was estimated to be about 10 or 11 leagues from Carteret's Island. Gower's Island was thought to be about 2½ leagues long on its western side. A landing was made on this island. There were a number of islanders here, whom Carteret supposed to have come from Carteret's Island. Carteret considered these islands to be a new discovery. From here Carteret continued on to the north-west and on 24 August 1767 fell in with nine low flat islands estimated to stretch north-west by west and south-east by east about 15 leagues, in latitude 4° 36' S., eight of them small, one of them larger. At 11 o'clock that night they came to a large, flat, green island of considerable extent, where they saw many fires. It was thought to be in latitude 4° 50' S. and to bear west 15 leagues from the northernmost of the 'Nine Islands'. This island they called Sir Charles Hardy's Island. Next morning, 25 August 1767, they discovered another large island which, rising in three considerable hills, had at a distance the appearance of three islands, about 10 leagues south-east of Sir Charles Hardy's Island. To this high island they gave the name Winchelsea's Island. The next morning they saw another large island to the north, which Carteret took to be Schouten's Saint John. Soon afterwards high land was seen to the west, which Carteret identified with Dampier's Nova-Britannia (see section 24).

Gower's Island, Carteret's Island, and Simpson's Island, discovered 2 days after leaving Ndeni, were Ndai, the northern end of Malaita, and the islet of Manaoba, in the Solomons. The latitudes and topography agree with Carteret's observations. Malaita had been discovered by Ortega on Mendaña's first voyage (see section 10). Carteret was the discoverer of Ndai. Continuing on to the north-west, Carteret ran parallel with the main Solomon Islands without being aware of them until he encountered the Kilinailau Islands (Nine Islands), on 24 August 1767. They are an atoll with six islands, some coral rocks and sand-keys. This was a

new discovery. That night Carteret saw Nissan, the large eastern
island of the Green Islands (Sir Charles Hardy's Island), discovered
by Le Maire (see section 16). The next morning, 25 August 1767,
Carteret discovered Buka (Winchelsea's Island), the northernmost
of the main Solomon Islands, lying some 36 miles south-east of
Nissan, and rising to 1,300 feet. Carteret then passed the Feni
Islands, correctly recognized as the St. John of Le Maire's expedition (see section 16). He then came to the eastern coast of New
Ireland, not as far west as Nova-Britannia, except in the sense that
New Britain and New Ireland were thought by Dampier to be
continuous (see section 24).

Carteret describes the islanders seen at Ndai as being like those
of Ndeni, but their canoes were of a different structure and much
larger.

Carteret was swept by a current into a bay which he recognized as
Dampier's 'St. George's Bay' (see section 24). He could not get the ship
out, and had hopes from the inward current that the 'bay' was in
fact a strait. This proved to be the case. On 9–11 September 1767
Carteret passed through a strait which he called Saint George's Channel,
a name which it still retains. He gave the name New Ireland to the
newly established island north of the Channel. He steered north-east
along its inner coast, seeing the nearer off-shore islands. He found that
New Ireland itself terminated in a strait, to which he gave the name
Byron's Strait, known now as Byron Strait. He gave the name New
Hanover to the newly established island north of this strait.

Carteret was thus the discoverer of Saint George's Channel and
Byron Strait, thereby establishing that New Britain, New Ireland,
and New Hanover were separate islands.

Having passed south of the Admiralty Islands—so named by him—
Carteret, on the evening of 19 September 1767, came past some low
land, level and green, which was seen only from the mast-head, in
about latitude 1° 14' or 16' S., called by him Durour's Island. During
the night Carteret coasted another island, which seemed to be about
6 miles long, where numbers of the inhabitants were seen running
along the beach. It ran east by north and west by south, and its latitude
was considered to be about 1° 45' S. This Carteret called Matty's
Island. These islands were about 4 days from Manus in the Admiralty
Islands. Five days later the ship reached the Schouten Eilanden in the
Geelvink Bay area of western New Guinea.

The descriptions, latitudes, and relative sailing times show that Durour's Island and Matty's Island were Aua and Wuvulu, the south-westernmost of the islands lying to the west of the Ninigo group. The latitude of Wuvulu, an island about 5 miles long, some 18 miles south-west of Aua, is 1° 43' S. These islands may have been seen by Saavedra (see section 5), or Retes (see section 7), or Vries (see section 19).

While passing from the Mapia Islands, north-west of the Schouten Islands, to the Philippines, Carteret, on 28 September 1767, encountered an island, seen to the south from the mast, the latitude given being about 2° 50' N. An accompanying profile sketch shows that this was Tobi, the southern island of the western Carolines.

This is the first clear record of Tobi, although it may have been seen by the Portuguese (see section 4) and by Woodes Rogers (see section 25).

Carteret's contributions to the discovery of the Pacific Islands were as follows: On 2 July 1767 he discovered Pitcairn, to the south of the Tuamotu Archipelago. On 11 July 1767 he discovered Tematangi, and on 12 July 1767, two of the three Duke of Gloucester Islands, in the Tuamotu Archipelago, a landing being made on one of the Duke of Gloucester Islands. On 12 August 1767 he made the first firm observation of Vanikoro, in the Santa Cruz group, although it is probable that it had been seen by Barreto (see section 12). On 20 August 1767 he discovered Ndai, on 24 August 1767 he discovered the Kilinailau Islands, and on 25 August 1767 he discovered Buka, all in the Solomon Islands. On 9-11 September 1767 he discovered St. George's Channel dividing New Britain from New Ireland. On 12 September 1767 he discovered Byron Strait dividing New Ireland from New Hanover. He was the first clearly established observer of Aua and Wuvulu, to the south-west of the Ninigo group, although they may have been seen by Saavedra (see section 5), or Retes (see section 7), or Vries (see section 19). He was the first clearly established observer of Tobi, in the western Carolines, although it may have been seen by the Portuguese (see section 4), and by Woodes Rogers (see section 25).

32. Louis Antoine de Bougainville

Two French ships, the *Boudeuse* and the *Étoile*, crossed the Pacific under the command of Louis Antoine de Bougainville in 1768. A narrative by Bougainville, with accompanying charts, was published in 1771.[1] This is supplemented by reference to his unpublished log[2] where this gives significant details clarifying obscurities in the published narrative and accompanying charts.

Coming out of the Strait of Magellan on 26 January 1768, the expedition, on 22 March 1768, came to four islets (Les Quatre Facardins) and another small island (Isle de Lanciers) which were visible from the ships at the same time, the four islets being towards the south-east. Some people were seen on the Isle des Lanciers, but no landing place could be found. Bougainville's accompanying sectional chart shows these islands between latitudes $18\frac{1}{4}°$ and $18\frac{1}{2}°$ S. The next day, 23 March 1768, they came to an island with a lagoon, of an estimated length south-east and north-west of 10 to 12 leagues, with some canoes in the lagoon. Bougainville called it, from its shape, Isle de la Harpe (Harp Island). In the chart it is shown between latitudes $18\frac{1}{2}°$ and $18°$ S. The next day, 24 March 1768, having left Harp Island from its north-west part, they saw some low land running from the south-west of the ships to the north-east, but their view of it, according to Bougainville's log, was fitful owing to bad weather. They bore north-west and then west, continuing to pass among low overflowed islands until 27 March 1768. Bougainville then struck south for a time in order to get clear of this dangerous archipelago of low islands. Bougainville says that while passing through it he did not go farther north than latitude 17° 40′ S., and that eleven low islands in all were seen, all inaccessible. His sectional chart of this passage shows four pieces of land west of Harp Island, incomplete on the sides farther from the ship's track, two of them north of the track and east and west of each other in $17\frac{1}{4}°$ S., two of them south of the track and east and west of each other in or about 18° S., the date of passing between them being shown as 26 March 1768. This sectional chart is cut short on the west and shows only ten islands in all, namely the four islets of Les Quatre Facardins, the Isle des Lanciers, the Isle de la Harpe, and the four pieces of land referred to. Bougainville's log relates that these four pieces of land were seen

---

[1] Bougainville, L. A. de, *Voyage autour du monde* (Paris, 1771).

[2] Microfilm in Alexander Turnbull Library of Bougainville's unpublished log in French National Archives.

fitfully as the ships passed between them, and that beyond them his second vessel the *Étoile* signalled land to the south-west on 26 March, but that no close sight of this land was got, and that they decided to turn south to get clear of these dangerous islands.

From these data, as will be seen from a map, there can be no doubt that Les Quatre Facardins, the Isle des Lanciers, and the Isle de la Harpe were Vahitahi, Akiaki, and Hao respectively, in the Tuamotu Archipelago. The latitudes of Vahitahi and Akiaki are respectively 18¼° and 18½° S., Akiaki being some 23 miles west-north-west of Vahitahi and 85 miles east of Hao. Hao had been discovered by Quiros (see section 14). Several low islets can be seen in Vahitahi's lagoon.[1] The first two pieces of land shown south and north of each other, between which the ships passed after coming from the north-west part of Hao, seeing the southern one for the first time on 24 March, were the north-eastern part of Marokau and the south side of Hikueru, lying 65 to 80 miles from the north-west of Hao. The further two pieces of land lying south and north of each other between which the ships then passed were the north side of Reitoru and the south side of Haraiki, Reitoru being some 20 miles west-south-west of Hikueru and Haraiki about 35 miles north-west of Reitoru. The waters between these four islands extend over an east–west distance of about 65 miles between latitudes 17¼° and 18° S. It has been seen that Bougain-ville's sectional chart stops short on the west side, and shows only ten of the eleven low islands he mentions in his text. Only one low island in fact lies to the west of Reitoru and Haraiki, namely Anaa, and Reitoru and Haraiki, like Marokau and Hikueru, lie on either side of latitude 17° 40′ S., which Bougainville says was the farthest latitude he attained to the north. James Cook, when coming west from Reitoru in 1769 (see section 33), and Domingo de Boe-nechea, when coming west from Haraiki in 1772 (see section 35), both came on Anaa, which is 85 miles from Haraiki. That the eleventh island was in fact Anaa is confirmed by Bougainville's log, which shows that further land was seen west of Haraiki and Reitoru from the *Étoile* on 26 March. Bougainville thus discovered Vahitahi and Akiaki on 22 March 1768, Marokau on 24

[1] *Pacific Islands Pilot*, vol. iii, p. 97.

March 1768, Hikueru, Reitoru, and Haraiki between 24 and 26 March 1768 (the precise dates as between the log and the sectional chart being uncertain), and Anaa on 26 March 1768, the last-named being sighted only from the *Étoile*.

After going south for a time and then coming north again, Bougainville rediscovered after Wallis Mehetia and Tahiti. On 16 April 1768 he came up towards the north-east from Tahiti, and then towards the north-west, seeing an island to leeward of which the native name was given by Bougainville's Tahitian interpreter as 'Oumaitia'. This appeared like three islands but was only one, as they saw in due course, the appearance of three islands being given by its peaks. It appeared to be of medium height, was visible at an estimated distance of 8 or 10 leagues, and it was thought that other land could be seen farther off. Bougainville's sectional chart of Tahiti and environs shows two islands 'Oumaitia' under the name 'Oumaitia' north of Tahiti in about latitude 17° S. It also shows an island 'Heeri' immediately west of Tahiti.

It is plain from these details, and confirmed by Bougainville's log, that he did not see anything of Tetiaroa, a low atoll to the north of and near Tahiti. Tubuai Manu, which lies 40 miles west of Moorea, which lies immediately west of Tahiti, if it were the land supposed to have been seen farther off, had been discovered by Wallis, as had Moorea (see section 30). Whether in fact Tubuai Manu, some 800 feet high, was seen, or whether the two islands of Oumaitia and 'Heeri' were all parts of Moorea's ramified mountain system, is therefore academic in the present context.

Bougainville, having rediscovered after Roggeveen (see section 27) the Manua Islands and Tutuila in the Samoa group, left Tutuila for the New Hebrides on 5 May, and then saw the eastern end of Upolu, which then became enveloped in fog and was seen no more. This makes it plain that he did not see Savaii. Six days later, on 11 May 1768, Bougainville saw at a distance to the west-south-west an island (L'Enfant Perdu) which at first seemed like two separate islands. A calm kept them from it all day. The following day they concluded that it was only one island, the two high parts of which were joined by low land which appeared to curve in an arc forming a bay open to the north-east. The big lands ran towards the north-north-west. An adverse wind prevented the ships from getting nearer to L'Enfant

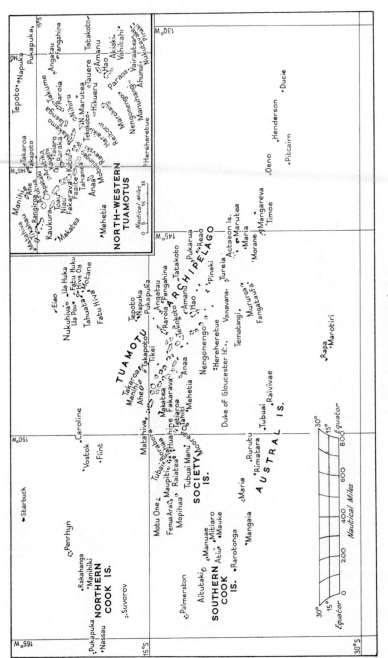

MAP 4. Eastern Polynesia

Perdu than 6 or 7 leagues. The island is shown in Bougainville's chart in latitude $14\frac{1}{4}°$ S. The weather was bad from the 6th to the 20th of the month. On 22 May the expedition reached Maewo in the New Hebrides, 11 days after seeing L'Enfant Perdu.

The Horne Islands, consisting of two islands, Futuna and Alofi, divided by a channel a mile wide, are in the latitude given by Bougainville for L'Enfant Perdu. They are not in fact one island, but Bougainville did not see L'Enfant Perdu at close quarters. Rotuma is an island with high parts joined by low land. Its latitude is, however, $12\frac{1}{2}°$ S., as compared with Bougainville's figure of $14\frac{1}{4}°$ S., and it is plain from the latitudes in Bougainville's log before, at, and after L'Enfant Perdu that his published location is not a mistake. Furthermore Rotuma is about as far from Tutuila as from Maewo, which agrees much less reasonably with the sailing times than with the identification of the island or islands in question with the Horne Islands. It must therefore be concluded that L'Enfant Perdu was not Rotuma but the Horne Islands. The Horne Islands had been discovered by Le Maire (see section 16).

On 22 May 1768, Bougainville came in sight of a number of islands, and during the next 6 days passed among them. His accompanying chart shows that these were the northern islands of the New Hebrides, i.e. Maewo, Pentecost, Aoba, Malekula, Espiritu Santo, and the islands between the two latter.

All these islands may have been discovered by Quiros, Prado, and Torres (see section 14), and Maewo and Espiritu Santo certainly had. Bougainville was, however, the first to give a firm record of Pentecost and Aoba, on 22 May 1768, and of Malekula on 25 May 1768. He made landings on Aoba.

Bougainville describes the people that were seen on Aoba and the neighbouring islands as negroes with thick lips and fuzzy hair, and of unattractive appearance and physique. They had cloth with attractive designs, and wore fish-teeth and tortoise-shell ornaments. Their arms were bows and arrows, ironwood clubs, and stones. Their arrows were pointed with sharp bone, some with barbs. They also had ironwood lances.

Leaving Espiritu Santo on 29 May 1768, Bougainville ran west, encountering some of the reefs east of the Barrier Reef of Australia, and then north. He rediscovered some of the islands in the Louisiade Archipelago, which had been skirted from the east by Prado and Torres (see section 14). On 25 June 1768 Bougainville saw the high peaks of the eastern island of the Archipelago and beat round it the next day. This island was later named Rossel after a senior officer of d'Entre-casteaux's expedition (see section 54).

Rossel may have been a new discovery by Bougainville, although it is possible that Prado and Torres saw its high peaks in the distance from Tagula.

Striking towards the north, Bougainville, on 28 June 1768, saw two islands to the north-west, and a long high coast running from east-south-east to east-north-east. He saw an opening in this latter coast to the east, but could not see whether it was a passage or a bay, since there was land beyond it. In due course he found a passage between the northern part of this latter coast and another long coast on their left hand. It is not clear when this latter coast was first seen. The land on the right hand was named Choiseul. The ships, having passed through the strait, skirted the northern side of the land on the north side of the strait, seeing high peaks inward from the coast. Beyond it to the north they came to a smaller island, which was called Bouka from a word used by some natives in a canoe. This latter island was seen on 4 July 1768. Bougainville's accompanying sectional chart shows Choiseul and the land on the north side of the strait in latitudes 8° to 5° S., with some land south of Choiseul and detached from it (see Plate III).

These data indicate that on 28 June 1768 Bougainville saw two of the islands south of Bougainville, presumably the Treasury Islands (Mono and Stirling, which are close together) and Short-land Island; and Vella Lavella and Choiseul as two sectors of the long coast running from east-south-east to east-north-east. The farther coast of Choiseul seen between Vella Lavella and Choiseul evidently made it uncertain whether they were separate islands, as they are. Choiseul had been discovered from the south by Ortega on Mendaña's first expedition (see section 10), but the other islands seen as Bougainville approached Bougainville Strait were new discoveries. The long coast on the left hand north of Bougainville Strait was Bougainville. The precise date when it was first seen is not clear. Bouka was the modern Buka, which had, however, been discovered by Carteret (see section 31). All these islands are in the Solomons.

PLATE III

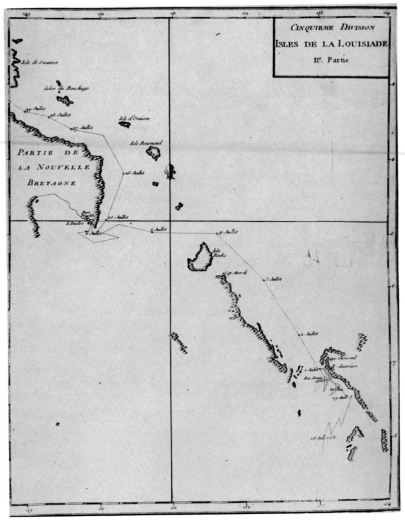

Bougainville's Chart of his Passage through the Northern Sector of the Solomons

From Buka Bougainville skirted New Ireland, New Hanover, and the Admiralty Islands, without seeing any islands which had not been previously discovered. On 8 August 1768 he passed a low inhabited island about 3 leagues long, divided into several parts surrounded by reefs and sand-banks. To this island, shown in his chart as in latitude 1° S., he gave the name Isle des Anachorètes. Three leagues to the west of it was another low isle, seen from the mast. On 9 August 1768 the ships passed an extended chain of low islands, named L'Échiquier, with a largish island to the east of it, named La Boudeuse, and after standing to for the night the westernmost of this chain was rounded from east to west on 10 August 1768. These islands are shown in the accompanying sectional chart as between latitudes 1° and 2° S. No more unknown islands were seen thereafter in the Pacific Islands area.

The latitudes, descriptions, and relative positions of these islands indicate that Bougainville came to Kaniet (Isle des Anachorètes) to the north-north-east of the Admiralty Islands, saw Sae beyond it, passed the Ninigo group (L'Échiquier) and Liot (La Boudeuse), and finally saw one of the islands south-west of the Ninigo group, probably Wuvulu. Some of these islands may have been seen by Saavedra (see section 5), by Retes (see section 7), and possibly by Vries (see section 19); and Wuvulu, if it were the last island seen, had been seen before by Carteret (see section 31). Bougainville, however, gave the first firm record of Kaniet, Sae, the Ninigo Islands, and Liot.

Louis Antoine de Bougainville's contributions to the discovery of the Pacific Islands may be summarized as follows: On 22 March 1768 he discovered Vahitahi and Akiaki, on 24 March he discovered Marokau, between 24 and 26 March 1768 he discovered Hikueru, Reitoru, and Haraiki, and on 26 March 1768 Anaa (the latter being seen by the *Étoile*), all these islands being in the Tuamotu Archipelago. Bougainville gave the first firm record of Pentecost and Aoba, on 22 May 1768, and of Malekula, on 23 May 1768, in the New Hebrides, although these islands may have been seen by members of Quiros's expedition in 1606 (see section 14). A landing was made on Aoba. On 25 June 1768 Bougainville may have discovered Rossel in the Louisiade Archipelago, although this island may have been seen from a distance by Prado and Torres in 1606 (see section 14). On 28 June 1768 Bougainville

discovered two of the islands south of Bougainville in the Solomons, presumably the Treasury Islands seen as one island and
Shortland Island, and Vella Lavella. At about this time he discovered Bougainville. On 8 August 1768 he gave the first firm
record of Kaniet and Sae, to the north of the Hermit Islands, and
on 9 August 1768 of the Ninigo Islands and Liot, some or all of
which may have been seen by Saavedra (see section 5), Retes (see
section 7), or Vries (see section 19).

33. James Cook's First Voyage

JAMES COOK, in command of the British naval vessel *Endeavour*,
made an exploration of the South Pacific in 1769–70. Cook's
journal[1] is the authority for the discoveries made on this voyage.

In the last days of January 1769 Cook entered the Pacific from the
east. On 4 April 1769 he came to a small inhabited island with a lagoon
(Lagoon Island), the latitude given being 18° 47′ S. On 5 April 1769
he came to another low small island (Thrum Cap), the latitude given
being 18° 35′ S. On 6 April 1769 he came to an inhabited island (Bow
Island) estimated to be about 12 or 15 leagues in compass, having a
bow-like shape, the latitude given being 18° 23′ S. On 7 April 1769
he saw land to the west which proved to be islands and reefs extending
north-west by north and south-east by south over an estimated distance
of 8 or 9 leagues, separated in the middle by a channel ½ mile broad,
named by Cook the Two Groups, the latitude of the southern one
being taken as 18° 12′ S. This was inhabited. Having passed it on the
south, they came to a small uninhabited island (Bird Island) on the
same day, the latitude given being 17° 48′ S. On 9 April 1769 Cook
came to some islands joined by reefs forming one oval-shaped chain-
like island (Chain Island), estimated to be about 5 leagues north-west
and south-east, and about 5 miles broad, the latitude of the middle of
it being given as 17° 23′ S. On 10 April 1769 he came to an island
recognized as Wallis's Osnaburgh Island (Mehetia), and on the 11th
to Wallis's King George's Island (Tahiti).

The sequence of islands encountered by Cook is clear from
these data, namely Vahitahi (Lagoon Island), Akiaki (Thrum

[1] *The Journals of Captain James Cook*, ed. Beaglehole, J. C., vol. i (Cambridge,
1955), pp. 1–479.

Cap), Hao (Bow Island), Marokau and Ravahere (Two Groups), Reitoru (Bird Island), and Anaa (Chain Island), all in the Tuamotu Archipelago. Cook had thus followed Bougainville's course (see section 32) with the exception that he passed south of Ravahere whereas Bougainville had passed north of Marokau. Quiros had discovered Hao (see section 14), as Cook himself surmised. Bougainville had discovered Vahitahi, Akiaki, Marokau, and Reitoru, and Anaa also was seen by Bougainville's second vessel. Cook was the discoverer of Ravahere, which Bougainville did not see.

After a long stay at Tahiti for the purpose of observing the transit of Venus, Cook, while standing to the north to get a nearer view of an island called 'Tethuroa', which had been seen previously from the hills of Tahiti, saw on 14 July 1769 an island called by his Tahitian interpreter 'Huaheine', to the north-west. On 16 July 1769, having reached 'Huaheine', three other islands were seen, namely 'Ulitea, Otaha, and Bolabola, so call'd by the Natives'. On 27 July 1769, while standing north from 'Bolabola', they discovered a low, small island called 'Tubai', some 4 or 5 leagues north by west or north-north-west of 'Bolabola'. On 30 July 1769 an island called 'Maurua' was seen to the west of 'Bolabola', with a high round hill in the middle. Landings were made on 'Huaheine', 'Ulitea', and 'Otaha'. To the islands 'Huaheine', 'Ulitea', 'Otaha', 'Bolabola', 'Tubai', and 'Maurua' Cook gave the name Society Isles.

These were the islands Huahine (Huaheine), Raiatea (Ulitea), Tahaa (Otaha), Borabora (Bolabola), Motu-iti (Tubai), and Maupiti (Maurua). The name Society Islands has since been extended to include Wallis's discoveries. Maupiti and Borabora had already been seen from a distance by Roggeveen (see section 27). Huahine, Raiatea, Tahaa, Borabora, and Tubai were new discoveries by Cook, as was Tetiaroa, the low island 'Tethuroa' seen to the north from the hills of Tahiti.

Cook says that the manners and customs of the islands to the west of Tahiti which were visited by him were much like those of Tahiti, of which he gives somewhat the same account as did Wallis.

While coming south from the Society Islands to New Zealand, Cook, on 14 August 1769, discovered an island called by his Tahitian interpreter Ohetiroa (meaning literally 'large high island'), the latitude given for it being 22° 27′ S. It was fairly high, and of an estimated circumference of 13 miles. The people were much like the Tahitians.

This was Rurutu, one of the Austral Islands. It rises to 1,300 feet, the latitude of the north-eastern part being 22° 26′ S. It was another of Cook's discoveries.

On 7 October 1769 Cook sighted New Zealand, the broad position of which was known from Tasman's discovery of the north-western parts. Between that date and 31 March 1770 Cook circumnavigated the main islands and sailed through the strait dividing the North and South Islands.

Leaving New Zealand on 1 April 1770, Cook went westward to the east coast of Australia, passing eventually through the waters dividing Australia from New Guinea, thus defining the eastern limits of Australia and the western limits of the South Pacific Ocean.

James Cook's contributions to the discovery of the Pacific Islands on his first voyage were as follows: On 7 April 1769 he discovered Ravahere in the Tuamotu Archipelago. On 14 July 1769 he sailed close to Tetiaroa, which had previously been seen from the hills of Tahiti. On 14 July 1769 he discovered Huahine, on 16 July 1769 Raiatea and Tahaa, and on 27 July 1769 Motu-iti, all in the Society Islands, landings being made on Huahine, Raiatea, and Tahaa. On 14 August 1769 Cook discovered Rurutu in the Austral Islands. Between 7 October 1769 and 31 March 1770 Cook circumnavigated New Zealand, proving its broad geography, and in particular that it was not a continent. He also defined the limits of Australia on the eastern side, and so of the Pacific Ocean on the west.

34. Duclesmeur

IN 1772 Nicholas Thomas Marion du Fresne, who had come to New Zealand from the west as the commander of two French ships, the *Marquis de Castries* and the *Mascarin*, was killed by the New Zealand natives. The command of the expedition was assumed by his second-in-command, called the Chevalier Duclesmeur in the accounts. Duclesmeur himself, and two of his officers, Julien Crozet and Jean Roux, left records of this voyage.[1]

Leaving the north part of New Zealand on 14 July 1772, the two ships came up to latitude 20° S., which, according to Crozet, they thought at the time was the latitude of Tasman's 'Roterdam' and 'Amsterdam' (see section 18), which were two islands in the south of the Tonga group, although Crozet says he found after his return to Europe that whereas the chart showed these in $20\frac{1}{2}$° S., Tasman's latitude for them was a degree farther south. Having reached a point considered to be east of these islands, the expedition turned west to pick them up. On 6 August 1772, as described by Crozet, they found themselves confronted with a chain of very low islands, appearing to be of broken coral, fringed with breakers, with coconuts planted by nature, the latitude when they were seen being taken at a little over 20° S. Roux says he could see fertile islands beyond these islands on their west side, where he thought there might be a port. Duclesmeur says that fires at night showed that there were inhabitants. Crozet, Duclesmeur, and Roux say that these islands were recognized as part of the archipelago discovered by Tasman. They then came north, skirting the archipelago for 2 more days, and seeing various islands. On 12 August 1772 they saw some more islands, judged to be in 16° S. No more islands were seen until they reached Guam.

These data show that Duclesmeur's ships, on 6 August 1772, came on the eastern islands of the central sector of the Tonga group in the vicinity of 20° S. Tasman had skirted this sector on its western side (see section 18). Duclesmeur then in the following days skirted the northern part of the Tonga group, but it is not possible to identify the precise islands seen. The islands seen on 12 August were presumably Tafahi and the Niuatobutabu cluster, situated in 16° S., but these were not new discoveries.

[1] Crozet, J., *Nouveau Voyage*, Rochon, A. (Paris, 1783); Duclesmeur's and Roux's manuscript accounts, in French National Archives, Paris, reproduced in microfilms in Alexander Turnbull Library.

35. Domingo de Boenechea and Tomas Gayangos

IN 1772 Domingo de Boenechea went from South America to Tahiti as commander of a Spanish vessel called variously the *Santa Maria Magdalena* or *Aguila*, returning to South America after leaving some Spanish priests at Tahiti. In 1774 Boenechea revisited Tahiti with a store-ship in addition to the *Aguila*, the name of the store-ship being the *Jupiter*. Boenechea died in Tahiti, and his successor, Tomas Gayangos, brought the ships back to South America in 1775. The journals of Boenechea and Gayangos are the authorities for the discoveries made on these voyages.[1]

Leaving Callao on 26 September 1772, Boenechea, on 28 October 1772, came to a low, flat, inhabited island, the latitude given being 17⅓° S. It was named by him San Simon y Judas. At noon on 30 October he continued to the west, and next morning, 31 October 1772, came on another low inhabited island, called San Quintin, the latitude given being about 17½° S. Like San Simon it was a lagoon island. On 1 November 1772, in the late afternoon, the ship came to an island with a lagoon in the middle, thought to be 17 leagues round, as compared with 5⅓ leagues for San Quintin and 3½ leagues for San Simon. This island, which was named Todos Santos, was considered to be in latitude 17° 24′ S. The accompanying plan of Todos Santos shows from its distinctive shape that it was Anaa in the Tuamotu Archipelago, which was discovered by the second ship of Bougainville's expedition (see section 32).

The identity of San Simon and San Quintin can be more easily established when considered in conjunction with the second voyage of Boenechea in 1774.

Leaving Callao on 20 September 1774, in company with the store-ship *Jupiter*, on his second visit to Tahiti, Boenechea, on 29 October 1774, came to a low inhabited island with a lagoon, the latitude given being 17° 26′ S. It was named San Narciso. Leaving it the next morning, 30 October, the ships, at 11 o'clock the following morning, came to the San Simon of the previous voyage, the latitude of the middle part being taken as 17° 27′ S. The distance from San Narciso was estimated

---

[1] *The Quest and Occupation of Tahiti*, ed. Corney, B. G. (London, 1913–18).

at 55 leagues. Leaving San Simon at 3 o'clock in the afternoon the course was resumed for the San Quintin of the previous voyage. Before coming to it, however, they saw just before noon the following day, 1 November 1774, two islands to the west-north-west and south-south-west. The latitude of the one to the north, named Los Martires, was taken as 17° 29′ S. It was thought to be 19½ leagues from San Simon. It consisted of a small wooded hummock, surrounded by a reef of which the greater part was overflowed by the sea. Towards this a current set with great force. The island to the south, named San Juan, was larger than Los Martires, the distance between them being estimated at 6⅓ leagues. On 2 November at 8.15 a.m. they sighted San Quintin, and leaving it at 6 p.m. under easy sail, they sighted Todos Santos next morning.

These details, as compared with charts of the Tuamotu Archipelago, show that San Quintin, Los Martires, San Juan, San Simon, and San Narciso were islands lying east and west of each other and east of Anaa, in the vicinity of latitude 17½° S., the distance from San Narciso to San Simon being much greater than from San Simon to Los Martires, Los Martires being smaller than San Juan and relatively near it, all of which indicates that the islands in question were respectively Tatakoto (San Narciso), Tauere (San Simon), Tekokoto (Los Martires), Hikueru (San Juan), Haraiki (San Quintin), and Anaa (Todos Santos). On the first voyage Tatakoto, Tekokoto, and Hikueru were not seen, and Tekokoto had meanwhile been discovered by Cook in the year 1773 during the course of his second voyage (see section 37). Hikueru and Haraiki had been discovered by Bougainville (see section 32). Tatakoto and Tauere were new discoveries by Boenechea.

The store-ship *Jupiter*, the captain of which was Joseph Andia y Varela, became separated from the *Aguila* before the latter reached Tatakoto, which Andia encountered the morning after Boenechea. The *Jupiter* then encountered Amanu while passing from Tatakoto to Tauere, reaching the latter island after Boenechea had left it. Amanu had already been discovered by Quiros (see section 14). Andia did not therefore make any new discoveries.

On 9 November 1774, while standing off Anaa waiting for the *Jupiter*, the *Aguila* was driven off the coast by storms and came in sight of land to the north-east. The ship ranged along this land with the head of the vessel to the east, at a distance of 3 to 4 leagues, until two hummocks were seen ahead, with a heavy sea breaking on them. These hummocks were thought to be 10 leagues distant from the other land seen, in latitudes 17° 9′ and 16° 53′ S.

These details show that Boenechea came in sight of the south coast of Tahanea some 40 to 45 miles north-east of Anaa, and later saw the two westernmost islets of Motutunga, which lies 10 miles south-east of Tahanea. Motutunga had already been discovered by Cook on his second voyage (see section 37). Tahanea was discovered by Boenechea.

A statement to the effect that when Boenechea's ship was near Anaa a cross near a wood was seen might appear to give support to the view that Anaa had previously been visited by Europeans. If a cross had in fact been erected by Europeans, it is unlikely that it was more than 50 to 75 years previously, since the life of cut timber in Anaa could not have been very long. It is plain that Cook did not land on Anaa, and that Bougainville's expedition after sighting it did not make close contact with it. In 1722 five members of Roggeveen's company deserted at Takapoto (see section 27), their subsequent fate and movements being unknown. Perhaps the most likely view of the origin of the supposed cross was that it was a post with a cross-arm on which things were hung by the islanders, such as is figured in some of the early drawings accompanying the records of exploration.

After the death of Boenechea in Tahiti, Tomas Gayangos became commander of the expedition, and returned to South America in company with the store-ship. The ships got clear of the south of Tahiti on 30 January 1775, and took a course to the south-east, lying to at night. On 5 February 1775 they came to an island, the latitude given being 23° 30′ S. The next day a boat was sent in, and made contact with the inhabitants at the shore edge, but a landing was not made. The people said that the name of their island was 'Oraibaba'. The Spaniards called it Santa Rosa.

This island was Raivavae, in the Austral Islands, some 360 miles south-south-east of Tahiti, in latitude 23° 52′ S.

Andia, the commander of the store-ship, has recorded in his journal the report of Bonacorsi, the officer commanding the *Aguila*'s boat which made contact with the islanders of Raivavae at the shore edge. The Tahitian interpreters who went with Bonacorsi could understand only an occasional word used by the islanders. The people were like those of Tahiti, some white, some mulatto-coloured, some more swarthy. They were tall and of good physique. Their ears were pierced and their hair was fastened in a tuft on the head. Their clothing was of wraps like the Tahitian, in various colours. They had double canoes with high bows and sterns. Their weapons were well-made short pikes and short cudgels, but the people appeared peaceable.

The *Aguila* made one more trip to Tahiti under the command of Cayetano de Langara, but no new islands were discovered, the only addition to those seen by Boenechea being a sight of North Marutea to the north-west of Tekokoto, North Marutea having been discovered by Cook in 1773 (see section 37).

The discoveries of Domingo de Boenechea were as follows: On 28 October 1772 he discovered Tauere. On 29 October 1774 he discovered Tatakoto. On 9 November 1774 he discovered Tahanea. All these islands are in the Tuamotu Archipelago.

Tomas Gayangos, on 5 February 1775, discovered Raivavae in the Austral Islands.

36. Felipe Tompson

IN 1773 Felipe Tompson, in a Spanish vessel named *Nuestra Señora de la Consolacion*, sailed from Manila to California via New Guinea.[1]

A late eighteenth-century Spanish chart shows the course of a vessel in 1773, which was apparently Tompson's, past a 'Ba. de S. Feliz' east-north-east of Morotai. The abbreviation 'Ba.' was common for Baxo or Baxos, meaning Bank or Reef.

Helen Reef, the uninhabited southern island of the western Carolines, consisting almost entirely of reefs, with one small islet,

[1] Espinosa, J., *Memorias* (Madrid, 1809), vol. ii, pp. 16–17; Duperrey, L. I., *Mémoire sur les opérations géographiques* (Paris, 1827), p. 64; Eilers, A., in *Ergebnisse der Südsee-Expedition 1908–1910. II. Ethnographie B Mikronesien*, vol. ix, part 2 (Hamburg, 1936), p. 2.

corresponds in position and description to the San Feliz Reef of the Spanish chart. The near-by island of Tobi might also correspond to the position, but scarcely to the description of a bank or reef. This may be taken as the first firm record of Helen Reef, although it may have been seen by Woodes Rogers (see section 25), and before him by the Portuguese (see section 4).

Coming north from New Guinea, Tompson, in June 1773, discovered a cluster of islands named Islas de la Passion, of which 'Los Valientes' were considered by him to be in latitude 5° 40′ N. Continuing north, Tompson encountered a reef or rock with one islet to the north-west of it, considered to be in latitude 7° 24′ N. and somewhat to the west of Los Valientes in longitude. To this islet Tompson gave the name S. Agostino, and to the reef or rock near it the name Baxotristo.

The only two islands corresponding to these data are the atolls of Ngatik and Oroluk, in the Caroline Islands. Ngatik consists of a number of islets in 5° 50′ N. Oroluk consists of reefs ringing a lagoon with an islet at the north-western extremity in latitude 7° 40′ N. and a rock a few feet high on its eastern side.[1] Ngatik may have been discovered by Saavedra (see section 5), and Oroluk may have been discovered by Arellano (see section 8).

Tompson thus gave the first firm report of Helen Reef, Ngatik, and Oroluk.

37. James Cook's Second Voyage

IN the years 1772–5 James Cook made a second voyage of exploration as commander of a British expedition of two ships, the *Resolution* and the *Adventure*, the latter of which became separated from the *Resolution* and returned to England without making any independent discoveries in the Pacific. The authority for this voyage is Cook's journal.[2] The voyage was the first in Pacific exploration in which methods of determining longitudes independently by lunar observations and chronometers were com-

[1] *Pacific Islands Pilot*, vol. i, p. 527.
[2] Cook, J., *A Voyage towards the South Pole* (London, 1777).

bined. Cook's positions are therefore given both with latitude and longitude.

Cook came from the west into the Pacific, and spent some time in New Zealand waters. On 7 June 1773 he left New Zealand and proceeded east. Finding no land, he came west making for the Society Islands, and passed through the Tuamotu Archipelago. On 11 August 1773, at daybreak, land was seen to the south, judged to be about 2 leagues in extent, in the direction of north-west and south-east, in latitude 17° 24′ S., longitude 141° 39′ W. This island Cook called Resolution Island. Continuing to the west, at 6 o'clock the same evening land was seen from the mast-head bearing west by south, the position given being latitude 17° 20′ S., longitude 141° 38′ W. This island was named Doubtful Island. Steering during the night west by north in order to pass the north of this island, at daybreak the next morning, 12 August 1773, another low, half-drowned island was found. It was a low coral shoal appearing to be about 25 leagues in circuit, of which only a small part was land, consisting of small islets along the north side, connected by sand-banks and breakers. The ships passed the south side, seeing in the middle a lake or inland sea, in which was a canoe under sail. The position given for this island, which was named Furneaux by Cook, was latitude 17° 5′ S., longitude 143° 16′ W. They brought to overnight and at dawn the next day, 13 August 1773, saw another low island, the position given being latitude 17° 4′ S., longitude 144° 30′ W. That evening at 5 o'clock Cook came to the Chain Island of his previous voyage, namely Anaa (see section 33).

These details show that on 11 August Cook encountered Tauere (Resolution) and Tekokoto (Doubtful), on 12 August North Marutea (Furneaux), and on 13 August Motutunga, reaching Anaa the same evening. This sequence of islands agrees with Cook's stated positions and sailing times, while the description of Furneaux conforms closely with North Marutea's distinctive topography.[1] Tauere had been discovered the previous year by Boenechea. Tekokoto, North Marutea, and Motutunga were new discoveries.

After some time in the Society Islands, Cook set out to the west, accompanied by two Tahitians, of whom one was later returned to Tahiti, while the other, called Omai by Cook, accompanied Furneaux in due course to England in the *Adventure*,

---

[1] *Pacific Islands Pilot*, vol. iii, p. 103.

and was brought back to the Society Islands by Cook on his third voyage.

On 23 September 1773 Cook discovered two or three small islets, connected together by breakers, lying in triangular form, and appearing to be about 6 leagues in circuit. No signs of inhabitants were seen as they passed. The position given was latitude 19° 18′ S., longitude 158° 54′ W. Cook named it Hervey's Island. On 1 October 1773 he reached the southern islands of Tonga.

Hervey's Island was the atoll usually now known as Manuae, in the southern Cook Islands. It actually consists of two islets on a reef encircling a lagoon. The position of the north-west of Manuae is latitude 19° 21′ S., longitude 158° 58′ W.

From Tonga Cook sailed south again to New Zealand, where the *Adventure* became separated from Cook in the *Resolution*. From New Zealand he came south and east as far as the pack ice, without finding any trace of a great southern continent in the extensive areas traversed by him.

After visiting Easter Island, Cook set out for Mendaña's discoveries in the Marquesas group (see section 12). On 6 April 1774, the position being taken as latitude 9° 20′ S., longitude 138° 14′ W., an island was seen bearing west by south at 9 leagues. Four more islands were subsequently seen to the south, and were recognized as Mendaña's discoveries. This indicated to Cook that the first island seen by him was a new discovery, which he named Hood's Island.

Hood's Island was Fatu Huku, lying 19 miles north-north-west of Hiva Oa.

From the Marquesas Cook came to Byron's King George's Islands, Takaroa and Takapoto (see section 29), on the northern fringe of the Tuamotu Archipelago. The day after leaving Takapoto, namely on 19 April 1774, Cook, having steered 'south-south-west, half west, and south-west by south', came to another lagoon island, the position given being latitude 15° 26′ S., longitude 146° 20′ W. It appeared to be 5 leagues long in the direction north-north-east and south-south-west, and about 3 leagues broad. Near the south end another low island was seen from the mast-head bearing south-east, distant about 4 or 5 leagues, but they could not fetch it because it was to windward. Soon afterwards a third island appeared, bearing south-west by south, the position of the east end being taken as latitude 15° 47′ S., longitude 146° 30′ W. This island appeared to be 7 leagues long west-north-west and east-south-east, but not more than 2 leagues broad. As they passed the north coast they saw inhabitants. Drawing near the west end, they saw a fourth island bearing north-north-east distant 6 leagues. These four islands Cook called Palliser's Isles. He was not sure whether any of these had been discovered by the Dutch navigators.

A comparison of these details with the map will show that Cook, sailing south-west from Takapoto, first came to Apataki, and, rounding it on the south, saw Toau to the south-east, then Kaukura to the south-west by south. The eastern end of Kaukura is in latitude 15° 49′ S., longitude 146° 28′ W., agreeing almost precisely with the position as stated by Cook. Finally Arutua was seen to the north-north-east. Of these four islands Apataki and Arutua had been discovered by Roggeveen (see section 27). Toau and Kaukura were new discoveries.

From the Tuamotus Cook went to the Society Islands. On 5 June 1774 he left Raiatea for Tonga. He passed Mopihaa, and saw nothing more of interest until 16 June 1774, when another reef island was discovered, composed of five or six woody islets connected with sand-banks and breakers, with a lake in the middle. From its southern to its northern extremity was about 2 leagues. No sign of inhabitants was seen. The position given was latitude 18° 4′ S., longitude 163° 10′ W. To this island Cook gave the name Palmerston.

This was the modern Palmerston Island, a detached atoll in the Cook group. The *Pacific Islands Pilot* says it consists of six sandy islets covered with coconut palms on a coral reef, which extends about 7 miles north and south and 5 miles east and west.[1] Its position is precisely as given by Cook.

From Palmerston Island Cook proceeded west, and 4 days later, on 20 June 1774, came to an inhabited island of moderate height on which landings were made, when the land proved to be of coral overgrown with trees and bushes. The island was of round form and appeared to be about 11 leagues in circuit. The position given for it was latitude 19° 1′ S., longitude 169° 37′ W. To this island Cook gave the name Savage Island.

This was the modern Niue, a detached coral island some 200 feet high, between the Cook Islands and Tonga, in the position stated by Cook.

[1] *Pacific Islands Pilot*, vol. iii, p. 86.

Cook did not see very much of the Niue Islanders, who resisted
his landings. They appeared to be of good physique, were naked
except round the waists, and some of them had their faces, breasts,
and thighs painted black. The canoes were like those of Tongatabu
in Tonga. Both the islanders and their canoes, said Cook, agreed
with Bougainville's descriptions of the Samoans.

After some time in the Tonga group, Cook came west from Tofua,
On 2 July 1774 a small island was discovered, not quite a league in
length north-east and south-west, and not half that in breadth. A
landing was made on this island, when inhabitants were seen at a
distance. Its position was given as latitude 19° 48' S., longitude
178° 2' W. This island was called Turtle Isle. South-west from it at
about 5 or 6 miles was a large coral shoal. Cook continued west and
saw no more land until 15 July.

Turtle Isle was Vatoa, in the southern sector of the Fiji Islands,
answering in all details to Cook's data, including having a detached shoal on its south-west side. Vatoa, as the map will show,
is in such a position to the south of the main Fiji group that a
vessel encountering it on a passage to the west would miss the
other islands of the group. This was a new discovery.

On 15 July 1774 Cook reached the northern islands of the New
Hebrides, known to him from the discoveries of Quiros and Bougainville (see sections 14 and 32). On 20 July 1774 Cook discovered an
island which was later named to him by the natives of the near-by
Malekula as Ambrim. On 21 July 1774 he saw off the south end of
Ambrim an elevated island, and after that another, still higher, with a
peaked hill, the names given to these two islands by Cook's informants
being Apee and Paoom. It was thought later by Cook that Paoom
might be two islands. On 24 July 1774 Cook discovered a large number
of islands to the south of Apee. The nearest were one about 4 leagues
in circuit remarkable for its three peaks, for which reason Cook named
it Threehills, and a group of small islands off the south-east point of
Apee east of Threehills which were named Shepherd's Isles. Cook now
saw lands or islands in every direction. On 25 July 1774 he continued
south, passing a high peaked rock named Monument, and a small
island with two peaked hills separated by a low strip of land, named by
Cook Twohills. Apart from Monument there were people on all the
islands they found. At noon the observed latitude was 17° 18' 30" S.
At 5 p.m. they drew near the southern lands seen by them previously,
and found them to consist of one large island and a number of smaller

ones on its north side, some of the latter being called by Cook Montagu and Hinchinbrooke Isles, the large island being named Sandwich. Sandwich Island made a delightful prospect, with woods and lawns, agreeably diversified, the hills, which were of moderate height, sloping gently to the sea-coast. On 27 July 1774 a new island was seen to the south. It took them 3 days to come near this because of adverse winds, calms, and currents, during which time they saw an elevated land to the south. When Cook later made contact with the people of this latter island, they told him that its name was Tanna, that the name of the previous island which he took 3 days to gain was Erromango, that the name of a high table island to the east of Tanna was Erronan or Footoona, that the name of a small island near by was Immer, and that the name of another island to the south-east of Tanna was Annatom. Footoona and Immer were discovered by Cook on 5 August 1774. Cook does not say precisely when Annatom was first seen. Landings were made on Erromango and on Tanna. The middle of Erromango was placed in latitude 18° 54' S., longitude 169° 19' E., and the position of Annatom in latitude 20° 3' S., longitude 170° 4' E. Apee was considered to be scarcely 5 leagues from Ambrim, Threehills 5 leagues south from Apee, Sandwich 9 leagues south from Threehills, Erromango 18 leagues south from Sandwich, and Tanna 6 leagues from Erromango. Immer, Erronan or Footoona, Erromango, and Annatom could all be seen from Tanna. Cook, having traversed these islands from north to south, then traversed the New Hebrides, so named by him, in the reverse direction, making contact with some of the islanders on the north coast of Espiritu Santo, at the north end of the group.

These details record Cook's discovery of the southern islands of the New Hebrides. Ambrim was the island of that name, situated 12 miles north of Epi, Cook's Apee. Near by are Paama and Lopevi, 'Paoom' being, as Cook suspected, two islands. To the south of Epi is Emae, an island with three conspicuous peaks—Cook's Threehills. South-east of Epi are the Shepherd Islands, so known from Cook's name, of which Tongoa is the chief. Twohills was Mataso, an island with two hilly portions joined by a low narrow isthmus, with a high rock near it. Sandwich was Efate, and Montagu and Hinchinbrooke Isles were some of the small islands near Efate's north coast. Erromango was Eromanga, some 56 miles south-south-east of Efate. Tana lies 23 miles south of Eromanga. Aniwa or Immer is 11 miles east-north-east of Tana, Erronan, more commonly known today as Futuna, is a table-

topped island to the east of Tana, and Aneityum, Cook's Annatom, the southernmost of the New Hebrides, is 35 miles south-
east of Tana.

Cook gives numbers of details of the people of Eromanga, Tana,
and the neighbouring islands, and makes some interesting com-
parisons of them with one another, with the people he met at
Malekula and Espiritu Santo to the north, and with some of the
Polynesian peoples to the east. Cook and Forster, the naturalist of
the expedition, had acquired a fair knowledge of Polynesian
words.

The people met with at Eromanga appeared to be of a different
race from those at Malekula, and spoke a different language. Thus
the people of the north-east part of Malekula, where Cook stayed
for a time, were the ugliest, most ill-proportioned and ape-like
people Cook ever saw, and of about eighty words collected by
Forster, hardly one had any affinity with any speech at any of
the places Cook had visited. The people of Eromanga were of
middle size, had a good shape, and tolerable features. Their
colour was very dark and their hair curly, and the men, like the
Malekulans, were in a manner naked, having only a belt round
the waist and a piece of cloth or leaf used as a wrapper. The
women had a kind of petticoat made of palm leaves or something
like that. The Eromangans lived in houses covered with thatch,
and their plantations were laid out by line and fenced round.
They were armed with darts, stones, and bows and arrows, the
arrows being pointed with hard wood. The Malekulans, who
were armed in much the same way, tipped their arrows with a
gummy substance which apparently had some poisonous property. No canoes were seen in any part of Eromanga.

At Tana, where Cook's ship stayed for some time, close contact
of a relatively friendly nature was established with numbers of
the islanders after some degree of mutual confidence had been
attained. The people spoke two languages, one of which they
ascribed to the near-by Futuna, the other language spoken by the
people of Tana, as also, Cook understood, the people of Eromanga and Aneityum, being properly their own, and different
from any that Cook and his associates had met with before,

including that of Malekula, so that it seemed to Cook that the people of Tana, Eromanga, and Aneityum were a distinct people. The language ascribed to Futuna, however, was nearly, if not exactly, that spoken at Tonga. From this Cook considered it more than probable that Futuna was peopled by Tongans, and that, by long intercourse with Tana and the other neighbouring islands, each had learnt the other's language. Some few men, women, and children were seen who had hair like the European, whereas the great majority had crisp curly hair, but it was obvious the minority were of a different people, and came, Cook thought he had been given to understand, from Futuna. Cook thought the majority showed little affinity with either the Tongans or Malekulans, except in the hair, which was rather like that of the Malekulans. Malekula, Epi, and even Efate were entirely unknown to the people of Tana, says Cook, who adds that he took no small pains to know how far their geographical knowledge extended, and found it did not exceed the limits of their horizon. The people of Tana appeared to live off the products of the land, their fishing being apparently confined to the shores and shoals, no fishing tackle other than darts being seen, and no off-shore fishing. Cook understood that Immer was chiefly inhabited by fishermen, and that the canoes which frequently passed to and from that island were fishing canoes. These were poorly made outrigger canoes with paddles and lateen sails. The produce of Tana was 'breadfruit, plantains, cocoa-nuts, a fruit like a nectarine, yams, terra, a sort of potato, sugar-cane, wild figs, a fruit like an orange, which is not eatable, and some other fruit and nuts whose names I have not. . . . Hogs did not seem to be scarce, but we saw not many fowls: these are the only domestic animals they have.' Both sexes were of a very dark colour, but not black, nor had they the least characteristic of the negro about them. The men wore nothing but a belt, and the wrapping leaf as at Malekula. The women had a kind of petticoat made of the 'filaments of the plantain-tree, flags, or some such thing'. Their ornaments were bracelets, earrings, necklaces, and amulets. Their stone hatchets, at least all Cook saw, were not in the shape of adzes, as at other islands, but more like an axe, in the thick handle being a hole into which the stone was fixed. Apart from the cultivation of the ground the people of Tana had few arts worth mentioning. They made a coarse kind of matting, and a coarse cloth of the bark of a tree. Their weapons were fairly well-made clubs, spears or darts, bows and arrows, and stones. They were very expert in the use of spears and darts.

Cook's contacts with the people of the north coast of Espiritu Santo made him think they were of another people from those of Malekula. They named the numerals as far as five or six in the language of Nomuka in Tonga, and understood Cook and his associates when asked the names of the adjacent lands in that language. Some had black short frizzled hair like the natives of Malekula, but others had it long, tied up on the crown of the head, and ornamented with feathers, like the New Zealanders. Their other ornaments were bracelets and necklaces. Their canoes were made like those of Tana.

Leaving Espiritu Santo on 29 August 1774, Cook came south and south-west, and on 3 September 1774 discovered more land. This proved on closer examination to be a large mountainous island, named by Cook New Caledonia, estimated to be about 87 leagues long, but not anywhere more than 10 leagues broad, lying between latitudes 19° 37′ to 22° 30′ S., and longitudes 163° 37′ to 167° 14′ E., with some small islands to the south of it, one of which, discovered on 26 September 1774, Cook called the Isle of Pines. Landings were made on New Caledonia at a district on the east coast called Balade, where the ship stayed for 10 days. Cook did not have time to examine the west coast, part of which was seen from a hill in the interior.

These islands were the modern New Caledonia and the small islands close to it on the south, of which latter the main one, Kunie, was Cook's Isle of Pines.

The people of the Balade district of New Caledonia, says Cook, seemed to be a race between the people of Tana and Tonga, or between those of Tana and New Zealand, or all three, their language, in some respects, being a mixture of them all. The people were robust, nearly of the same colour as those of Tana, but with better features. They wore large wooden combs in their hair. The men were naked apart from the same type of wrapper as at Tana and Malekula, the women's dress being a very short petticoat. The general ornaments of both sexes were ear-rings of tortoise-shell, necklaces or amulets made of shells and stones, and bracelets made of large shells worn above the elbow. They had earthenware pots. While they appeared a peaceable people, they had weapons such as clubs, spears, darts, and slings for throwing stones. Their houses were circular, something like a bee-hive, with low entrances. They grew sugar cane, plantains, yams, and taro, the latter by two methods, one in flat patches, the other in ridges. Their vessels were large, clumsy, double canoes made of two dug-out logs with a platform between, and one or two lateen sails made of matting.

On 10 October 1774 Cook, while making for New Zealand, discovered an island of good height, appearing to be about 5 leagues in circuit. Its position was taken as latitude 29° 2' 30" S., longitude 168° 16' E. A landing was made, when the island was found to be uninhabited. A type of spruce pine grew in great abundance. This island Cook named Norfolk Island.

This was Norfolk Island, a detached island in the position given by Cook, and answering to Cook's description.

Cook, having come south to New Zealand, returned to England round South America.

On this voyage James Cook on 11 August 1773, discovered Tekokoto, on 12 August 1773 North Marutea, and on 13 August 1773 Motutunga, in the Tuamotu Archipelago. On 23 September 1773 he discovered Manuae, in the southern Cook Islands. On 6 April 1774 he discovered Fatu Huku in the Marquesas group. On 19 April 1774 he discovered Toau and Kaukura in the Tuamotu Archipelago. On 16 and 20 June 1774 he discovered Palmerston in the Cook group, and Niue. On 2 July 1774 he discovered Vatoa in the Fiji Islands, a landing being made. On 20 July 1774 he discovered Ambrim; on 21 July 1774 Epi, Paama, and Lopevi; on 24 July 1774 the islands south of Epi as far as Efate; on 27 July 1774 Eromanga, landings being subsequently made; between that date and 30 July 1774 Tana, landings being subsequently made; on 5 August 1774 Aniwa and Futuna, and on the same day or thereabouts, Aneityum; all these islands being in the New Hebrides group. On 3 September 1774 he discovered New Caledonia, landings being made, and on 26 September 1774 Kunie, to the south of New Caledonia. On 10 October 1774 he discovered Norfolk Island, to the north-west of New Zealand, a landing being made. On this voyage Cook also proved that there was no great continent in the South Pacific between Australia and America north of the Antarctic pack ice.

38. James Cook's Third Voyage, and Charles Clerke

IN the years 1777–9 James Cook was again in the Pacific, on his third and last voyage, this time as the commander of an expedition of two ships, the *Resolution* and the *Discovery*. After his death in the Hawaiian Islands on 14 February 1779 Charles Clerke assumed the command. Under him the expedition made the first firm record of some islands. The authorities for this voyage are the journal of Cook until shortly before his death, and thereafter the journal of James King, a senior officer of the expedition.[1]

Having come to New Zealand from the west, Cook, on 25 February 1777, sailed for the Society Islands. The winds were variable, and it was not till 29 March 1777 that land was seen. It proved to be a small inhabited island, appearing to be about 5 leagues in circuit, of moderate height. Omai, Cook's Tahitian interpreter, had some conversation with some of the inhabitants in a canoe and at the shore edge. The name given by them to the island was Mangya or Mangeea. Its position was taken as latitude 21° 57′ S., longitude 201° 53′ E.

This was Mangaia, in the southern Cook Islands, corresponding in position and topography to Cook's detail.

The little that was seen of the Mangaians appeared to show that they were like the Tahitians and Marquesans, their language being a dialect of the Tahitian, although, like the New Zealand, more guttural in pronunciation. One house seen near the beach resembled those of Tahiti. The islanders did not have pigs or dogs, but knew their names. They said they had plantains, bread-fruit,

[1] Cook, J., and King, J., *A Voyage to the Pacific Ocean* (London, 1784).

and taro. They saluted strangers by rubbing noses as in New Zealand, with the additional ceremony of taking the hand of the other person and rubbing it on their nose and mouth. The only canoe seen was a narrow one, and was paddled. A man with a scar on his face said he had sustained the wound in fighting with people from an 'island' to the north-east who sometimes invaded them, but since the usual Tahitian words were used indifferently for people, islands, or lands, and there are no historical records of contacts between Mangaia and islands to the north-east, the reference was presumably to internal warfare with the north-eastern sector of Mangaia, which is well documented by later references.[1]

Leaving Mangaia on 30 March and proceeding north, the next day, 31 March 1777, Cook discovered another island, with a smaller island to the north-west. The larger island was about 6 leagues in circumference, and was a beautiful spot, with a surface composed of hills and plains. Its name was given as Wateeo by the islanders. The position was taken as latitude 20° 1' S., longitude 201° 45' E.

This was Atiu in the southern Cook Islands, the small island being Takutea, 10 miles to the north-west of Atiu.

A landing party including Omai went ashore at Atiu. The people had, in addition to the products mentioned at Mangaia, pigs, but not dogs. Red feathers were worn by the people of rank, also necklaces of two small bone balls on a cord. Both sexes practised tattooing. Their general dress was a piece of cloth or mat wrapped round the waist, but some wore a sort of jacket without sleeves, and others a conical cap of coconut core, interwoven with small shelly beads. Some of the men were armed with clubs and spears of varying sizes. Both single canoes with outriggers, and double canoes, were seen, some with elaborate black markings in squares and triangles. The visitors were entertained to a repast of baked plantains and pig, and Omai drank a ceremonial draught of kava with the chiefs.

A landing was made on Takutea, where no inhabitants were found.

[1] Williams, J., *Missionary Enterprises* (London, 1837), pp. 242-4; Gill, W. W., *Life in the Southern Isles* (London, 1876), pp. 148-9.

Cook came west from the Cook group to Tonga. Here, on 16 May 1777, he gave the first firm record of the eastern islands of the Haapai sector, Uoleva, Lifuka, Foa, and Haano, some or all of which were probably seen by Duclesmeur as he skirted the group on its west side (see section 34).

From Tonga Cook came east for the Society Islands. On 8 August 1777 an island with hills was discovered. Its greatest extent in any direction was not above 5 or 6 miles. Its position was taken as latitude 22° 15' S., longitude 210° 37' E. Some men in canoes said the name of the island was Toobouai.

This was Tubuai in the Austral Islands, answering in position and description to Cook's data.

The men in the canoes were of the same people and language as the Tahitians. They had only a loincloth as covering, but some of those seen on the beach were entirely clothed with a kind of white garment. Some of the islanders wore pearl-shell necklaces. One kept blowing a large conch shell. Their canoes, which appeared to be about 30 feet long, were single paddling canoes with outriggers, well carved, the sides being decorated with flat white shells disposed nearly in concentric semicircles with the curve upward. No weapons were seen.

After some time in the Society Islands, where Omai remained, the expedition set out for the North Pacific, where Cook had instructions to look for a passage to the Atlantic. On 24 December 1777 a low lagoon island was discovered. Landing parties found it uninhabited. It appeared to be crescent-shaped, and about 15 or 20 leagues in circumference. On the west side the position given was latitude 1° 59' N., longitude 202° 30' E. Cook called it Christmas Island.

This was Christmas Island, in the mid-Pacific area, a detached atoll answering to Cook's position and other details.

On 2 January 1778 Cook resumed his course to the north. There was a gentle breeze at east and east-south-east till the latitude of 7° 45' N., then one calm day, succeeded by a north-east by east and east-north-east wind which freshened as they advanced to the north. On 18 January 1778 two high islands were seen. The next day, 19 January 1778, when Cook was some distance to the south of the second of these islands, a third was seen to the west-north-west. The ships anchored at the second island, the native name of which was stated by the inhabitants to be Atooi. The name of the first island seen on 18 January

1778 was Woahoo, the latitude according to Cook being 21° 36' N.
There were actually three islands near Atooi on the west side, called
by the people of Atooi Oneeheow, Oreehoua, and Tahoora, all of
which were seen by Cook, and of which Oneeheow, being much the
largest, must have been part or all of the land seen as the third island
on the 19th. Just when the smaller islands Oreehoua and Tahoora were
first seen is not clear. The five islands seen by Cook were placed by him
between latitudes 21° 30' and 22° 15' N., and longitudes 199° 20' and
201° 30' E.

These were the islands Oahu (Woahoo), Kauai (Atooi), Niihau
(Oneeheow), Lehua (Oreehoua), and Kaula (Tahoora) in the
Hawaii group.

After visiting Niihau as well as Kauai, Cook went north and explored
the North American and Behring Strait area. He returned south, and
on 25 November 1778, at daybreak, land was seen to the south. At
8 a.m. the ships were 2 leagues distant from its northern coast. The
summit of an elevated saddle hill appeared above the clouds. The ships
sailed west along the northern coast. At noon they were near a low
flat like an isthmus. Here the position was taken as latitude 20° 59' N.,
longitude 203° 50' E. They did not go farther west, having made contact with some islanders in canoes. In the evening, the horizon being
clear to the west, the westernmost land in sight was judged to be a
separate island. Cook came back east along this coast. On 30 November
1778 another island was discovered. The name given by the inhabitants
was Owhyhee, and to the island first seen on the 25th, Mowee. Snow
lay on the high land of Owhyhee. Having rounded this island on the
east and south sides, the ships anchored in a bay on its west coast
called by the inhabitants Karakakooa.

Mowee was Maui in the Hawaii group. The *Pacific Islands Pilot*
says it consists of two sectors joined by a low, flat isthmus, and
that the crater of Haleakala in the eastern sector, rising to 10,025
feet with a large gap or opening on its northern side, is often seen
above the clouds. The position given by Cook when near the low
flat like an isthmus is a point close to the north side of the low
isthmus between the two sectors of Maui. Molokai, an island about
$7\frac{1}{2}$ miles north-west of Maui, rises to 4,970 feet.[1] It is evident,
therefore, that Cook, having come to the eastern part of Maui
and seen Haleakala, sailed west as far as the low, flat isthmus

---

[1] *Pacific Islands Pilot*, vol. iii, pp. 240, 246, 256.

which divides the two high parts of Maui, and saw Molokai to the west. There is no reason to believe that Lanai, which lies west-south-west of the north-western part of Maui, was seen at this time. Owhyhee was the island of Hawaii, about 26 miles south-west of Maui, Karakakooa, where the ships anchored on the west side of Hawaii, being Kealakakua Bay.

Cook's journal ends at the arrival at Kealakakua Bay on 16 January 1779, and King takes up the story.

Cook, on 4 February 1779, left Kealakakua Bay and made north, intending to finish the survey of the island of Hawaii. The ships made slow progress on that day and the next because of calm weather. Before they were past the north-west of the island the foremast of the *Resolution* was found to be sprung by bad weather, and on 8–10 February 1779 they made back to Kealakakua Bay. Here Cook, on 14 February 1779, was killed, being succeeded in the command by Charles Clerke. On 22 February 1779 the expedition left for Maui. On 24 February 1779, as King relates, they passed a small barren island called Tahoorawa 7 or 8 miles south-west of Maui and stood for the passage between Maui and an island called Ranai. At noon the position was taken as latitude 20° 42′ N., longitude 203° 22′ E., with Tahoorawa, Ranai, and Morotai in sight. During the day people came off in canoes and traded produce to the ships. The only further point of relevance in the expedition's further traverse of the Hawaii group under Clerke was a contact with Oahu, where after sailing round its north-east and north-west coast a brief landing was made on the north-west side on 27 February 1779. On what he saw King considered this to be the finest island in the group.

Tahoorawa, Ranai, and Morotai were Kahoolawe, Lanai, and Molokai. Molokai had been seen on 25 November 1778 from the north coast of Maui. Kahoolawe is an island with peaks of nearly 1,500 feet 6 miles west-south-west of the south-western extremity of Maui, and about 36 miles from the north-western part of Hawaii, while Lanai, which lies about 15 miles north-west of Kahoolawe, reaches a height of 3,370 feet.[1] Whether Kahoolawe, and possibly Lanai also, were seen when the expedition came north the first time from Kealakakua Bay under Cook is not clear. The first firm record of them is King's reference under date 24 February 1779.

[1] *Pacific Islands Pilot*, vol. iii, pp. 252–4.

Cook and King between them give copious details of the people of the Hawaiian Islands—called by Cook the Sandwich Islands—derived from the expedition's contacts, either on land or with people who came out in canoes or both, at Kauai, Niihau, Maui, Hawaii, and Oahu.

The appearance, language, arts and crafts, and ways of life of the people in all these islands were substantially the same, and there were many indications that they communicated freely with one another both in friendly exchanges and in warfare. In these things the Hawaiians showed a close similarity to the people of the Society Islands, Tonga, and New Zealand.

The foods of the commoners were principally fish, yams, sweet potatoes, taro, plantains, sugar cane, and bread-fruit, to which the people of higher rank added the flesh of pigs and dogs. Flesh food was salted for taste and not preserving. Fowls were also used for food but were not much esteemed. A sour taro pudding was used as at Tonga. The Hawaiians did not have the art of preserving bread-fruit in a sour paste as at Tahiti, and the Englishmen showed them how to do this. The cooking was of like manner to that at the southern islands. Kava was extensively drunk by the chiefs.

One thing in which the Hawaiians resembled the people of New Zealand rather than those of Tonga or the Society Islands was in living together in villages, although there were also straggling houses. The houses of the villages were built close together without any order. The houses had low sides and low entrances, the only light coming through the latter. They were kept very clean, with dried grass on the floor, on which sleeping mats were spread. A kind of bench at one end held their few utensils, consisting of gourds, some of which were very big, and some lacquered, and wooden bowls and plates, often well carved. There were wooden pillows.

The Hawaiian mats and cloth, the latter made from the bark of trees, were beautifully worked in a variety of patterns and colours, being in King's opinion unexcelled anywhere else in the world.

The Hawaiian fish-hooks were ingeniously made of mother-of-pearl, bone, or wood, pointed and barbed with small bones or tortoise-shell. A common type was made in the form of a small fish with feathers attached. The lines, cordage, and nets, made from bark or coconut fibre, were very strong.

The adzes were of the same pattern as those of the southern islands, and either made of the same sort of blackish stone, or of a clay-coloured one.

The men wore the *maro* or loincloth. They used beautifully manufactured mats as a protection in war, drawn round the shoulders and in front. Striking helmets and mantles were used as ceremonial dress by the chiefs, the helmets, made of covered wickerwork fitting the head closely, and with a ridge from back to front which would act protectively against blows, being like those formerly worn by the Spaniards, the mantles being magnificently feathered in red or yellow, or in white with variegated borders. The ordinary dress of the women resembled that of the men, but they sometimes wore loose pieces of fine cloth over their shoulders in the evening, and the younger women frequently wound thin, fine cloth several times round the waist so that it looked like a full short petticoat.

Both sexes wore necklaces made of strings of variegated shells, also neck pendants in the form of a handle of a cup, or a small human figure made of bone, hung on a cord. Fly-flaps of coconut fibre or feathers tied to the top of a handle were used, the most valuable form of handle being the arm or leg bone of an enemy slain in battle. Bracelets of shell, black wood, pigs' or boars' teeth were worn. The women wore wreaths of dried flowers of the mallow, and another beautiful ornament called *eraie* (*lei*), generally about the neck, sometimes round the hair, sometimes both made like a ruff, of very small feathers so close together that they resembled velvet, the ground being generally red, with alternate circles of green, yellow, and black. An ornament of shells or dogs' teeth or red berries was tied round the arm or ankle or below the knee when dancing, so that it made a noise during the movements. A kind of mask made of a large gourd, with holes for the eyes and nose, was seen on two occasions, being apparently worn for fun.

The weapons were wooden spears, daggers, clubs, and slings. One sort of spear about 6 to 8 feet in length tapered to a point

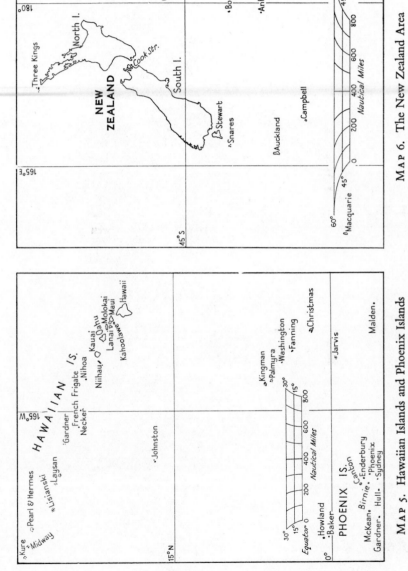

MAP 5. Hawaiian Islands and Phoenix Islands

MAP 6. The New Zealand Area

furnished with four or six rows of barbs; another was 12 or 15 feet long and not barbed. The daggers, 1 to 2 feet long, had a string through the handle whereby they were hung from the arm.

The canoes consisted of a base of a single piece or log of wood hollowed out to the thickness of 1 or 1½ inches, with three boards as sides. They were not more than 15 or 18 inches broad, and were either provided with an outrigger or fastened together in pairs. They were rowed by paddles and sometimes had a light triangular sail. The head chief of Hawaii had a double canoe 70 feet in length, 3½ feet in depth, and 12 feet in breadth, each being hollowed out of one tree.

The men were frequently tattooed, the quantity of it varying considerably. Only at New Zealand and the Hawaiian Islands, according to King, did the people tattoo the face, and as between the two latter, the New Zealanders employed elegant spiral volutes, while the Hawaiians used straight lines at right angles.

Several *morai* (*marae*), or sacred enclosures, were inspected by Cook and King. They consisted of stone platforms, on which were pyramids covered with white cloth, wooden frameworks, and figures of gods and chiefs. Chiefs were buried here with the bodies of slain common people. The priests appeared to be a special hereditary order.

The chiefs were highly autocratic towards the commoners and to chiefs inferior to themselves, but the property of the people appeared to be protected by usage.

The making of canoes and mats was a chiefly occupation, the women were employed in making cloth, and the commoners in the plantations and fishing.

Many forms of recreation were indulged in. The people were expert swimmers, and the men competed in riding surf-boards. They had boxing and wrestling matches, although inferior to those at Tonga. No grand ceremonial dances such as those of Tonga were seen, although it seemed probable they had them on occasion. The Hawaiian music was also ruder than the Tongan. Neither flutes nor reeds nor instruments other than drums were seen. Their songs, in parts and with accompanying gentle motions of the arms, were very pleasing. The dances performed by women started gently and worked up into a climax like the New Zealand dances. The people had gambling games, and bet on racing matches between the boys and girls.

The people of Kauai and Niihau recognized iron. Only a piece of iron hoop about 2 inches long, fitted into a wooden handle, and another edge tool, was seen, at Kauai. Cook conjectured that the iron might have come from jetsam, such as hooped casks or bits of wreckage from the Spanish American coast. A bit of fir wood which was supposed to have come as jetsam was seen. Colour was later given to Cook's explanation by the fact that when the ships were again at Kauai after Cook's death, an islander showed them a bolt which appeared to be of some ship's timbers and was not of English make, and which, if they comprehended the islander aright, had come out of a piece of timber driven on the island since their previous visit. Cook and King were sure that if the Spaniards had known of the existence of Hawaii they would have used it as a stopover on their voyages to the East Indies.

James Cook's contributions to the discovery of the Pacific Islands on his third voyage were as follows: On 29 March 1777 he discovered Mangaia in the southern Cook Islands. On 31 March 1777 he discovered Atiu and Takutea in the southern Cook Islands, landings being made on both. On 16 May 1777 he gave the first firm record of the eastern islands of the Haapai sector of the Tonga Islands, namely Uoleva, Lifuka, Foa, and Haano, landings being made; some or all of these islands had probably been seen by Duclesmeur (see section 34). On 8 August 1777 Cook discovered Tubuai in the Austral Islands. On 24 December 1777 he discovered Christmas Island in the mid-Pacific area, landings being made. On 18 January 1778 he discovered Oahu and Kauai in the Hawaiian Islands, landings being subsequently made on Kauai. On 19 January 1778 he discovered Niihau, and on that day or shortly thereafter Kaula and Lehua, in the Hawaiian Islands, landings being subsequently made on Niihau. On 25 November 1778 he discovered Maui and Molokai in the Hawaiian Islands. On 30 November 1778 he discovered Hawaii in the

Hawaiian Islands, landings being subsequently made. Cook may have seen Kahoolawe or Lanai or both, also in the Hawaiian Islands, on 6–8 February 1779.

Charles Clerke having succeeded to Cook in command of the expedition, the first firm record of Kahoolawe and Lanai was given on 24 February 1779, and a landing was made on Oahu on 27 February 1779.

39. Francisco Antonio Maurelle

FRANCISCO ANTONIO MAURELLE, a Spanish captain, went with secret papers from the Philippines to North America in a vessel named *La Princessa* in 1780–1. It was the wrong time of the year for a passage by the ordinary North Pacific route and Maurelle tried unsuccessfully to reach the Americas through the South Pacific, finally having to come up to Guam and go on to North America from there. On this detour he made some discoveries. Maurelle's account of this voyage, secured by the French explorer La Pérouse (see section 40), was published with the latter's papers.[1]

On 7 January 1781 Maurelle, while making for New Ireland, passed an extensive cluster of small islands, twenty-nine of which were counted, with others in sight to the south. Maurelle identified these correctly as encountered by Bougainville (see section 32), namely the Ninigo Islands, which number some fifty islets in all. Quitting these islands, Maurelle, at 5 or 6 leagues, on 8 January 1781, saw two islets which he named Los Eremitanos (Hermits), and on the evening of the same day saw two islands to the north and west, distant 5 miles, which he identified with Bougainville's Anachorètes, the latitude being precisely the same, at the same moment seeing two small islands to the east, which he called Los Monges (The Monks). He passed south of them at midnight. On 10 January he passed a very large high island with smaller islands beyond it, which were plainly the Admiralty Islands including Manus.

[1] *Voyage of La Pérouse*, ed. Milet-Mureau, M. L. A. (London, 1798), vol. i, pp. cxv–clxiii.

These data show that between the Ninigo Islands and Manus Maurelle passed in succession the Hermit Islands, Sae, and Kaniet. The two latter atolls had been seen by Bougainville. Maurelle, however, gave the first firm record of the Hermit Islands, which are actually an atoll of some seventeen islands and islets, divided into two sectors by a channel when viewed from some aspects.[1] They were probably Retes's La Caimana (see section 7), and may have been seen before that by Saavedra (see section 5).

On 12 January 1781 Maurelle came to a large island with a very high mountain which he identified as Dampier's Matthias (see section 24), namely Mussau in the Bismarck Archipelago. He expected to find Dampier's Squally Island, namely Emirau. The night was very stormy, but next morning, 13 January 1781, despite fogs and showers, another island was seen at north-west by north at an estimated distance of 7 leagues. It seemed smaller than Squally as shown on Maurelle's chart and he judged it to be either Squally or a little island near it. The same day he came in sight of the high coast of New Hanover.

Whereas Mussau is high, Emirau, which lies 13 miles south-east of Mussau, and Tench, a small island 38 miles east of Emirau and 52 miles north-east of New Hanover, are both relatively low. It is evident that the island seen on the morning of 13 January 1781 was actually Tench Island.[2] It is a small island, as described by Maurelle, whereas Emirau is a fairly large island, and if it had been Emirau, one might expect that Tench would also have been seen.

Continuing south, Maurelle saw various islands which had been previously discovered, and Roncador Reef, which may have been Mendaña's Baxos de la Candellaria (see section 10). Being now far south he decided to continue on south to higher latitudes where he expected to find westerlies to take him to the American coast-line. On 26 February 1781 he saw a small island with a barren peak, which he called Amargura (Bitter). The following day, 27 February, an island with a very high mountain came in sight. When they got up to it some islanders who came out and traded with them said that its name was Latte. Other islands, not so high, but bigger, with channels,

[1] *Pacific Islands Pilot*, vol. i, pp. 491–2.
[2] This identification accords with that of H. Nevermann, in *Ergebnisse der Südsee-Expedition 1908–1910. II. Ethnographie A Melanesien*, vol. ii (Hamburg, 1933), p. 2.

were seen to the east-north-east at a distance thought to be 12 leagues. Maurelle went in to these and anchored at a large island with rising ground in the interior, shifting later to a port near by, inland from which were hills. He named these islands after Don Martin de Mayorga. The position given by him for the port on the west side of the group was latitude 18° 36' S., longitude 179° 52' E. (from Paris).

These data show that Maurelle, having passed Fonualei (Amargura) on 26 February, saw Late (Latte) and the western islands of the Vavau group (Don Martin de Mayorga) on 27 February. All these islands are in the Tonga group. Fonualei, a volcano, 38 miles north-west of Vavau, was a new discovery. Late, a high island west-south-west of Vavau, had been seen from the south by Tasman (see section 18). What islands in the Vavau group may have been seen by Duclesmeur (see section 34) is not clear.

Maurelle's latitude for Vavau is accurate, but his longitude shows an error of several degrees.

Maurelle and Tubau, the chief of Vavau, exchanged visits and became on very friendly terms. The visitors were presented with great quantities of pigs, fowls, bananas, coconuts, and other produce. At a feast the Tongans put on wrestling and boxing matches, and an old woman declaimed a song. The chief's wife, a young woman, and her attendants were attractive in appearance and dress, but when some of the attendants later joined in a boxing match they did so with such violence that the Spaniards begged that this should cease. The chief was treated with extreme deference by the islanders, including the sub-chiefs. The islands were very fertile, with neat cultivations and plantations. One shrub furnished a bark cloth used for cloaks or counterpanes, and for a kind of petticoat.

Maurelle was told that two frigates had put in to the islands, the captains of which, with some officers from each, had slept on shore, and given them chaplets of glass beads, hatchets, and adzes, and that at the time of the visit of Maurelle two vessels similar to his own were making sail to the north-west. Since Maurelle was unfamiliar with the language, these were presumably references to Cook's visits to Tonga in 1773 and 1777, and possibly

Duclesmeur's passage past the islands in 1772 (see sections 34, 37, and 38).

From Vavau Maurelle, on 20 March, continued south-east, traversing the Tonga group with the aid of guidance from some islanders who came out in canoes. Having got as far south as latitude 25° 52', he decided to turn back. He passed between the Haapai and Vavau sectors of the Tonga group. On 19 April 1781 he saw Late again to the north at a distance of some 6 leagues. He could not fetch Vavau. On 21 April 1781 he had two islands to the north-north-east and east-north-east respectively, which he called Consolación (Consolation) because he got supplies from islanders who came out in canoes. He resumed his course on 22 April, and on 24 April passed another island named Maurelle. On 3 May 1781, in latitude 6° S., he found a very low island surrounded by a sandy shore terminating in one impenetrable reef, over which even the islanders found difficulty in taking their canoes. The island, being covered with coconut trees, was named Cocal (Coconut Grove). Continuing on to the north-west, Maurelle, on 6 May 1781, saw an island lower but larger than the preceding one, and left it 6 leagues to the south-west. This island he named San Agostino.

The two islands called Consolación must have been Fonualei and Toku, and Maurelle must have been Niuafou. Toku, a low island, is 27 miles north-north-west of Vavau, Fonualei is a high island 11 miles north-north-west of Toku, and Niuafou is about 160 miles north-north-west of Fonualei. Consolación could not have been Niuatobutabu and Tafahi, the distance of 200 miles from south of Late being too far to have been accomplished in 2 days in relation to Maurelle's other sailing times, and being off course in relation to Niuafou, which is the only possibility for Maurelle. Toku was a new discovery. Fonualei, a high island, had been seen from a distance to the west when Maurelle was coming south, whereas Toku, being a low island, had evidently not been seen. Niuafou had been discovered by Le Maire (see section 16). On 3 May 1781 Maurelle came to Nanomana, and then on 6 May 1781 to Nanumea, in the Ellice Islands. Nanomana, the latitude of which is 6¼° S., is described by the *Pacific Islands Pilot* as a low coral island with coconut palms, fringed by a narrow reef with an unusually precipitous face on its seaward side.[1]

---

[1] *Pacific Islands Pilot*, vol. ii, pp. 433-4.

Nanumea is about 37 miles north-north-west of Nanomana, being the north-westernmost island of the Ellice group. These were the islands called respectively Cocal and San Agostino by Maurelle. They may have been previously discovered (see section 10).

Francisco Antonio Maurelle, on 8 January 1781, gave the first firm report of the Hermit Islands, which were probably Retes's La Caimana (see section 7), and may have been seen before Retes by Saavedra (see section 5). On 13 January 1781 he encountered Tench Island in the Bismarck Archipelago. On 26 February 1781 he discovered Fonualei in the Tonga group. On 27 February 1781 he gave the first firm record of the Vavau Islands in the Tonga group, landings being made then and subsequently; but what islands Duclesmeur may have seen there before him (see section 34) is not clear. On 21 April 1781 Maurelle discovered Toku in the Tonga group. On 3 and 6 May 1781 he sighted Nanomana and Nanumea respectively, in the Ellice Islands, this being the first firm report of these two islands, either of which may have been discovered by Mendaña (see section 10).

40. Jean François de la Pérouse

DURING the years 1786 to 1788 Jean François de la Pérouse, the commander of an expedition of two French vessels, the *Boussole* and the *Astrolabe*, made several discoveries.[1]

La Pérouse tells in his journal of how, on 4 November 1786, he discovered a small barren island with steep sides, the position given being latitude 23° 34' N., longitude 166° 52' W. (from Paris). He named this Necker. On 5 November 1786, to the west of Necker, he discovered some shoals.

The position and relative location of these, together with the topographical data, show that they were Necker Island and the French Frigate Shoals, in the northern sector of the Hawaiian Islands.

[1] *Voyage of La Pérouse*, ed. Milet-Mureau, M. L. A. (London, 1798), vol. i, pp. 235–9; vol. ii, pp. 158–203.

After 13 further months of voyaging round the Pacific area, the expedition made for the eastern islands of the Samoa group, of which they had Bougainville's account (see section 32). They came to the Manua Islands, which are described in unmistakable detail, and then to the north coast of Tutuila, where they were given by the islanders a number of local place-names which they supposed to be the names of separate islands, including Maouna, thought to be the native name for Tutuila, and Oyolava and Pola, thought to be the native names for two more islands to the west of Tutuila. They continued on to Upolu, which they identified with Oyolava, and on 17 December 1787 reached another island to the west of Upolu, from which it was separated by a channel which appeared to be about 4 leagues wide, cut by two islands, one of which was very low and wooded. The big island beyond this channel was skirted on its north side, its west point was rounded, and the expedition then passed south to the Tonga group.

The big island to the west of Upolu was Savaii, the western-most island of the Samoa group, separated from Upolu by a strait in which lie two relatively small islands, Manono and Apolima. Neither Roggeveen nor Bougainville had seen Savaii, Manono, or Apolima, the discoverer of which was thus La Pérouse, on 17 December 1787.

41. Thomas Gilbert and Captain Marshall

Two British sea-captains, Thomas Gilbert and one Marshall, commanded the *Charlotte* and the *Scarborough* respectively in the fleet which founded the British colony at Port Jackson in New South Wales, Australia, in 1788. They then agreed to keep in company on a voyage to Canton in China. Gilbert's own account was published, together with profile sketches,[1] and an account based on Marshall's data, with a chart and profile sketches, was also published.[2] Apart from Matthew Island, the first sight of which is conceded by Marshall to Gilbert, and the first sight of the Marshalls, which is conceded by Gilbert to Marshall, it would be impossible, and indeed academic, to say which of the islands

[1] Gilbert, T., *Voyage from New South Wales to Canton* (London, 1789).
[2] In *The Voyage of Governor Phillip to Botany Bay* (London, 1789).

seen were respectively discovered by each, since there is little agreement in their accounts on this and they were in any case together during the passage. Nor is there any clear-cut agreement in their accounts on the names given to the islands they saw, after the first discovery, Matthew Island. The following summary, therefore, omits the names given by Gilbert and Marshall after Matthew Island. The dates are taken from Gilbert, Marshall's dates varying somewhat because one account is in ship time and the other in civil time.

On 27 May 1788 Gilbert discovered a high rock seeming to be about 5 or 6 miles in circumference, the position given being latitude 22° 31' S., longitude 172° 16' E. There is a profile sketch showing the island's configuration. Gilbert called it Matthew's Rock.

This was the modern Matthew Island, a barren island to the south of the New Hebrides.

On 18 June 1788 three low islands were discovered, the position of the middlemost being given as latitude 00° 2' N., longitude 175° 54' E. by Gilbert. These were passed on the west on the following day. On 20 June 1788 they came to the first islands of what proved to be a further chain, which they passed on 20–22 June 1788. Marshall's chart indicates that the northernmost of these was in the vicinity of latitude 3° 50' N. A number of profile sketches of parts of these islands are given.

Abemama, Aranuka, and Kuria are three islands in the Gilbert group conforming closely to the positions given for the three islands seen on 18 June 1788, the identifications being confirmed by the profiles given by Marshall. The other data, which are confirmed here and there by recognizable features in Gilbert's and Marshall's profile sketches, show that on 20–22 June 1788 the ships passed the Gilbert atolls Maiana, Tarawa, Abaiang, Makin, and Makin Meang. It is improbable that Marakei, to the north-east of Abaiang, was seen. Marakei and Abaiang were probably discovered by Grijalva's ship (see section 6), and Makin Meang was discovered by Quiros (see section 14). Abemama, Aranuka, Kuria, and Maiana were new discoveries, and also Tarawa and Makin except in the unlikely event that one of them was the Acea of Grijalva's ship. It is not possible to relate the topographical descriptions in Gilbert's and Marshall's data in all particulars to the precise geography of the area as known today, since all these atolls are broken clusters of islets and reefs.

On the evening of 24 June 1788 Marshall saw more land. The next day this proved to be a number of islands, the southernmost of which was according to Marshall in latitude 5° 58′ N., longitude 172° 3′ E., the northernmost in latitude 6° 29′ N., longitude 171° 10′ E. On the morning of 26 June 1788 they found themselves on the north side of some more islands, between two of which they had drifted during the night. The position at noon, according to Gilbert, was about latitude 7° 19′ N., longitude 172° 30′ E. On the morning of 27 June 1788 they came to another cluster of small islands, the position at noon, according to Gilbert, being about latitude 7° 57′ N., longitude 172° 5′ E. Still another lot of islands was discovered on the morning of 28 June 1788, the position at noon, according to Gilbert, being latitude 9° 29′ N., longitude 171° 11′ E. The next day, 29 June 1788, they encountered two lots of islands, passing through a narrow channel dividing them. The day after, they saw more islands before turning east out of the Marshalls.

These data show that on 24 June 1788 Marshall saw part of the south-eastern sector of the Marshall Islands; that on 25 June 1788 Gilbert and Marshall saw at close quarters Mili and the small atoll close to it on its south-east side, Narikirikku To; that on 26 June 1788 they discovered Arno and Majuro, having drifted between the two; that on 27 June 1788 they discovered Aur; that on 28 June 1788 they discovered, or rediscovered after Villalobos (see section 7) or the *San Jeronimo* (see section 9), Maloelap; and that on 29 June 1788 they passed through the channel dividing Erikub and Wotje, of which they thus gave the first firm report, although they may have been discovered by Villalobos (see section 7) or by the *San Jeronimo* (see section 9). The islands north of Wotje, seen the following day, had been discovered previously (see section 8).

Gilbert and Marshall give a few notes on the islanders who came out to the ships here and there in the Gilbert and Marshall atolls. They were all much the same sort of people, sturdy and cheerful. Their canoes were 'proas', i.e. Micronesian single canoes with an outrigger.

The discoveries of Gilbert and Marshall may be summarized as follows: On 27 May 1788 Gilbert discovered Matthew Island, south of the New Hebrides. On 18 June 1788 Gilbert and Marshall discovered Abemama, Aranuka, and Kuria in the Gilbert Islands. On 20 June 1788 they discovered Maiana, and on 20–22 June 1788 gave the first firm report of Tarawa, Abaiang, and Makin. Abaiang had probably been discovered by Grijalva's ship, failing which either Tarawa or Makin may have been discovered by it (see section 6). On 24 June 1788 Marshall saw some land in the southern sector of the Marshalls, and on 25 June 1788 Gilbert and Marshall saw at closer quarters Mili and the small atoll close to it, Narikirikku To. On 26 June 1788 they discovered Arno and Majuro. On 27 June 1788 they discovered Aur. On 28 June 1788 they gave the first firm report of Maloelab, and on 29 June 1788 of Erikub and Wotje, which may have been discovered by Villalobos (see section 7) or by the *San Jeronimo* (see section 9).

42. Captain Sever

THE British vessel *Lady Penrhyn*, commanded by one Captain Sever, was one of those which took part in the founding of the British colony at Port Jackson in New South Wales, Australia, in 1788. The ship then came up to China via the Society Islands. The log, and an account made from the papers of Lieutenant Watts, one of the ship's company, with some sketches by Watts, give the story of this voyage.[1]

Leaving New South Wales on 5 May 1788, Sever went first to the Society Islands. On the way, on 31 May 1788, he discovered two islands, the position of the more northerly being given as latitude 30° 9′ S., longitude 180° 58′ 37″ E. These islands were about 5 leagues apart. The more southerly, called Curtis's Isles, consisted of two barren isles about ¼ mile apart. Sever landed on the more northerly with difficulty, since it was edged with cliffs. It was high at the west end and sloped down towards the north, and extended about 2½ miles east-south-east and west-north-west. There were no human inhabitants, but many mice and rats. This island was named Macauley's Island. Watts drew profile sketches of these islands.

[1] In *The Voyage of Governor Phillip to Botany Bay* (London, 1789).

These were the middle islands of the Kermadec group, Curtis and Macauley, as Watts's sketches alone would show.

From Huahine in the Society Islands, Sever set out on 29 July, and took a north-west course. On 8 August 1788 he passed a low flat island which he named Penrhyn's Island, the position given for it being latitude 9° 10′ S., longitude 202° 15′ E. They saw no more land until the Ladrones.

This island was the modern Penrhyn or Tongareva, in the northern Cooks, a detached island the position of which corresponds almost exactly with the stated position.

43. John Shortland

HAVING taken part in the establishment of the British settlement at Port Jackson in New South Wales, Australia, in 1788, John Shortland returned to England via Batavia in command of two ships, the *Alexander* and the *Friendship*. The authorities for the course are Shortland's log, two charts made by Shortland's son, and an account prepared from Shortland's papers.[1]

Having left Port Jackson on 14 July 1788, Shortland saw land in latitude 10° 32′ S., longitude about 161° 11′ E. on 31 July. This was San Cristobal in the Solomons. Shortland then skirted San Cristobal, Guadalcanal, and the Russell Islands, Pavuvu, the eastern island of the Russell Islands, being named Cape Marsh. Shortland's sight of Cape Marsh was made on 2 August 1788. It was the only new discovery made by Shortland in this part of his voyage. San Cristobal and Guadalcanal had been discovered by Ortega and Gallego of Mendaña's first expedition more than two centuries previously, but no mention of any land which might correspond to the Russell Islands is mentioned in those accounts.

Shortland continued to the north-west, and on 3 August 1788 more land was discovered. The position at noon on this day was taken as latitude 8° 55′ S., longitude 158° 14′ E. The land first seen appeared like islands, but they could not see a passage through them to the north. The ships stood off and on, on a north-westerly course, skirting this land on its west side. Some canoes came off to the ship on 6 August

[1] In *The Voyage of Governor Phillip to Botany Bay* (London, 1789).

1788, and indicated that their locale was named 'Simboo'. Shortland then found a passage to the north, the position given being latitude 7° 10' S., longitude 156° 30' E. From the position and topographical description this was Bougainville Strait, already traversed by Bougainville (see section 32). To all the lands he saw from San Cristobal to Bougainville Shortland gave the name New Georgia.

Shortland, as a comparison of his data with the map will show, had come north-west from the Russell Islands to the New Georgia group, which he skirted on its western side, rounding Simbo and the other islands south of Choiseul, and passing through Bougainville Strait. The southern islands of the New Georgia group, Gatukai and Vangunu, and the eastern island, New Georgia, had already been discovered by Ortega and Gallego (see section 10), from the east. Shortland was the discoverer of the western sector of the New Georgia group and of Simbo.

The people who came out from Simbo showed a friendly disposition, exchanging gifts with the Englishmen. They were of fine physique and appeared to have a good food supply. Their canoes were well constructed, with high bows and sterns like the Tahitians'. They had shells with feathers as head-ornaments, and large rings of white bone on their wrists. They were armed with lances.

John Shortland, on 2 August 1788, discovered the Russell Islands. Between 3 and 7 August 1788 he discovered the western islands of the New Georgia group north of Gatukai and Vangunu, and Simbo.

44. William Bligh's First Voyage and the *Bounty* Mutineers

IN 1788 William Bligh, in command of the British naval vessel *Bounty*, while *en route* to Tahiti to get bread-fruit plants, passed south of New Zealand. After getting a cargo of plants in Tahiti, he came west. Between the Tonga and Fiji Islands a mutiny occurred, as a result of which Bligh and some of his company were sent off in the ship's launch. They eventually reached Timor in the East Indies. The authorities for this voyage are a published narrative by Bligh,[1] and two plans or charts of his voyages through the Fiji Islands,[2] since found among Bligh's papers. (See Plate IV for plan of his first traverse.)

On 19 September 1788 Bligh discovered a cluster of small rocky islands, the position given being latitude 47° 44′ S., longitude 179° 7′ E.

These were the Bounty Islands, a detached group of uninhabited islands in the stated position, to the south-east of New Zealand.

Later in the voyage Bligh, having left the Society Islands with the intention of coming west to Tonga, on 11 April 1789, discovered an island of moderate height with a number of low keys. A canoe with four men in it came off and, according to Bligh, said the name of the largest island was 'Wytootackee'. It was considered to be about 10 miles in circuit, its latitude from 18° 50′ to 18° 54′ S., longitude 200° 19′ E.

This was Aitutaki, in the southern Cook Islands, conforming in position and topography to Bligh's data—a new discovery.

According to Bligh the four men he met at Aitutaki spoke the same language as at Tahiti with no great variation. They were tattooed on the arms and legs, but not the loins or buttocks like the Tahitians. They said they had fowls but not pigs, although they evidently knew the Tahitian name for the latter.

Shortly after the ship left Nomuka in the Tonga Islands, the mutiny occurred. The mutineers took the ship east, to Tubuai and Tahiti, returning later west (see below). Bligh and his companions in the launch first made for Tofua, on the north-western fringe of the Tonga group. Bligh had instruments for observing latitudes, but his longitudes, made by dead reckoning, are unreliable from this point on.

Bligh left Tofua on 2 May 1789, at 8 p.m. On 4 May 1789, just before noon, he discovered a small flat island of moderate height, his observed latitude being 18° 58′ S. Soon after noon other islands appeared, and at 3.15 eight could be counted. Bligh kept a course to the north-west by west between these islands. At 6 o'clock that evening

---

[1] Bligh, W., *A Voyage to the South Sea* (London, 1792).
[2] In Henderson, G. C., *The Discoverers of the Fiji Islands* (London, 1933).

PLATE IV

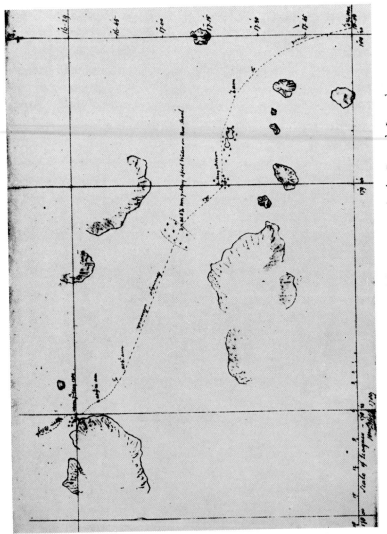

Bligh's Plan of his Traverse of the Fiji Group in the *Bounty's* Launch

he saw three other small islands to the north-west, and, steering south of them, took a west-north-west course for the night under a reefed sail. The islands he had passed were considered by Bligh to lie between the latitudes of 19° 5' S. and 18° 19' S. The largest island was estimated at about 6 leagues in circuit. Bligh says he made a sketch of these islands. The latitude at noon next day, 5 May 1789, was 18° 10' S., according to Bligh. About 6 o'clock in the afternoon he discovered two more islands. At daylight, 6 May 1789, a number of other islands were in sight from south-south-east to the west, and round to north-east by east. He decided to pass between those in the north-west. At noon, in an observed latitude of 17° 17' S., he passed a small sandy island or key. Before reaching this he had passed ten islands, the largest of which he judged to be 6 or 8 leagues in circuit, much larger lands appearing in the south-west and north-north-west, between which he directed his course. He says he made a sketch of these islands. Those which were near appeared fruitful and hilly, some very mountainous, all of a good height. At 6 o'clock, when the boat was passing between islands of considerable extent, woody and mountainous, at about 6 leagues from each shore, an extensive coral bank with only 4 feet of water, which Bligh says he showed in his sketch, lay beneath them. At dawn, 7 May 1789, more land was discovered from west-south-west to west-north-west, and another island north-north-west, the latter a high round lump of little extent, the southern land that they had passed in the night being still in sight. The land in the west had some extraordinarily high rocks, the country appearing to be agreeably interspersed with high and low land. Off the north-east part lay some small rocky islands, between which and an island 4 leagues to the north-east the boat passed. The latitude at noon was given as 16° 29' S. Bligh conjectured they had passed through the 'islands called Feejee', since they conformed with the description of those islands given to him by the Tongans.

The two charts of Bligh's passage through the Fiji Islands which have since been found among Bligh's papers are presumably the two sketches referred to by him in his published narrative. It does not matter, since they have a high degree of conformity with the modern charts and topographical data in themselves, no less than with the written data in the published narrative. These data leave no doubt of the identity of the islands seen by Bligh. On 4 May 1789 he passed north of Yangasa and south of Mothe, seeing the other islands immediately west of them. That night he came into the inner sea of the Fiji group. The following day,

5 May 1789, he discovered Ngau and Nairai. On 6 May 1789 he discovered Viti Levu and Koro and the numbers of smaller islands lying between, and passed between Viti Levu and Vanua Levu, seeing below him the shallows in between. Vanua Levu had been discovered from the east by Tasman (see section 18). On 7 May 1788 Bligh discovered the Yasawa Islands, which form the western fringe of the Fiji group, and passed through the northern part of these.

On 14 May 1789 Bligh came to four islands, one of them much larger than the others, and all of them high and remarkable. At noon he saw a small island and some rocks to the north-west by north, and another island to the west, the four he had first seen being still in sight, the latitude given being 13° 29' S. At one in the morning, 15 May 1789, he saw another island bearing west-north-west, which at 8 a.m. was north-east. These islands were placed by Bligh between latitudes 13° 16' and 14° 10' S.

These details show that Bligh came upon the north-eastern sector of the Banks Islands. The four islands first seen were Vanua Lava, Gaua, Mota, and Saddle Island, the island and rocks seen at noon were the Reef islets, the island to the west was Ureparapara, and the island seen in the morning of 15 May was Vatganai. Gaua, Vanua Lava, and Ureparapara had been discovered by Quiros (see section 14), but no land which might correspond to Mota or Saddle Island is mentioned in the accounts of that expedition. Bligh can therefore be credited with the discovery of Mota, Saddle Island, the Reef islets, and Vatganai.

The discoveries of William Bligh on his first voyage were as follows: On 19 September 1788 he discovered the Bounty Islands to the south-east of New Zealand. On 11 April 1789 he discovered Aitutaki in the southern Cook Islands. On 4 May 1789 he discovered Yangasa and Mothe and the islands immediately west of them, on 5 May 1789 he discovered Ngau and Nairai, on 6 May 1789 he discovered Viti Levu and Koro and the islands lying between them, and on 7 May 1789 he discovered the Yasawa Islands, all the islands named being in the Fiji group. On 14 May 1789 he discovered Mota, Saddle Island, and the Reef Islands, and on 15 May 1789 he discovered Vatganai, all in the Banks group.

The evidence for the discoveries made by the *Bounty* mutineers while coming west from Tahiti to Tonga and Fiji before proceeding to Pitcairn consists of memories of a big ship captained by one 'Makore' which were recorded by Maretu, a Rarotongan who was educated by the early missionaries in the Cook Islands; similar references gleaned by John Williams, an early missionary who visited Rarotonga in and after 1823; and references to a visit to an island between Tahiti and Tonga by 'Jenny', a Tahitian woman on the *Bounty* at the time, and to another island to the west of Tonga by the same witness.[1]

Maretu, who died in 1880, and was obviously not a direct witness, recounted circumstantial details to the effect that when the big ship with 'Makore' on board came to Rarotonga, no landing was made, that the islanders did a bit of barter in canoes, that one Maia, one of the Rarotongans who visited the ship, stole a large box containing oranges and *mautini* (pumpkins?), from which the Rarotongans established these plants, and that a chief named Tamarua saw on board numbers of European goods and also taro, banana, and bread-fruit plants. Williams was told of the visit of this ship by the Rarotongans in or about 1823, and worked out that the date of the visit would be about the time of the *Bounty*. William Wyatt Gill, a later missionary, had no doubt that the *Bounty* was referred to and considered the name 'Makore' to be the native rendering of McCoy, one of the *Bounty* leaders. No other vessel than the *Bounty* would be likely to have possessed the plants referred to by Maretu, and to have had a motive not to report the discovery. 'Jenny' referred to a visit to an island between Tahiti and Tonga by the *Bounty* when some of the mutineers were looking for somewhere to settle.

It can be accepted on this evidence that this island was in fact Rarotonga, a new discovery.

From Rarotonga the *Bounty* mutineers proceeded to Tonga and thence west. From the statement made by 'Jenny', the Tahitian woman on the *Bounty*, that the Tongan island at which the *Bounty* called was one where some horned cattle left by Cook were still living, the island in question can be taken to have been Tongatabu, since Cook left cattle at this island only, i.e. in 1777 on his third voyage (see section 38).

[1] *Journal of the Polynesian Society*, vol. xx, p. 192; Williams, J., *Missionary Enterprises* (London, 1837), pp. 199–200; Narrative of 'Jenny', in *Bengal Hurkaru*, 2 Oct. 1826, cited by Maude, C. E., *Journal of the Polynesian Society*, vol. lxvii, p. 121.

A few days' sail to the west, the *Bounty* came to a small low island with inhabitants, and evidently with a lagoon, where a landing was made.[1]

The small island must have been either Vatoa or Ono-i-Lau, which are the only two detached lagoon islands to the west of the southern Tonga islands. Vatoa had been discovered by Cook (see section 37). Ono-i-Lau, if it were the island, had not been previously reported.

45. Captain Douglas

CAPTAIN DOUGLAS, of the British vessel *Iphigenia*, while proceeding north-west from Niihau in the Hawaiian Islands, discovered, on 19 March 1789, an island or rock in the form of a saddle, covered with verdure on the south, but on the north, west, and east sides barren rock, with very steep sides.[2]

The topographical description of this island,[3] and its location in relation to Niihau, show that it was Nihoa, 116 miles north-west of Niihau, in the Hawaiian Islands.

46. Captain Wilkinson

CAPTAIN WILKINSON, of the British vessel *Indispensable*, while on a passage from New South Wales to China in 1790, passed between two islands to the south of the main Solomon Islands. Other vessels in due course reported contacts with islands in this vicinity. The British hydrographer Arrowsmith, in his chart of 1798, showed two islands in this area north-west and south-east of each other, the north-western one being named Bellona, the other unnamed. In due course as the geography of the area became better known, it became established

---

[1] Narrative of 'Jenny' in *Sydney Gazette*, 17 July 1819, and *Bengal Hurkaru*, 2 Oct. 1826, cited by Maude, C. E., *Journal of the Polynesian Society*, vol. lxvii, pp. 125–6 (Maude's analysis is followed).

[2] Meares, J., *Voyages* (London, 1790).

[3] *Pacific Islands Pilot*, vol. iii, pp. 293–4.

that there are in fact only two islands there, namely Bellona and Rennell.[1]

These facts may be considered to establish that Wilkinson discovered Rennell and Bellona in 1790.

47. Edward Edwards and Oliver

IN 1791 Edward Edwards made an extensive search in the South Pacific in the British naval vessel *Pandora* for the *Bounty* mutineers (see section 44). A petty officer named Oliver, in charge of a prize crew in a small schooner built by the mutineers in Tahiti, became separated from Edwards in the Samoan Islands, and made a separate traverse of the Pacific from there to the south coast of New Guinea, rejoining Edwards later in Java. An account of the voyage was given in an official report by Edwards, to which some details are added in an account by the surgeon, George Hamilton. These accounts make a few references to Oliver's separate traverse.[2]

Coming from the east, Edwards first encountered Ducie, to the southeast of the Tuamotu Archipelago, and then an island stated to be in latitude 21° 31' S., longitude 135° 32' 30" W., and about 8 miles long, which was evidently Marutea in the Tuamotus. Both these islands had been discovered by Quiros (see section 14). Edwards then discovered another low lagoon island, called by him Carysfort's Island, thought to be 5 miles long, the position given being latitude 20° 49' S., longitude 138° 33' W. Hamilton says the date was 19 March 1791.

This is the position of Tureia, in the Tuamotu Archipelago, an island with no others very close to it.

After capturing some of the *Bounty* mutineers in the Society Islands, Edwards, accompanied by Oliver in the tender, as the mutineers' locally built ship is called in the accounts, came west to Aitutaki and Palmerston, in the southern Cooks. He then went to look for Byron's Duke of York's Island, namely Atafu in the Tokelau Islands (see section 29). On 6 June 1791 he came to a lagoon island, on which a landing

---

[1] Arrowsmith, A., *Chart* (London, 1798); Findlay, A. G., *A Directory for the Navigation of the Pacific Ocean* (London, 1851), vol. ii, p. 1017.

[2] Both are in *Voyage of H.M.S. Pandora*, ed. Thomson, B. (London, 1915).

party found huts and other signs of human visitors, the position given being latitude 8° 34′ S., longitude 172° 6′ W., and on 12 June 1791, found another lagoon island on which people were seen, the position given being latitude 9° 9′ 30″ S., longitude 171° 30′ 46″ W. A landing party found that the inhabitants appeared to have left the island after seeing the ships. Edwards called this second island Duke of Clarence's Island, having concluded that the first was in fact Byron's Duke of York's Island.

The position of the first island corresponds closely to that of Atafu, Byron's Duke of York's Island. It would appear from the latitude given for the second island, and the probabilities from the course in relation to Atafu, that it was Nukunonu in the Tokelau Islands. This was a new discovery.

Edwards then spent some time in the Samoan Islands, where he became separated from Oliver, and then at Tonga, after which he came to Uvea, known from Wallis's discovery (see section 30).

Leaving Uvea on 5 August 1791, Edwards, on the evening of 8 August 1791, came to more land, which the next morning proved to be rather high, well populated, about 10 miles long, with islands at its west end joined to it by a reef. This island he named Grenville Island, the position given being latitude 12° 29′ S., longitude 183° 3′ W.

This was Rotuma, a large detached island north of the Fiji Islands, conforming with Edwards's data. This was a new discovery, the thought that Bougainville's L'Enfant Perdu might have been Rotuma being untenable.

A great number of paddling canoes came off from Rotuma to the ship. No sailing canoes or double canoes were seen. The people said they were in contact with the Tongans. They were tattooed distinctively, with fish, birds, and other things marked on their arms. Their language appeared to bear some resemblance to that of the Tongans.

On 12 August 1791 Edwards saw a small island with 'two high hummocks and a steeple rock', named Mitre Island, which appeared uninhabited. The position given was latitude 11° 49′ S., longitude 190° 4′ 30″ W. This he named Mitre Island. Soon afterwards another island, high but small, and well cultivated, was seen, the position given being latitude 11° 37′ S., longitude 190° 19′ 30″ W. This was named Cherry Island.

These data show that the two islands were Fataka and Anuta, two detached islands lying west of the Santa Cruz Islands. They correspond closely with Edwards's positions and descriptions.

Oliver, after his separation from Edwards, according to Hamilton, came down to Tofua in Tonga. Edwards says that Oliver, after leaving Tofua, steered 2 days to the westward, and fell in with an island which Edwards supposed to be one of the Fiji Islands, where he waited for Edwards for 5 weeks, and then proceeded through Endeavour Straits, between Australia and New Guinea. Hamilton says that Oliver and his company were attacked at Tofua, and were 'obliged to be much on their guard afterwards, at those islands which were inhabited', and that 'after much diversity of distress, and similar encounters', they at last made the reef between Australia and New Guinea.

It must therefore be presumed that Oliver saw one or more of the Fiji Islands, and probably other islands between them and the Torres Strait area. So far as the islands between Fiji and Torres Strait are concerned, all had already been discovered with the exception of the Torres Islands to the west-north-west of the Banks Islands, and the position of the latter is such that on Oliver's course from the south-east the possibility of his having seen them can be virtually ruled out, since the Banks Islands are so placed in relation to them that sailing vessels coming from the south-east would be likely to pass well to the east or south-east of the Torres Islands. Any discoveries that Oliver may have made, therefore, may reasonably be regarded as in the Fiji Islands, and Tasman, Cook, and Bligh had already discovered most of these. Some of those Fiji Islands which had not in fact been discovered by these previous explorers might however have been discovered by Oliver.

The islands discovered by Edward Edwards were Tureia, in the Taumotu Archipelago, on 19 March 1791; Nukunonu, in the Tokelau Islands, on 12 June 1791; Rotuma, north of Fiji, on 8 August 1791; and Fataka and Anuta, on 12 August 1791.

Edwards's associate Oliver may have discovered one or more of the islands in the Fiji group which had not been discovered by previous explorers.

48. Joseph Ingraham and Étienne Marchand

IT has been seen that Mendaña discovered the four southernmost islands of the Marquesas group (see section 12), and that Cook discovered Fatu Huku (see section 37).

In 1791 Joseph Ingraham, of the American trading vessel *Hope*, traversed the Marquesas group. The relevant extracts from his journal were published by the Massachusetts Historical Society in 1793 and reprinted in 1810.[1]

Coming north-north-west from Hiva Oa (Mendaña's Dominica), on 19 April 1791, Ingraham, at 4 p.m., saw two islands, one northwest by north and the other to the west, which he called Washington's Island and Adams's Island, Washington's Island being reckoned to be 35 leagues from Dominica. At 5 p.m. two more islands were seen, one of them, called Federal Island, being between Washington's Island and Adams's Island, the other, called Lincoln's Island, being a small island bearing about south of Adams's Island. All four of these islands could be seen at once when sailing towards them from the east. The situations of these four islands were given as follows: Washington's—latitude 8° 52′ S., longitude 140° 19′ W.; Adams's—9° 20′ S., 140° 54′ W.; Lincoln's—9° 24′ S., 140° 54′ W.; Federal—8° 55′ S., 140° 50′ W. Ingraham says that the position of Federal Island was most liable to a small mistake, since he saw it late in the afternoon and had no opportunity to work out its distance by angle. On 20 April, while they were close to Washington's Island, a canoe with three men came out to them. This island was considered to be about 10 leagues in circuit, of moderate height, diversified with hills and valleys, well wooded, and of very pleasant appearance. At noon on this day Ingraham bore away for another island seen bearing west by north at a distance estimated at about 10 leagues. At 6 p.m. they passed within 2 leagues of this latter island, which was much higher than Washington's Island, but appeared to be about the same extent. Its north-east part was much divided, its summits terminating in ridges and peaks like pyramids. It was inhabited, since they saw fires on it. Its position was taken as latitude 8° 45′ S., longitude 140° 49′ W. This island Ingraham called Franklin's Island. He then steered north till 6 a.m. the following morning, 21 April 1791, when two more islands were encountered, which Ingraham named Hancock's Island and Knox's Island. The

[1] *Collections of the Massachusetts Historical Society*, vol. ii (Boston, 1810), pp. 20–24.

positions given for them were respectively latitude 8° 3' S., longitude 141° 14' W., and latitude 8° 5' S., longitude 141° 8' W. Hancock's Island appeared to be about 5 leagues in circuit, with good verdure. Knox's Island appeared to be about 6 or 7 leagues in circuit, to be fertile and pleasant, and to be inhabited, since habitations were seen on it.

These data plainly show that Ingraham first saw Ua Pou (Adams's Island) and Ua Huka (Washington's Island), and then Nukuhiva (Federal Island), beyond and between Ua Pou and Ua Huka, and the small island of Motu Oa close to the south side of Ua Pou. He then came up to Ua Huka, and saw to the west by north of it at an estimated distance of 10 leagues the island called by him Franklin's Island, a large island like Ua Huka, higher than the latter, with pyramidal peaks. This was the north part of Nukuhiva, answering closely in relative position and topography to Ingraham's detail. Its height is 3,600 feet as compared with Ua Huka's 2,800 feet. Ingraham, having seen the south part of Nukuhiva the previous afternoon at a long distance, did not realize that his Federal Island and Franklin's Island were the south and north aspects of the same large island. That night Ingraham came north without seeing Motu Iti (23 miles west-north-west of the west side of Nukuhiva), the loftiest part of which is 720 feet high, and which consists of three islets, all of which bears no resemblance to Ingraham's detail of Franklin's Island. On 21 April 1791 Ingraham discovered two more islands in addition to his discoveries of Ua Pou, Motu Oa, Ua Huka, and Nukuhiva on 19 April 1791. These were Eiao (Knox's Island), and Hatutu (Hancock's Island), some 60 miles north-north-west of Nukuhiva.

Ingraham gives a few details of the canoe and men who came out to the ship at Ua Huka. With the exception of one young man, who had his hair stained white at the ends, as was common at the Hawaiian Islands, they resembled the people of the islands to the south, as did the canoe, which was curved at each extremity. They paddled in shore after receiving a few cents and nails, giving the Americans a song as they did so.

Only one discovery of any consequence in the Marquesas Islands still remained to be made. This occurred only a month or two after Ingraham had traversed the group. Étienne Marchand, of the French trading vessel *Solide*, made this discovery during the course of a voyage across the Pacific in 1791, the story of which, given by Marchand himself, was published in 1798–1800.[1] Since Ingraham's account of his own discoveries was not yet well known, it seemed that Marchand had discovered numbers of islands, but a collation of the two accounts shows that Ingraham had in fact anticipated Marchand in all these discoveries with the exception of one.

Coming north-west from Hiva Oa, Marchand, after rediscovering Ua Pou, Motu Oa, and Nukuhiva, saw two small islands to the west of the latter which he called Les Deux Frères. The date of their discovery was 23 June 1791.

This was Motu Iti, a cluster of rocky islets 23 miles west-north-west of Nukuhiva.

49. George Vancouver and William Robert Broughton

GEORGE VANCOUVER was the commander of an expedition of two British naval ships, the *Discovery* and the *Chatham*, William Robert Broughton being in command of the latter vessel. While rounding the south of New Zealand, in 1791, the two ships became separated, and made independent passages to Tahiti. Vancouver wrote a detailed narrative of both these passages.[2]

Vancouver, on 24 November 1791, came to a small cluster of seven craggy islands south of New Zealand, the position given being latitude 48° 3′ S., longitude 166° 20′ E. These he called the Snares, a name they still retain. Actually they had been discovered by Broughton the previous afternoon, as will appear later. Continuing on his way, Vancouver, on 22 December 1791, discovered an island of romantic appearance, with high steep mountains, the position being given as

[1] Marchand, É., *Voyage autour du monde* (Paris, 1798–1800).
[2] Vancouver, G., *A Voyage of Discovery* (London, 1798).

latitude 27° 54′ S., longitude 215° 58′ E. The natives appeared to call it Oparo, although Vancouver was not sure of this. No landing was made on the island itself.

This was Rapa, a detached island in the Austral group answering closely to Vancouver's details.

Vancouver's contacts with the islanders who came out in canoes were friendly. He saw in the canoes spears, clubs, and slings. The people appeared to him to be like the Tongans. Some of the hills seemed to be fortified, with redoubts and outer palisades. There were double canoes and single canoes with outriggers, but they had no sails. The people appeared well fed, hospitable, and cheerful. None of them seemed to be tattooed. Their only clothing was a 'wreath made of a broad long-leaved green plant, worn by some about the waist'.

Broughton's report of his own experiences after the separation is reproduced by Vancouver. On the afternoon of 23 November 1791 Broughton discovered a cluster of small islets and rocks, to the largest of which he gave the name Knight's Island, the position given being latitude 48° 15′ S., longitude 166° 44′ E.

These were the Snares, so named by Vancouver when he encountered them the following day.

Making sail to the north-east, Broughton, early on the morning of 29 November 1791, saw some low land lying north-east to east-north-east. He ran that day along the north coast, which extended for about 12 leagues, seeing several peaked hills which at a distance had the appearance of islands, and also a 'range of retired hills'. The northernmost part of this coast was placed in latitude 43° 48′ S., longitude 183° 2′ E. Two small islands lay off this north coast. Broughton landed on the large land, to which he gave the name Chatham. Over the eastern termination more land was seen to the southward, but the weather became so hazy that it was impossible to discover how far it extended to the southward.

These were the Chatham Islands, to the east of New Zealand. The main island, Chatham, has another island, Pitt, close to it on the south-east.

Broughton recorded a number of details of the Chatham Islanders. Their vessels were of some light substance interwoven and bound together with plant fibre in the manner of basketwork, about 3 feet wide, 9 feet long, and flat-bottomed. Their fishing nets were ingeniously made, some in the form of a purse with the rim kept open by wood of the supplejack kind, others in the form of scoop nets. They had long spears, cudgels, and also stones fashioned like the hand clubs of New Zealand. They had mantles and half-cloaks of seal-skin and well-woven mats of fine texture. They had no markings on their skins, and appeared clean. Their hair was black, their general colour was dark brown, their features were plain, and their teeth in general bad. They were cheerful and laughed a lot. After a time they made an attack on the landing party, and were repulsed with musket shots.

George Vancouver discovered Rapa in the Austral Islands on 22 December 1791. William Broughton discovered the Snares, south of New Zealand, on 23 November 1791; and the Chatham Islands, east of New Zealand, on 29 November 1791, making a landing on the main island.

50. John Hunter

IN 1791 John Hunter, while coming north in the *Waaksamheyd* from Sydney, discovered five islands, to the east of the main Solomons chain, the position given being latitude 8° 26′ S., longitude 163° 18′ E. He called them Stewart's Islands. The two largest appeared to be about 3 miles in length.[1]

This was the atoll known as Stewart Island. It has five islands or islets, two of which, Sikaiana and Faore, are larger than the others.

[1] Hunter, J., *An Historical Journal* (London, 1793), pp. 219–20.

51. William Bligh's Second Voyage

WILLIAM BLIGH made a second voyage in the Pacific (see section 44 for his first voyage) in 1792, as commander of two naval ships, the *Providence* and the *Assistant*. The relevant extracts from Bligh's log in the Public Records Office, London, together with a chart by Bligh, are the authorities for his further discoveries or possible discoveries, all of them in the Fiji Islands between 5 and 12 August 1792.[1]

Bligh's aforesaid chart gives the islands, locations, and tracks both of his 1789 and 1792 traverses of the Fiji group. The new islands which were seen by him in 1792 can therefore easily be distinguished. Coming west from Late in the Tonga group, Bligh, on 5 August 1792, saw his previous discovery, Mothe, from the north-east, slightly north of his 1789 track. In doing so he saw Oneata, near Mothe on the latter's north side. Bligh had not seen Oneata in 1789. Bligh then came on a north-west course, seeing the Lakemba–Yathata sector, and also the high points of Moala to the south from the mast. These islands also had not been seen in 1789. Lakemba was first seen on 6 August 1792. In this vicinity some men came out to the ships in a canoe. Moala was seen on 7 August 1792. On this latter day a high island was seen towards the north, and other lands to the north-west and south-west. The high island was Taveuni, discovered by Tasman (see section 18), the others were Vanua Levu, also discovered by Tasman and seen by Bligh in 1789, and Ngau, discovered by Bligh in 1789. A distant view of one of the westernmost parts of the Exploring Isles far to the east was also seen by Bligh, this being another additional island over and above those islands seen in 1789. On 8 August 1792 Bligh came south-west past Viti Levu and the off-shore islands on its east side, which he had seen in 1789. Finally he saw Kandavu on 9 August 1792, which he had not seen in 1789. The additional islands thus seen by Bligh in 1792, over and above those discovered by him in 1789, were the Oneata–Lakemba–Yathata sector, Moala, the westernmost part of the Exploring Isles, and Kandavu. Of these islands Bligh gave the first firm record. Whether any of them had been seen by Oliver in the *Pandora*'s tender in 1791 (see section 47) is not known.

Bligh gives some interesting details of the men who came out in canoes to the ships near Lakemba, and again of Ngau, close to

[1] In Lee, I., *Captain Bligh's Second Voyage* (London, 1920), and Henderson, G. C., *The Discoverers of the Fiji Islands* (London, 1933).

which he sailed. Of the men near Lakemba, one plaited his hair 'in tails loaded with black grease', another wore it 'short and lime-burnt'. They had few marks of tattooing. One of their ears was elongated and pierced. One man wore a 'pretty pearl oyster shell at his breast'. The canoe was of the outrigger type. The spears seen were 'common for striking fish', and the clubs were identical with those of Tonga. Ngau was a fine cultivated island with numerous inhabitants. Some of the people on the shore waved to them with white cloths as they sailed past. In general they had a piece round their heads, and a lance or spear in their hands. Fine plantation walks of coconut and other trees were rendered more picturesque by the dwellings among them. These were all thatched round the sides or top, with an opening. Three canoes came off from the island. In the first were seven men of a very dark colour, almost black, their heads bound round with white cloth, and with pearl oyster shells pendent from the neck. They wore a strip of clothing round the hips. The black colour of these men Bligh considered to be certainly artificial, as at Tonga, since in the other canoes the people were 'rather lighter coloured than the Otaheitians'. Their hair was bushy. They had double canoes and canoes with outriggers.

52. Matthew Weatherhead

In 1792 a British vessel named the *Matilda*, Captain Weatherhead in command, was wrecked in the Tuamotu Archipelago. The survivors reached Tahiti, where William Bligh heard of and recorded some details of the disaster. The wreck occurred on 25 February 1792, on a long reef, the position as recorded by Bligh being latitude 22° S., longitude 139° 45' W. 'Matilda Rocks' in due course appeared on the charts, being shown by the English cartographer Arrowsmith in his chart of 1798 in latitude 22° S., longitude 141⅓° W.[1]

The latitude given by Arrowsmith accords very closely with that of Mururoa in the Tuamotu Archipelago. Confirmation that

[1] Lee, I., *Captain Bligh's Second Voyage* (London, 1920), pp. 39–41; Arrow-smith, A., *Chart* (London, 1798).

Matilda Rocks was in fact Mururoa was given by the British explorer Beechey in 1826 (see section 108), when he found there the wreckage of a vessel, including anchors, corresponding to what would be expected from the *Matilda*.

53. Essex Henry Bond

ON 15 December 1792 Essex Henry Bond, of the British vessel *Royal Admiral*, while coming north from Australia, discovered two small islands close together in the western sector of the Marshalls, in latitude $5\frac{2}{3}°$ N. These Bond called Baring's Islands. The following day, 16 December 1792, to the north of Baring's Islands, he came to a cluster of some twenty low islets, called by Bond the Muskillo Islands, which from their position and description must have been the islets of Namu Atoll, previously discovered by Mendaña (see section 10).[1]

These details show that Baring's Islands were the two islets of Namorik Atoll, on the western fringe of the Marshalls. They lie south of Namu in the stated latitude.

54. Antoine Raymond Joseph de Bruni d'Entrecasteaux

IN the years 1791-3 two French ships, the *Recherche* and the *Espérance*, under the command of Antoine d'Entrecasteaux (so spelled ordinarily), searched the western Pacific for the missing expedition of La Pérouse (see section 40). It was not until 1793 that any new discoveries were made. There are two main accounts. A later editor, E. P. E. Rossel, prepared an account based on d'Entrecasteaux's own journal, and Labillardière, the expedition's

[1] Collins, D., *An Account of the English Colony in New South Wales*, vol. i (London, 1798), pp. 236, 244; Arrowsmith, A., *Chart* (London, 1798); Findlay, A. G., *A Directory for the Navigation of the Pacific Ocean* (London, 1851), vol. ii, p. 1069.

naturalist, wrote another account accompanied by a large-scale chart showing the expedition's course.[1] Rossel's account is followed except where Labillardière is specifically cited.

On 15 March 1793 d'Entrecasteaux, while going from New Zealand to Tonga, discovered a high rock to the south of a cluster recognized by him as Sever's Curtis's Islands (see section 42). The position given for this rock was latitude 31° 27′ 30″ S., longitude 178° 45′ E. from Paris. On 17 March 1793, to the north of Sever's Macauley's Island, another island, named Raoul, was discovered, the position given being latitude 29° 16′ 45″ S., longitude 179° 35′ 40″ E. from Paris. It was almost triangular in shape, high and steep.

The rock was Esperance Rock, and the island Raoul, in the Kermadec group.

On 17 April 1793, while going from the New Hebrides to New Caledonia, d'Entrecasteaux discovered a number of reefs with three low islands, the position given for the northernmost being latitude 20° 15′ 30″ S., longitude 163° 50′ E. from Paris. This cluster was given the name îles Beaupré.

This was the modern Atoll Beautemps-Beaupré, slightly north of the Loyalty Islands.

On 11 June 1793 d'Entrecasteaux came to the Louisiade Archipelago, and in the following days skirted it on the north side. He passed Rossel, which had been encountered by Bougainville, and on 13 June came to some low islands called the îles Renard. Upon this day they also saw a high island to the north-west, which was named Saint-Aignan. Passing north of this, on the next day, 14 June 1793, the ships came to some islands which they named the îles de Boynes. Beyond these again, on 15 June 1793, the expedition came to another cluster of islands called by them the îles Bonvouloir. The next day high land was seen, appearing to extend towards the north. The expedition kept passing these islands till 20 June 1793, when some low islands of great extent, which were named îles Trobriand, were encountered. Beyond these to the west, on 22 June 1793, they encountered some more low islands and reefs. Having at last got clear of these reefs and islands on 26 June 1793, the mountains of New Guinea were seen.

These data show that d'Entrecasteaux discovered the Renard Islands on 13 June 1793, Misima (Saint-Aignan) on the same day,

[1] *Voyage de Dentrecasteaux*, ed. Rossel (Paris, 1808); Labillardière, J. J. de, *Relation du voyage à la recherche de La Pérouse* (Paris, 1800).

the Deboyne Islands on 14 June 1793, and the Bonvouloir Islands on 15 June 1793, these islands being the northern islands of the Louisiade Archipelago. He then discovered the D'Entrecasteaux Islands on 16 June 1793, and the Trobriand Islands on 20 June 1793, and passed among the islands and reefs lying between the Trobriand Islands and the coast of New Guinea in the days 22–26 June 1793.

Antoine d'Entrecasteaux's discoveries were as follows: On 15 and 17 March 1793, respectively, he discovered Esperance Rock and Raoul Island in the Kermadec group. On 17 April 1793 he discovered the Atoll Beautemps-Beaupré, to the north of the Loyalty Islands. On 13, 14, and 15 June 1793, respectively, he discovered the Renard Islands and Misima, the Deboyne Islands and the Bonvouloir Islands, on the north side of the Louisiade Archipelago. On 16 June 1793 he discovered the D'Entrecasteaux Islands, on 20 June 1793 the Trobriand Islands, and on 22–26 June 1793 the islands between the Trobriand Islands and New Guinea.

55. Captain Musgrave

IN 1793 Captain Musgrave, of the British vessel *Sugar Cane*, while coming north from Australia, made a discovery in the Caroline Islands area, shown in Arrowsmith's chart of 1798 as two small islands close together, in latitude $6\frac{1}{4}°$ N., longitude $159\frac{1}{4}°$ E., on which many inhabitants were seen. Coming west from these islands, Musgrave saw a cluster of seven islands, shown by Arrowsmith as being in latitude $6°$ N., longitude $157\frac{1}{2}°$ E.[1]

Pingelap is an atoll consisting of two islands in latitude $6\frac{1}{4}°$ N., longitude $160\frac{3}{4}°$ E. Ngatik is an atoll consisting of seven or eight islands in latitude $6\frac{1}{4}°$ N., longitude $157\frac{1}{4}°$ E. Ngatik's distinctive topography and the relative location of Pingelap and Ngatik help to confirm that the two islands first seen by Musgrave were the islets of Pingelap, and the second cluster was Ngatik. Ngatik had

[1] Collins, D., *An Account of the English Colony in New South Wales*, vol. i (London, 1798), p. 315; Arrowsmith, A., *Chart* (London, 1798).

been reported by Tompson (see section 36). Musgrave's report of Pingelap is the first firm record of that island, although it is not impossible it was seen by Saavedra on his first attempt to return to North America (see section 5).

Arrowsmith's chart of 1798 also shows 'land seen' in latitude $5\frac{2}{3}°$ N., longitude 161° E. Since it is placed close to Musgrave's track on the south side, it presumably represents a report by Musgrave.

The latitude given corresponds to that of Kusaie, an island 144 miles east-south-east of Pingelap with peaks of 2,000 feet. The longitude of Kusaie is, however, 163° E., not 161° E. Since, however, Musgrave's longitude for Pingelap was also well to the west of its true position, the disparity is not fatal to a possible identification with Kusaie.

56. William Raven

DAVID COLLINS, a New South Wales official, in his memoirs of the early years of that colony published in 1798, says that William Raven, of the British vessel *Britannia*, made trips from New South Wales to India and back. On the first of these, Raven left New South Wales in August 1793, and arrived back in June 1794. On the second he left in June 1795, and arrived back in May 1796. No further trips on this northern course were made by Raven before the publication of Collins's references. Raven, according to Collins, said in 1796 that some islands, called by Raven the Loyalty Islands, were situated between New Caledonia and the New Hebrides, and extended from about latitude 21° 30' to 20° 50' S., and from longitude 168° to 167° E.[1]

These details correspond closely to the modern Loyalty Islands, of which Raven was thus the discoverer. It is not clear from Collins's data whether they were discovered by Raven on his first or second voyage. In Arrowsmith's chart of 1798 the date of this discovery is given as 1703.[2] Since 9 is frequently confused with 0 by printers, it seems probable that the date of Raven's discovery was 1793, on his first voyage to India.

[1] Collins, D., *An Account of the English Colony in New South Wales*, vol. i (London, 1798), p. 477.   [2] Arrowsmith, A., *Chart* (London, 1798).

57. Captain Butler

ON 17 November 1794 Captain Butler, of the British vessel *Walpole*, discovered a small island appearing to be about a mile in extent and 200 feet high, with sheer cliffs, the position given being latitude 22⅔° S., longitude 169¼° E. It was named Walpole's Island.[1]

This was the modern Walpole Island, a relatively detached island south-east of the Loyalty Islands, corresponding to Butler's position and description.[2]

58. Captain Mortlock

IN 1795 Captain Mortlock, of the British vessel *Young William*, discovered some islands in the Caroline Islands area. Arrowsmith, in his chart of 1798, shows them in latitude 5¼° N., longitude 153½° E.[3]

These were the Nomoi Islands, a detached group of three small atolls close together on the southern fringe of the Carolines. Mortlock gave the first firm report of them. It is possible they were discovered by Saavedra (see section 5).

Later in the same voyage a low island was seen to the east in about latitude 7⅓° N., longitude 149° E., as shown by Arrowsmith.

This must have been either Puluwat or Pulap in the Caroline group. Pulap had been discovered by Arellano (see section 8).

59. Thomas Dennet

IN 1797 Thomas Dennet, of the British vessel *Britannia*, while passing from Australia to China, encountered a sequence of four islands named by him Hunter, Lambert, Ross, and Princess. Hunter was a small island to the south of Lambert, Ross was close to Lambert on the north-west, and Princess was a small island close to Ross on the west side.

[1] Arrowsmith, A., *Chart* (London, 1798); Findlay, A. G., *A Directory for the Navigation of the South Pacific Ocean* (London, 1851), vol. ii, p. 822.

[2] *Pacific Islands Pilot*, vol. ii, p. 131.

[3] Arrowsmith, A., *Chart* (London, 1798).

The position given for Hunter was latitude 5° 43' N., longitude 169° E., and for Lambert was latitude 7° 52' N., longitude 168° E.[1]

It is evident from these data that Hunter was Kili, Lambert was Ailinglapalap, Ross was Namu, and Princess was Lib, in the western chain of the Marshalls, these being the only sequence of islands corresponding in relative position and size to the details given. Lib had been discovered by Arellano (see section 8), and Namu may have been visited by the *San Jeronimo* in 1566 (see section 9), or, if not, was discovered by Mendaña in 1568. Ailinglapalap may have been discovered by the *San Jeronimo*, but Dennet was the first to give a firm report of it. Kili was a new discovery by Dennet.

60. James Wilson

JAMES WILSON was the captain of the British ship *Duff*, which took out to the Pacific a number of missionaries, making a traverse of that ocean in 1797. A published narrative, in which the nautical data are taken from Wilson's papers, and which is accompanied by charts, is the authority for this voyage, the main author being William Wilson, a member of the ship's company.[2]

While going from Tonga to the Marquesas Islands, the *Duff*, on 19 May 1797, came to a low crescent-shaped island, 6 or 7 miles round, with a higher island to the north-west, the position given being latitude 23° 22' S., longitude 225° 30' E. The ship came up towards the higher island, which was seen to be inhabited, and was of considerable extent, with high hills. The centre of this island was estimated to be in latitude 23° 12' S., longitude 225° E. To these islands the name Gambier's Islands was given.

These were Timoe, a crescent-shaped small island, and Mangareva, a larger island near Timoe on the north-west, in the stated positions on the south-eastern fringe of the Tuamotu Archipelago. These were new discoveries.

[1] Purdy, J., *The Oriental Navigator* (London, 1816), pp. 693–6; Krusenstern, A. J., *Atlas de l'Océan Pacifique. Hémisphère boréal* (St. Petersburg, 1827).

[2] *A Missionary Voyage to the Southern Pacific Ocean* (London, 1799).

On 26 May 1797 the *Duff* came to a low lagoon island, without sign of inhabitants, the position given being latitude 21° 36′ S., longitude 224° 36′ E., which was thought, no doubt correctly, to be Edwards's Lord Hood's Island, namely Marutea (see section 47). On 28 May 1797 another low island was discovered, the position given being latitude 18° 18′ S., longitude 223° E. On this island a landing was made. No inhabitants were seen. It was named Serle's Island.

This was evidently Pukarua, a relatively detached island on the eastern fringe of the Tuamotu Archipelago—a new discovery.

Later in the year the *Duff* came west from Tongatabu in the Tonga Islands, leaving it on 7 September 1797. On 8 September 1797 the *Duff*'s company saw two other islands, one with a flat table top and the other towards the north-west, with other islands beyond the latter. These were correctly identified as those seen by Bligh after leaving Tonga during his first voyage (see section 44), namely Yangasa, Mothe, and the islands near them.

An accompanying chart shows that Wilson at this time saw Ongea and Fulanga to the south of Yangasa. Neither of these islands had been seen by Bligh, but the possibility that Oliver had seen them cannot be ruled out (see section 47). Wilson gave the first firm record of them.

From Yangasa Wilson came north, seeing no islands that had not been seen by Bligh either on his first or second voyages until 12 September 1797. On that day Wilson saw a large island, called by him Sir Charles Middleton's Island, with a number of other islands round it.

The accompanying chart shows that these were the Exploring Isles in the eastern or Lau sector of the Fiji group. The biggest of the Exploring Isles, which was no doubt Wilson's Sir Charles Middleton's Island, is Vanua Mbalavu. Bligh had seen the western-most part of the Exploring Isles on his second voyage (see section 51), but was too far off to see as far as Vanua Mbalavu. Any or all of these islands may have been seen by Oliver. Wilson, however, gave the first firm record of Vanua Mbalavu and the islands close to it.

From here Wilson came up to the north-eastern sector of the Fiji group which had been discovered by Tasman (see section 18). He passed between the islands east of Taveuni and the Nanuku Reef, and so between Vanua Levu and Thikombia to the open sea.

After passing the Duff Islands and other previously discovered islauds, the *Duff*, on 25 October 1797, came to a low island in a position given

as latitude 7° 22′ N., longitude 146° 48′ E. Some of the inhabitants came
off to the ship in canoes without showing fear, and kept saying a word
like 'Capitaine', which made the people of the *Duff* think they had been
acquainted with Europeans before. Two men, William Tucker and
John Connelly, elected to chance their fate with the islanders, from
which circumstance the island was called Tucker's Island. On 26
October 1797, about 10 leagues farther to the west, the *Duff* came to a
cluster of six islands, where another of the ship's company, Andrew
Lind, a Swede, was received by the islanders with joy as a resident.
On 27 October 1797 another low island, appearing from the east like
two islands, was passed, the position given being latitude 7° 14′ N.,
longitude 144° 50′ E. A few hours after passing it they saw another
island. In the morning of 28 October 1797 they came to a cluster of
some thirteen islands, in latitude 7° 16′ N., longitude 144° 30′ E.,
according to their observations. Here great numbers of canoes came
off. On 5 November 1797 they reached the Palaus. Some of the indi-
vidual islands seen after Tucker's Island are named in the accompanying
chart Swede and Haweis, but no systematic sequence of names is
given either in the narrative or the chart.

These islands, all in the vicinity of latitudes $7\frac{1}{4}°$ and $7\frac{1}{3}°$ N., can
be identified by working back from the Palaus. The Palaus were
reached eight days after the cluster of some thirteen islands, which
had another island close to them on the east, the latter island having
another island close to it on the east which appeared from the
east like two islands. These three were plainly Woleai, Ifalik,
and Elato, the first of these atolls consisting of many islets, and
Elato being in fact two atolls north and south of each other, with
Ifalik to the west, their relative locations and their latitudes all
conforming closely to the given details and sailing times. Oli-
marao, an atoll very close to Elato, was apparently not seen; its
later discovery is obscure owing to its close proximity to Elato
and the other islands near by. The cluster at which the Swede
Lind was left, and Tucker's Island to the east of it, which were
thought to be about 10 leagues apart, were Lamotrek and Satawal,
about 38 miles west and east of each other, Lamotrek being broken
into several islets and Satawal an island on a reef. All these islands
are in the western Carolines. These islands were new discoveries.

The Caroline Islanders in the canoes which came out to the *Duff*
were of a dark copper colour, with lively dispositions. Their canoes

were raised high at each end, and painted red; they had outriggers and sailed either end foremost. Their sails resembled those of the single sailing canoes of Tonga. The supposed use of the word 'capitaine' may be fanciful, or previous contacts with the Spanish in other islands may have made the Spanish word 'capitan' known. It cannot be taken as evidence of previous European contact with the islands seen by the *Duff*.

James Wilson's contributions to the discovery of the Pacific Islands were as follows: On 19 May 1797 he discovered Timoe and Mangareva in the Tuamotu Archipelago. On 28 May 1797 he discovered Pukarua in the Tuamotu Archipelago. On 8 September 1797 he encountered Ongea and Fulanga, and on 12 September 1797 Vanua Mbalavu and the islands immediately contiguous to it, these being the first firm records of these islands, although it is possible that they might have been seen by Oliver (see section 47). On 25, 26, 27, and 28 October 1797, respectively, he discovered Satawal, Lamotrek, Elato and Ifalik, and Woleai, in the western Carolines.

61. Captain Fearn

IN 1798 Captain Fearn, of the British vessel *Hunter*,[1] discovered an island reported to be in latitude 22° 24' S., longitude 171° 50' E., which he called Hunter's Island. That this was different from Matthew's Rock, discovered by Gilbert (see section 41), was shown when Fearn found a rock corresponding to the latter some 14 leagues to the west.

The position and relative location of Hunter's Island in relation to Matthew Island show that it was the modern Hunter Island, south-east of the Loyalty Islands.

Fearn discovered in the same year another island, the position given being latitude 0° 20' S., longitude 167° 10' E. It was of considerable size, well inhabited by a stout race of men with canoes of moderate dimensions, and with reefs projecting from its north and south extremes. To this island he gave the name Pleasant Island.

This was Nauru, a detached island in the west of the Gilbert group.

[1] Purdy, J., *The Oriental Navigator* (London, 1816), pp. 697-8; Horsburgh, J., *India Directory*, vol. ii (London, 1827), pp. 593-4.

62. Edmund Fanning

EDMUND FANNING, an American trading captain, made some discoveries in the *Betsey* in 1798. He gave an account of this voyage in a published book.[1]

While coming north-west from the Marquesas Islands, Fanning, on 11 June 1798, came to an island which appeared to be of some extent, and to consist of three islands, the north and south about 9 miles in length each, the eastern about 6, the whole three forming a bay into which Fanning went in the ship's boat, making a landing for fish and coconuts. The position given for these islands was latitude 3° 51′ 30″ N., longitude 159° 12′ 30″ W. He gave them the name Fanning's Islands. Leaving them at 7 p.m., he discovered another island a little before noon the following day, 12 June 1798. This was somewhat higher than Fanning's Islands, and north-west by west of them, the position given being latitude 4° 45′ N., longitude 160° 8′ W. To this island Fanning gave the name Washington. On 14 June 1798 Fanning came on a coral reef or shoal, the position given being latitude 6° 15′ N., longitude 162° 18′ W. Fanning says he went aloft and could plainly see land to the south of this reef. He identified this land with Palmyra's Island. This latter island had been reported a few years later than Fanning's voyage (see section 68).

Fanning's Islands and Washington's Island were the modern Fanning Island, a large broken atoll, and Washington Island, in the mid-Pacific area. They correspond in position and topography to Fanning's details. The reef was evidently the modern Kingman Reef, the northern part of which is in latitude 6° 27′ N., longitude 162° 24′ W. Since Palmyra is 30 miles south-east of Kingman Reef, and Fanning was slightly north of the latter at the time when he thought he saw land to the south, he could scarcely have seen Palmyra, which is a low wooded atoll. Perhaps he saw a mirage of one of the islands to the south of Kingman Reef.

Edmund Fanning was the discoverer of Fanning Island, Washington Island and Kingman Reef, in the mid-Pacific area, on 11, 12, and 14 June 1798, respectively.

[1] Fanning, E., *Voyages round the World* (New York, 1833).

63. Juan Ibargoitia

IN 1799, and again in 1801, Juan Ibargoitia, master of a Spanish Philippines vessel, passed through the western Caroline Islands. In a Spanish chart of Ibargoitia's voyage of 1801, which the French explorer Duperrey procured on his own voyage (see section 94) and collated with his own traverse of the Carolines in 1824, the three islets of Pulap were shown under the name Los Martires, the name commemorating Arellano's discovery of Pulap with the loss of two of his men at the hands of the islanders (see section 8). Close to the south of Pulap, islands were shown under the names Kata and Bartolomé. To the north-north-east of Pulap Ibargoitia encountered an island in latitude 8° 36' N. This island received the name Anonima. The island Bartolomé was evidently identical with an island seen by Ibargoitia on his voyage of 1799.[1]

From the relative locations of these islands it is evident that Bartolomé (apparently encountered in 1799), Kata, and Anonima were respectively Pulusuk, Puluwat, and Onon. Puluwat may have been the low island seen by Mortlock (see section 58), but Ibargoitia gave the first firm record of it, and was the discoverer of Pulusuk and Onon.

64. Captain Bishop

IN 1799 Captain Bishop, of the British vessel *Nautilus*, passed through the Gilbert–Marshall area on his way north from Australia. A chart of the voyage by Roger Simpson and George Bass, who were in charge of the ship's trading activities, was published by the English hydrographer Alexander Dalrymple. The vessel passed a large island called Drummond with shoals on its south-west side, and a cluster of islands to the north-west of it called Sydenham. These ranged from latitude 1° 30' S. to 0° 37' S. The French explorer Duperrey in 1824 recognized these islands from data given him by the Russian hydrographer Krusenstern, who had seen Simpson's and Bass's chart, and Krusenstern, in his Atlas of 1824,

---

[1] Duperrey, L. I., *Mémoire sur les opérations géographiques* (Paris, 1827), p. 70; Espinosa, J., *Memorias* (Madrid, 1809), vol. ii, pp. 28–33.

figured them in relation to the northern islands of the Gilberts, discovered by Gilbert and Marshall (see section 41).[1]

These data show that the two atolls encountered by the *Nautilus* were Tabiteuea and Nonouti in the Gilberts. Tabiteuea may have been discovered by Byron (see section 29). The *Nautilus*, however, gave the first firm report of it. Nonouti was a new discovery, being to the south of the islands discovered by Gilbert and Marshall, and north of Tabiteuea.

65. Henry Waterhouse

IN 1800 Henry Waterhouse, of the British naval vessel *Reliance*, while proceeding from New South Wales to England, discovered an island which, from its nearness to the Antipodes of London, he named Penantipode Island. Its position was given as latitude 49° 49′ 30″ S., longitude 179° 20′ E.[2]

This was the modern Antipodes Island, a detached island in the given position to the south of New Zealand.

66. George Bass

THE discovery in 1800 of Marotiri, an atoll with four islets east-south-east of Vancouver's Oparo (see section 49), i.e. Rapa in the Austral Islands, is attributed by nineteenth-century hydrographers to George Bass.[3]

[1] Collins, D., *An Account of the British Colony in New South Wales*, vol. ii (London, 1802), pp. 110–11; Duperrey, L. I., *Mémoire sur les opérations géographiques* (Paris, 1827), pp. 46–50; Krusenstern, A. J., *Atlas de l'Océan Pacifique. Hémisphère austral* (St. Petersburg, 1824).

[2] Collins, D., *An Account of the English Colony in New South Wales*, vol. ii (London, 1802), p. 287; Scott, E., *Life of Matthew Flinders* (London, 1914), pp. 77, 163.

[3] Findlay, A. G., *A Directory for the Navigation of the Pacific Ocean* (London, 1851), vol. ii, p. 799.

67. Flint's Island

AN island called Flint's Island was discovered in 1801. The position assigned to it in early nineteenth-century references is close to that of the modern Flint Island.[1]

Since Flint Island is a detached island in the mid-Pacific area, its identity with Flint's Island can be regarded as reasonably established.

68. Captain Sawle

IT has been seen that Edmund Fanning's claim to have discovered Palmyra Island in the mid-Pacific area in 1798 is scarcely acceptable (see section 62). The continued attribution by hydrographers of this discovery to Captain Sawle of the *Palmyra*, on 7 November 1802, after Fanning made his claim in 1833, may therefore be regarded as sustained.[2]

69. John Buyers

JOHN BUYERS, a trading captain, in command of the British vessel *Margaret*, made some discoveries in the Tuamotu Archipelago in 1803. The story of this voyage is given in an account by an associate of Buyers, John Turnbull.

While going north from the Duke of Gloucester Islands, Buyers, on 10 March 1803, discovered an inhabited atoll, the position given being latitude 16° 24′ S., longitude 143° 57′ W. This was named Phillips's Island. It appeared to be about 6 or 7 miles in circumference. To another atoll in the neighbourhood, the position given being latitude 16° 12′ S., longitude 143° 47′ W., they gave the name Holt's Island.

---

[1] e.g. Krusenstern, A. J., *Atlas de l'Océan Pacifique. Hémisphère austral* (St. Petersburg, 1824).

[2] Findlay, A. G., *A Directory for the Navigation of the Pacific Ocean* (London, 1851), vol. ii, p. 1051.

Buyers, while coming west for Tahiti, came to another atoll on 13
March 1803. This atoll had a large lagoon, enclosed by land except for a
narrow channel in the leeward (west) end, through which tide rips
came. The ship reached Mehetia in the Society Islands on 16 March
1803.[1]

The positions of Phillips's Island and Holt's Island correspond
precisely with those of Makemo and Taenga. When Turnbull
said that the circumference of Makemo was 6 or 7 miles he was
no doubt referring to the northern land area, the southern part
of the atoll being reef ŋearly covered by the sea. The atoll with
the large lagoon was evidently Faaite, lying west of Makemo
between the latter atoll and Mehetia. The *Pacific Islands Pilot* says
that Faaite has a break in the reef at the north-western end of the
atoll giving access to the lagoon for small vessels, through which
the outgoing tidal stream sets very strongly.[2] Makemo, Taenga,
and Faaite were new discoveries.

70. The *Ocean*, 1804

THE British vessel *Ocean* reported seeing in 1804 a high island called
Ocean Island, in latitude 0° 48' S., longitude 170° 49' E., a group called
Margaret in latitude 8° 52' N., longitude 166° 15' E., a group called Lydia
in latitude 9° 4' N., longitudes 166° 15' or 165° 58' E., and a group
called Catharine in latitude 9° 14' N., longitude 166° 2' or 167° 2' E.,
according to different authorities.[3]

The position for the high island Ocean Island is that of the
modern Ocean Island, which is a detached island of moderate
height in the Gilbert group. This was a new discovery.
The position for Margaret is close to that of Lae, a small atoll
in the western chain of the Marshalls. The positions given for

---

[1] Turnbull, J., *A Voyage Round the World* (London, 1805).

[2] *Pacific Islands Pilot*, vol. iii, p. 110.

[3] Horsburgh, J., *India Directory*, vol. ii (London, 1827), pp. 594–5; Krusenstern, A. J., *Atlas de l'Océan Pacifique. Hémisphère boréal* (St. Petersburg, 1827);
Findlay, A. G., *A Directory for the Navigation of the Pacific Ocean* (London, 1851),
vol. ii, p. 1069.

Lydia correspond with the south of Ujae, a large atoll about 27 miles west of Lae. Catharine was presumably either the north-western sector of Kwajalein or a distant view of the northern islets of Ujae, but the issue is academic so far as the discovery of Kwajalein is concerned, since Kwajalein had been discovered by previous Spanish voyagers (see sections 7 and 8). The *Ocean* can be credited with the first firm reports of Lae and Ujae, although either may have been discovered by Villalobos (see section 7) or by the *San Jeronimo* (see section 9).

71. Samuel William Boll

IN the summer of 1804 Samuel William Boll, of the *Maria*, an American vessel, sailed from Guam into the western Caroline Islands in search of trepang. He was accompanied by Luis de Torres, a Spanish official at Guam, who gave details to the Russian explorer Kotzebue and his naturalist Chamisso when Kotzebue visited Guam on his first voyage (see section 83). The following details were obtained from Torres by Chamisso.[1]

Torres had detailed information of the western Caroline Islands from voyagers who came to Guam to exchange their native products for iron. On the visit of the *Maria*, he made contact with the islanders of 'Guliai', the position of which was given by Torres as latitude 7° N., longitude 144° E. This was Woleai, discovered by Wilson (see section 60). Another island seen was 'Farruelap', discovered by Rodriguez (see section 23). Its position is latitude 8° 35′ N., 144° 36′ E. This was presumably the 'Pik' or 'Lydia' reported by the vessel *Lydia* in 1801.[2] Torres also gave the positions of two small islands 'Fallao' and 'Piguelao', described as desert islands, namely latitude 8° 5′ N., longitude 146° 45′ E., and latitude 8° 6′ N., longitude 147° 17′ E.

These were the two western Caroline Islands West Fayu and Pikelot, of which Boll was the discoverer.

[1] In Kotzebue, O. von, *A Voyage of Discovery* (London, 1821), vol. iii, pp. 112–13.
[2] Cf. Meinicke, C. E., *Die Inseln des Stillen Oceans* (Leipzig, 1888), vol. ii, p. 357.

72. James Cary

IN 1804 James Cary, of the American whaling vessel *Rose*, while on the way to Canton in China, discovered an inhabited island placed by him in latitude 2° 33′ S., longitude 176° 9′ 30″ E., named Rose Island.[1]

The position given is almost precisely that of Tamana, the south-westernmost of the Gilbert Islands. Had Cary's Rose Island been Arorae, some 52 miles east of Tamana in latitude 2° 40′ S., it might be expected that he would have seen others of the Gilbert Islands on his conjectural north-west course. Rose Island can reasonably be regarded as Tamana, a new discovery by Cary.

73. Captain Crozer

THE French explorer Duperrey, in his geographical memoir of 1827, cited an account from the *Moniteur* of 1 February 1806, of the seeing by an American captain Crozer, commanding the *Nancy* of Boston, from a distance of 11 leagues, of a high island named Strong Island, on 20 December 1804, the position given being latitude 5° 21′ N., longitude 160° 37′ 40″ E. of Paris. Duperrey concluded from the close correspondence of this position with his own observations of 'Oualan' in the eastern Carolines, in 1824, that this was the same island.[2]

This was Kusaie, alternatively known as Ualan, a detached high island in the stated position. This may have been the high land shown in Arrowsmith's chart, presumably reported by Musgrave of the *Sugar Cane* (see section 55).

[1] Stackpole, E. A., *The Sea-Hunters* (Philadelphia–New York, 1953), p. 341, citing log of the *Rose*, 1803–4.

[2] Duperrey, L. I., *Mémoire sur les opérations géographiques* (Paris, 1827), p. 54.

74. Urey Lisianski

UREY LISIANSKI, in command of the Russian vessel *Neva*, traversed the Pacific from North America to China in 1805.[1] On the night of 15 October 1805 he grounded temporarily on a reef, and the next day found he was near a small island beset with reefs. The position given was latitude 26° 2¾′ N., longitude 173° 42½′ W. The island, on which Lisianski landed, was low and arid. It was named Lisianski's Island.

The position and description show that this was Lisianski Island, in the northern part of the Hawaii group.

75. Juan Baptista Monteverde

IN February 1806 Juan Baptista Monteverde, of the Spanish vessel *La Pala*, while passing through the Caroline Islands on his way from Manila to Peru, encountered two islands. One of them was identified by him with Tompson's San Agostino, i.e. Oroluk (see section 36). The other, discovered on 18 February 1806, and named Dunkin by Monteverde, was placed by him in latitude 3° 27′ N., longitude 155° 48′ E.[2]

Dunkin was evidently Nukuoro, a large detached atoll in latitude 3° 50′ N., longitude 155° E. Monteverde's latitudes show a tendency to be too low. Monteverde was thus the discoverer of Nukuoro.

76. Abraham Bristow

ROSS, the Antarctic explorer, in his account of his own voyage, gives a note on the discovery of the Auckland Islands by Abraham Bristow in the British vessel *Ocean*. This was a whaler belonging to Enderby's of London. The ship's log was shown to Ross by one of the Enderbys.[3]

---

[1] Lisianski, U., *A Voyage Round the World* (London, 1814).
[2] Espinosa, J., *Memorias* (Madrid, 1809), vol. ii, p. 21.
[3] Ross, J. C., *A Voyage of Discovery* (London, 1847), vol. i, pp. 137-8.

On 18 August 1806 land of moderate height was seen, the position at noon of this day being latitude 50° 48′ S., longitude 166° 42′ E. The north end appeared to afford good harbourage. The latitude was judged to be 50° 21′ S. The greatest extent of the land was in a north-west and south-east direction. Bristow gave the name Lord Auckland's Island to this land.

This is the first record of the Auckland Islands, to the south of New Zealand, corresponding in position and topography to the data in Bristow's log.

77. Charles James Johnston

ON 14 December 1807 Charles James Johnston, of the British naval vessel *Cornwallis*, found two small islands surrounded by a reef, the position given being latitude 16° 53′ N., longitude 169° 31′ 30″ W. They were called the Johnston or Cornwallis Islands.[1]

The stated position is that of the modern Johnston Island, a detached atoll consisting of two islets, to the south-west of Hawaii. It is possible, although not probable, that Johnston Island was seen by Huydecoper (see section 13). One or other of the Spanish vessels which had been passing from Mexico and California to Guam and Manila for $2\frac{1}{2}$ centuries may have seen it. Johnston, however, must be credited with the first firm record of it.

78. Captain Patterson

IN 1809 Captain Patterson, of the British vessel *Elizabeth*, coming north from the Ellice Islands, discovered a small island named by him Hope, the position given being latitude 2° 43′ S., longitude 177° E. The English hydrographer Purdy, who recorded Patterson's positions, changed the name to Hurd's Island, to differentiate it from another Hope's Island, a name given to Kusaie. After traversing a number of already discovered atolls in the Gilberts, Patterson discovered some islets and banks in the western Marshalls forming an island called by

[1] Purdy, J., *Tables of Positions* (London, 1816), p. 156; Horsburgh, J., *India Directory*, vol. ii (London, 1827), p. 595.

him G. Bonham's Island, in latitude 5° 48′ 18″ N. This was later considered by the French explorer Duperrey to be the southern part of an atoll which he himself encountered in 1824 (see section 94), and which from his careful observations and topographical data was evidently Jaluit Atoll in the western chain of the Marshalls. Patterson encountered more islands to the north-west of Bonham, which the Russian hydrographer Krusenstern later identified, no doubt correctly, with Dennet's Lambert, i.e. Ailinglapalap, and other previously discovered islands in the western chain of the Marshalls (see section 59). Duperrey, from a comparison of a number of Patterson's positions with his own observations, considered that Patterson's longitudes by chronometer showed a consistent error of 11′ E.[1]

The position for Hope is slightly east of that of Arorae in the southern sector of the Gilbert Islands. In the light of Duperrey's comment on Patterson's longitudes, it is reasonable to accept that Patterson was the discoverer of Arorae. Bonham was plainly Jaluit, another discovery, its latitude and its location in relation to Ailinglapalap agreeing with the data given.

79. Frederick Hasselbourgh

IN 1810 Frederick Hasselbourgh, of the New South Wales vessel *Perseverance*, found two islands called by him Campbell's Island and Macquarie's Island. Immediately after the return of the *Perseverance* to New South Wales, Captain Smith, of the American whaling vessel *Aurora*, knowing their positions from Hasselbourgh, went and found these islands again, reporting them as being respectively in latitude 52° 32′ S., longitude 169° 30′ E., and latitude 54° 20′ S., longitude 159° 45′ E. Hasselbourgh and Smith reported wreckage on Macquarie's Island, described by Smith as several pieces of a large vessel, apparently very old and high up in the grass.[2]

These islands were Campbell Island and Macquarie Island, two detached islands to the south of New Zealand. While Hasselbourgh was the discoverer of Campbell's Island, apparently the

[1] Purdy, J., *Tables of Positions* (London, 1816), pp. 153–4; Duperrey, L. I., *Mémoire sur les opérations géographiques* (Paris, 1827), pp. 45–53; Krusenstern, A. J., *Atlas de l'Océan Pacifique. Hémisphère boréal* (St. Petersburg, 1827).
[2] McNab, R., *Murihiku and the Southern Islands* (Invercargill, 1907), pp. 119–21.

company of the wrecked vessel had seen Macquarie's Island before him. Since numbers of vessels had passed round the south of New Zealand since the settlement of New South Wales in 1788, the most probable view of the origin of the wrecked vessel was that it was a late European one. It does not seem likely that the wreckage was merely jetsam, since several pieces of one vessel are referred to.

80. Captain Henry

THE discovery of Rimatara in the Austral Islands in 1811 is attributed by J. A. Moerenhout, a European trader of Tahiti in the early nineteenth century who himself visited numbers of the surrounding islands, to Captain Henry of Tahiti, a well-known local ship's master. It is evident that this information was conveyed to Moerenhout by Henry himself, since Moerenhout mentions making visits to islands in the Tuamotu Archipelago in company with Henry.[1]

There being no previous record of Rimatara, it can be concluded that Henry was its discoverer.

81. David Laughlan

ON 16 August 1812 David Laughlan, of the British vessel *Mary*, discovered a group of six or seven islands which appeared to be surrounded by reefs and to have an extent east-south-east and north-north-west of $3\frac{1}{2}$ or 4 leagues, the south-east extremity being placed in latitude 9° 20′ S., longitude 153° 45′ E. They were named Laughlan's Islands.[2]

The position and description of these islands show that they were the Nada Islands, to the north of the Louisiade Archipelago. They are an atoll of eight low islands.[3]

[1] Moerenhout, J. A., *Voyages aux îles du Grand Océan* (Paris, 1837), vol. ii, p. 346.

[2] Horsburgh, J., *India Directory*, vol. ii (London, 1827), p. 588.

[3] *Pacific Islands Pilot*, vol. i, p. 194.

82. Mikhail Lazarev

IN 1814 Mikhail Lazarev, of the Russian vessel *Suvorov*, discovered an uninhabited island in the mid-Pacific area, the position given being latitude 13° 20′ S., longitude 163° 30′ W.[1]

This is very close to the position of the modern Suvorov Island, a detached island in the northern Cooks, which was no doubt the island discovered by Lazarev.

83. Otto von Kotzebue's First Voyage

OTTO VON KOTZEBUE was the commander of a Russian expedition of two ships, the *Rurick* and the *Nadeshda*. He wrote a detailed narrative of this voyage.[2]

While passing through the Tuamotu Archipelago, Kotzebue, on 25 April 1815, discovered a number of small coral islands connected by reefs from north-north-east to south-south-west. There was a large lake in the middle, in which was a wooded island which, says Kotzebue, made it easily recognizable. The position of the middle point of this island, which Kotzebue named Krusenstern, was taken as latitude 15° S., longitude 148° 41′ W. A large island lay to the south-east, separated by a narrow passage from Krusenstern.

This island was Tikahau, in the north-western sector of the Tuamotu Archipelago, a large atoll close to Rangiroa on the latter's west side. Le Maire discovered Rangiroa (see section 16), but no record of an island corresponding to Tikahau is given in the accounts of Le Maire's voyage or of intervening visits to the Tuamotus.

Later in the voyage Kotzebue visited the Marshall Islands, where he was told of an island 'Bigar' in the north-east of the Marshall Islands visited by the native voyagers. From the information of

---

[1] Krusenstern, A. J., *Recueil de mémoires hydrographiques*, vol. i, p. 16; *Atlas de l'Océan Pacifique. Hémisphère austral* (St. Petersburg, 1824).

[2] Kotzebue, O. von, *A Voyage of Discovery* (London, 1821).

these voyagers he constructed a chart including the position of 'Bigar' in relation to the contiguous islands of the Marshalls. When he left the Marshalls and proceeded north, he decided to make 'Bigar' but could not sight it because of the wind. In this search he had the assistance of one of the islanders from the near-by Marshall Islands. This was on 14–15 March 1817.

This was the island of Bikar, in latitude 12° 15′ N., longitude 170° 6′ E., 55 miles north of Utirik in the north-eastern sector of the Marshalls. Krusenstern included it in his Atlas of 1827. Its final discovery is obscure.[1]

84. Captain Henderson

IN 1825 the British explorer Beechey visited islands shown on the charts as Elizabeth Island, Pitcairn Island, and Oeno Island, south-east of the Tuamotu Archipelago. These were the modern Henderson Island, Pitcairn Island, and Oeno Island. Beechey stated that the island then known as Elizabeth Island, so called after a vessel named *Elizabeth*, had in fact been discovered by Captain Henderson of the British vessel *Hercules*, which encountered the island and reported it to the people of Pitcairn very shortly before the *Elizabeth* arrived at Pitcairn and reported it. Beechey goes on to say that Captain Henderson also discovered Oeno, the latter name being subsequently given to it by the master of a whale-ship of that name who supposed it had not been seen before. The *Elizabeth*'s encounter with Elizabeth Island was in 1819.[2]

Elizabeth or Henderson Island had in fact been discovered by Quiros (see section 14). Captain Henderson would, however, appear to have been the discoverer of Oeno.

---

[1] Krusenstern, A. J., *Atlas de l'Océan Pacifique. Hémisphère boréal* (St. Petersburg, 1827); Meinicke, C. E., *Die Inseln des Stillen Oceans* (Leipzig, 1888), vol. ii, p. 327.

[2] Beechey, F. W., *Narrative of a Voyage* (London, 1831), vol. i, pp. 64, 137–8; Krusenstern, A. J., *Atlas de l'Océan Pacifique. Hémisphère austral* (St. Petersburg, 1824).

85. Captain De Peyster

IN 1819 Captain De Peyster, of the ship *Rebecca*, made a passage from Valparaiso to India. In doing so De Peyster discovered a cluster of about fourteen low islands and sand keys. These islands De Peyster called Ellice's Group. The next morning another group of about seventeen low islands was discovered, to which the name of De Peyster's Islands was given. The position of their southern extremity was taken as latitude 8° 5' S., longitude 181° 43' W.[1]

The only two clusters of islands which conform with the latitudes, descriptions, and relative positions of these groups are Funafuti and Nukufetau, two large atolls in the Ellice Islands, Nukufetau being 43 miles north-west of Funafuti.

86. George Barrett

GEORGE BARRETT, of the American whaling vessel *Independence*, on 6 November 1821 came to an inhabited group of islands with coconut trees, a landing being made the following day. The position given was latitude 9° 18' S., longitude 179° 45' E. Barrett called these islands Mitchell's Group. On 8 November 1821 a small, low, uninhabited island about 1 mile long, guarded all round by a coral reef, was seen. This island was named Rocky or Independence Island. Its position was taken as latitude 9° 6' S., longitude 179° 48' E.[2]

The positions of these islands correspond closely with those of Nukulaelae and Nurakita, the two southernmost of the Ellice Islands. Nukulaelae is a large atoll with numbers of islets, while Nurakita appears as a single island, and is beset with reefs. Nurakita was discovered by Mendaña (see section 12). Nukulaelae was a new discovery.

[1] Horsburgh, J., *India Directory*, vol. ii (London, 1827), p. 595; Stackpole, E. A., *The Sea-Hunters* (Philadelphia–New York, 1953), p. 280, citing *Nantucket Inquirer*, 22 Oct. 1822.

[2] Stackpole, E. A., *The Sea-Hunters* (Philadelphia–New York, 1953), pp. 279–81, citing *Nantucket Inquirer*, 22 Oct. 1822; Reynolds, J. N., Report of 1828, in Doc. No. 105, House of Representatives, Navy Department, 23rd Congress, 2nd Session (Washington, 1835).

87. Joseph Allen

JOSEPH ALLEN, of the American whaling vessel *Maro*, on 2 June 1820 discovered an island or rock, 150 feet high with two detached humps, the position given being latitude 25° 3′ N., longitude at 3 miles away 167° 40′ W. He named it Gardner's Island.[1]

This was Gardner Island, a barren, rocky island with a smaller pinnacle rock on its north-western side,[2] in the north-western sector of the Hawaiian Islands.

88. Thaddeus Bellingshausen

THADDEUS BELLINGSHAUSEN was the commander of a Russian exploratory expedition of two ships, the *Vostok* and the *Mirnyi*. Bellingshausen wrote a detailed account of his voyage with charts.[3]

Coming north from Amanu in the Tuamotu Archipelago, Bellingshausen, on 10 July 1820, came to an inhabited island, the position given being latitude 15° 51′ 5″ S., longitude 140° 49′ 19″ W., called by him Count Arakcheev Island.

This was Angatau, in the stated latitude north of Amanu. It may have been discovered by Magellan (see section 2), but Bellingshausen gave the first firm record of it.

Sailing west from Angatau, Bellingshausen came past Takume and Raroia, and on 13 July 1820 saw two more islands. The first was a small island called 'Nihera' by some islanders who came aboard. Its position was taken as latitude 16° 42′ 40″ S., longitude 142° 44′ 50″ W. The other island lay to the north-west of it.

These two islands were Nihiru and Taenga. Nihiru was a new discovery.

Having continued to the west past Makemo, Bellingshausen was

---

[1] Stackpole, E. A., *The Sea-Hunters* (Philadelphia–New York, 1953), p. 269, citing *New Bedford Mercury*, 8 June 1821.

[2] *Pacific Islands Pilot*, vol. iii, p. 299.

[3] *The Voyage of Captain Bellingshausen*, ed. Debenham, E. (London, 1945).

informed almost immediately that two more islands were in sight from the mast, one south-west by south, and the other west by south. The ship could not fetch an island called by Bellingshausen General Raevski Island because of the head wind. It was judged to be in latitude 16° 43′ S., longitude 144° 11′ W. This was on 15 July 1820.

These were the Raevski Islands, a cluster south-west of Makemo —another new discovery.

The first island to be sighted after General Raevski Island, also on 15 July 1820, was judged to be 12½ miles long and 6⅓ miles wide. Two narrow openings into the lagoon were noted. The position given was latitude 16° 28′ 35″ S., longitude 144° 17′ 33″ W. Bellingshausen called it Graf Osten-Saken Island.

This, as might be expected from the map, was Katiu, a large atoll 9 miles north-north-west of the Raevski Islands.

The next day, 16 July 1820, Bellingshausen saw Tahanea and Faaite, neither of which were new discoveries, and more land to the north-west of Faaite. The next day this latter land was inspected more closely. The position given for its northern point was latitude 16° 9′ 20″ S., longitude 145° 33′ 55″ W. Bellingshausen called it Count Wittgenstein Island.

This was Fakarava, north-west of and close to Faaite—another new discovery.

Beyond Fakarava Bellingshausen came to two islands which he surmised correctly were two of Cook's Palliser Islands (see section 37)—Toau and Kaukura.

On 18 July 1820, at daylight, Bellingshausen found himself near a small island, higher than the others, the position given being latitude 16° 11′ 18″ S., longitude 146° 15′ 50″ W. The diameter was thought to be 5½ miles. This was named Admiral Greig Island. Here a landing was made.

The small island was Niau, which lies 18 miles west of Toau and Fakarava. The *Pacific Islands Pilot* says that it is 5½ miles long and consists of a crater with a lagoon, being about 26 feet high, all of which agrees with Bellingshausen's topographical details. Niau was another new discovery.[1]

Bellingshausen now sailed to Tahiti past Makatea. From Tahiti he came north again to the north-western Tuamotus, encountering

[1] *Pacific Islands Pilot*, vol. iii, p. 115.

Tikahau, which he recognized as Kotzebue's Krusenstern Island (see section 83). He then came west, and at a distance from Tikahau thought to be 22 miles, he passed an island judged to be 5½ miles long and 2 miles wide, apparently uninhabited. The position given was latitude 14° 56' 20" S., longitude 148° 38' 30" W. This island, which Bellingshausen called Lazarev Island, was seen on 30 July 1820.

This was Matahiva, 22 miles west-north-west of Tikahau, 5 miles long and 3 miles wide—another new discovery.

During his passage through the Tuamotus, Bellingshausen saw numbers of islanders, some of whom occasionally attacked the ship. The only close contact was at Nihiru, where a chief of Anaa who was visiting the island, accompanied by a woman, came aboard and was entertained to dinner by Bellingshausen.

On 1 August 1820 another island was discovered. It was considered to be little more than ⅓ mile long in a north-west by north direction, and in width less than ½ mile. The position given was latitude 10° 5' 50" S., longitude 152° 16' 50" W. It was named Vostok.

This was the modern Vostok. It may have been discovered by Magellan.

From Vostok Bellingshausen came past Rakahanga, Pukapuka, and Vavau to the Fiji Islands. On 19 August 1820 he saw three islands. The first two were small islands about 6½ miles apart, the position given for the more easterly being latitude 21° 1' 35" S., longitude 178° 40' 13" W. Bellingshausen called this Mikhailov, and the other, to the north-west of it, Simanov. North-west of the latter, high land was seen. This proved to be a cluster of small high islands, the centre judged to be in latitude 20° 39' S., longitude 178° 40' W. Here they made contact with the inhabitants, who told them the name of the cluster was Ono.

These were the south-easternmost islands of the Fiji group, Tuvana-i-Tholo (Mikhailov), Tuvana-i-Ra (Simanov), and Ono-i-Lau (Ono). These are south of Oliver's course to the west from Tofua (see section 47). Ono-i-Lau may have been discovered by the *Bounty* mutineers (see section 44).

At Ono the Russians had friendly contacts with the chief Fio and his people. They got many fine artifacts, drawings of which were included with Bellingshausen's account, together with impressive portraits of the chiefs.

Bellingshausen's contributions to the discovery of the Pacific

Islands were as follows: On 10 July 1820 he gave the first firm record of Angatau in the Tuamotu Archipelago. This island may have been discovered by Magellan (see section 2). On 13 July 1820 Bellingshausen discovered Nihiru, on 15 July 1820 the Raevski Islands and Katiu, on 16 July 1820 Fakarava, on 18 July 1820 Niau, and on 30 July 1820 Matahiva, all in the Tuamotu Archipelago. On 1 August 1820 Bellingshausen gave the first firm report of Vostok Island. On 19 August 1820 Bellingshausen discovered Tuvana-i-Tholo and Tuvana-i-Ra, and either discovered, or rediscovered after the *Bounty* mutineers (see section 44), Ono-i-Lau, in the Fiji Islands. Landings were made on Niau and Ono.

89. Captain Browne

CAPTAIN BROWNE, of the British vessel *Eliza Francis*, on 21 August 1821 discovered a small island, 5 miles in circumference, and took its position as latitude 0° 23′ S., longitude 159° 46′ W.[1]

This is almost precisely the position of the modern Jarvis Island, a detached small coral island in the mid-Pacific area, which was no doubt the island discovered by Browne.

90. Captain Patrickson

IN October 1822 Captain Patrickson of the British vessel *Good Hope* discovered two low islands near each other, abounding in coconut trees, named by him Reirson's Island and Humphrey's Island respectively. The positions given were, for Reirson's Island, latitude 10° 6′ S., longitude 160° 55′ W., and for Humphrey's Island, latitude 10° 30′ S., longitude 161° 2′ W. As the ship passed Reirson's Island a number of inhabitants were seen, and it was conjectured that Humphrey's Island, being to leeward, was inhabited likewise.[2]

[1] Krusenstern, A. J., *Supplémens* (St. Petersburg, 1836), p. 22; Royal Geographical Society, *Journal* (London, 1837), p. 227.
[2] Horsburgh, J., *India Directory*, vol. ii (London, 1827), p. 596.

These islands were Rakahanga (Reirson's Island) and Manihiki (Humphrey's Island), in the northern Cooks. They are close to Patrickson's positions, but owing to slight errors in longitude he reversed their positions leeward and windward of each other in relation to the prevailing south-east wind. Rakahanga had been discovered by Quiros (see section 14) and seen again by Bellingshausen (see section 88), but Patrickson was the discoverer of Manihiki.

91. The *Pearl* and *Hermes*, 1822

ON 26 April 1822 two British whaling ships, the *Pearl* and the *Hermes*, were wrecked on the same night on a large reef in latitude 27° 46' N., longitude about 176° W. This land was named the Pearl and Hermes Reef.[1]

This position is almost precisely that of the modern Pearl and Hermes Reef. This is actually a large atoll with a barrier reef and a number of low arid islets, to the north-west of the main Hawaiian islands.[2]

92. The *Abgarris*, 1822

IN 1826 Captain Renneck, of the British vessel *Lyra*, found a chain of low islands and sand-banks connected by a reef, the north part being placed in latitude 3° 9' S., longitude 154° 22' E. On the south side there was a detached shoal with a reef, placed in latitude 3° 33' S., longitude 154° 37' E. Most of the islands were inhabited. This was considered by later hydrographers to confirm the report of the whaleship *Abgarris* of Abgarris Island, seen in 1822 in the same position.[3]

[1] Horsburgh, J., *India Directory*, vol. ii (London, 1827), p. 596; Krusenstern, A. J., *Atlas de l'Océan Pacifique. Hémisphère boréal* (St. Petersburg, 1827).

[2] *Pacific Islands Pilot*, vol. iii, p. 303.

[3] Krusenstern, A. J., Note of 1834, cited in Royal Geographical Society, *Journal* (London, 1837), p. 408; Findlay, A. G., *A Directory for the Navigation of the Pacific Ocean* (London, 1851), vol. ii, p. 1023; Meinicke, C. E., *Die Inseln des Stillen Oceans* (Leipzig, 1888), vol. i, p. 140.

This was Nuguria, to the east of the main islands of the Bismarck Archipelago. It consists of two contiguous groups of islets, sandbanks and reefs in the stated positions.[1]

93. The *Britomart*, 1822

THE British vessel *Britomart* reported seeing an island in 1822 in latitude 19° 52′ S., longitude 145° 23′ W. The British hydrographer Findlay, in his 1851 Directory, considered that this island had not been seen since, although he mentioned that Ringgold of the U.S. Exploring Expedition of 1838–42 had seen an island 'San Pablo' in latitude 19° 50′ S., longitude 145° W., which is about the same position as that of Britomart Island.[2]

The latitude given for Britomart Island is precisely that of Hereheretue, on the western fringe of the Tuamotu Archipelago. The longitude of the west extremity of Hereheretue is 145° W., which again agrees very closely with the longitude of Britomart Island. This would not in itself be sufficient to differentiate Britomart Island if it were not that the nearest islands to it are not in the precise latitude of Hereheretue and that given for Britomart Island, and that if the *Britomart* had in fact been farther to the east among the closer Tuamotuan islands, it is probable that she would have reported more than one. It would appear that the *Britomart* discovered Hereheretue and that Ringgold merely confirmed it.

94. Louis Isidor Duperrey

LOUIS ISIDOR DUPERREY, the commander of the French vessel *Coquille*, made an exploration of the Pacific in 1823 and 1824. Duperrey wrote a memoir of this voyage, including his

[1] *Pacific Islands Pilot*, vol. i, p. 432.

[2] Findlay, A. G., *A Directory for the Navigation of the Pacific Ocean* (London, 1851), vol. ii, pp. xv, 855–6; Wilkes, C., *Narrative of the United States Exploring Expedition* (Philadelphia, 1845), vol. iv, p. 266.

own views of the relationship of the islands encountered by him to the discoveries of his predecessors.[1]

On 22 April 1823, coming from the east, Duperrey discovered a large low inhabited island in the Tuamotu Archipelago, to which he gave the name Clermont-Tonnerre. The position given for its northern point was latitude 18° 28' 10" S., longitude 138° 46' 50" W. from Paris. It lay east-south-east and west-north-west. Its northern part consisted of a wooded island with a fine sandy beach, the southern part was only a bank covered with rocks and islets, and there was a lagoon in between.

These data establish Clermont-Tonnerre as Reao, on the eastern fringe of the Tuamotu Archipelago, agreeing in position and topography with Duperrey's details. This was a new discovery.

The next encounter by Duperrey which there is any reason to believe might have been a new discovery did not occur until 20 May 1824, when the expedition took careful observations of the position of certain islands which Duperrey thought had been discovered by Gilbert and Marshall (see section 41). Included among them was an island named Matthews, in the Gilberts. The position of the northern part of this island was given by Duperrey as latitude 2° 4' 30" N., longitude 170° 56' E. from Paris.

This position agrees with that of Marakei and can be taken as the first firm record of it. Marakei is the most likely candidate for identification as the Acea of Grijalva's ship (see section 6).

Later again in the voyage, Duperrey, on 18 June 1824, discovered some islands which were named Iles Duperrey. They were three in number, on the same reef, with an internal lagoon, the names given to them by the inhabitants who came out to the ship being 'Ongai', 'Mougoul', and 'Aoura'. The position of the south point of 'Mougoul', the middle of the group, was taken as latitude 6° 39' N., longitude 157° 29' 25" E. from Paris.

This was Mokil in the eastern Carolines, consisting of three islands on a reef, the atoll being named after Mokil (Duperrey's 'Mougoul'), one of the islands. Mokil may have been seen by Saavedra on his first attempt to return to North America (see section 5), but Duperrey gave the first firm report of it.

[1] Duperrey, L. I., *Mémoire sur les opérations géographiques* (Paris, 1827).

The men of Mokil who came out to Duperrey's ship in a sailing canoe were tall, strong, and well made. Their fine wavy hair came down to their shoulders. They had a cheerful air and a softness in their faces which, says Duperrey, showed them to be a happy healthy people with no reason to envy the rest of the world.

On 23 June 1824, in the evening, Duperrey came to a small low island called by him d'Urville, of which the north point was taken to be in latitude 7° 5' 18" N., longitude 150° 16' 52" E. from Paris. The approach of night prevented their getting a plan of it. Next morning they came to Truk.

D'Urville Island was evidently a sight of Losap-Nama, two almost conjoined atolls forming one small cluster, close to Duperrey's stated position. This was the first firm record of Losap-Nama, which may, however, have been seen by Saavedra on his first attempt to return to North America (see section 5).

The contributions of Louis Isidor Duperrey to the discovery of the Pacific Islands were as follows: On 22 April 1823 he discovered Reao in the Tuamotu Archipelago. On 20 May 1824 he gave the first firm record of Marakei in the Gilberts, Marakei having, however, probably been discovered by Grijalva's ship (see section 6). On 18 and 23 June 1824, respectively, he gave the first firm records of Mokil and Losap-Nama in the Caroline group, either of which may have been discovered by Saavedra (see section 5).

95. John Williams and John Dibbs

IN 1823 the British missionary John Williams made an exploration of the southern Cook Islands in a hired British vessel named the *Endeavour*, the master of which was John Dibbs. While at Atiu Williams heard of two small near-by islands, Mitiaro and Mauke, and accordingly visited them. The nineteenth-century hydrographers[1] recorded the position of 'Mitiero' from Dibbs's information as latitude 20° 1' S.,

[1] Williams, J., *Missionary Enterprises* (London, 1837), pp. 86–8; Findlay, A. G., *A Directory for the Navigation of the Pacific Ocean* (London, 1851), vol. ii, p. 804. citing *Journal des voyages*, vol. xxviii (Paris, 1825).

longitude 157° 34' W., describing it as a low island measuring 3 to 4 miles from north to south and a mile from east to west, at a distance of 25 miles from Atiu, Mauke being an island near by.

These were Mitiaro, about 20 miles north-east of Atiu, and Mauke, about 22 miles south-east of Mitiaro, both of them new discoveries. The visit of the *Endeavour* to these islands was made in July 1823.

96. William Clark

WILLIAM CLARK, of the American whaling vessel *Winslow*, reported making contact in 1823 with two islands, the position given being latitude 15° 30' S., longitude 177° 10' W. The islands in question certainly existed, since Clark gave circumstantial details of contacts with the islanders. The islands were presumably in the area of the Tonga group. No land, however, exists in or close to the position given. The issue is only important as a demonstration of the unreliability of Clark's stated position, since all the islands in the vicinity had been discovered. This has a bearing on Clark's report of another island, called Clark's Island, the position given being latitude 3° 10' S., longitude 154° 30' W., also in 1823.[1]

Clark's Island, if it were an island, may have been Malden Island, in latitude 4° S., longitude 155° W. If so, Clark was its discoverer.

97. Obed Starbuck

OBED STARBUCK, an American whaling captain, made his first contribution to discovery as captain of the *Hero* in 1823. On 5 September in that year Starbuck discovered a desolate island estimated to be 8 or 10 feet in height and 2 miles wide by 10 miles long, with a very white beach. It lay in the form of an angle, the position given being latitude 5° 32' S., longitude 155° 55' W.[2]

[1] Stackpole, E. A., *The Sea-Hunters* (Philadelphia–New York, 1953), p. 349, citing *Nantucket Inquirer*, 23 Sept. 1826.

[2] Ibid., pp. 349–50, citing Morrell, M. E., MS. journal.

The position given is close to that of Starbuck Island, in the mid-Pacific area, and the description tallies with it. This was no doubt the island discovered by Obed Starbuck. By a coincidence Starbuck got its name, not from Obed Starbuck, but from Valentine Starbuck, who saw the island three months after Obed, naming it Volunteer Island. When at a later date George Anson Byron visited it and recognized it as the island reported by Valentine Starbuck,[1] it received the name Starbuck Island.

In 1825 Obed Starbuck made a traverse of the Pacific from north-east to south-west, during which time he made some more contributions to discovery. On this voyage he was master of the *Loper*. Details of these contacts were given in American newspaper reports, and by Jeremiah N. Reynolds in his report of 1828 to the U.S. Navy Department on American whaling discoveries.[2]

Starbuck's first encounter of significance on this traverse was with a small, low, barren island estimated to be not more than ½ mile in circumference, with dazzling white beaches, the position given being latitude 0° 11′ N., longitude 176° 20′ W. To this island he gave the name New Nantucket.

This is the position of Baker Island, a relatively detached island in the north of the Phoenix group, answering to Starbuck's topographical data. This was no doubt Starbuck's New Nantucket.

Later in his traverse Starbuck came to an island placed by him in latitude 6° 7′ S., longitude 177° 40′ E., named Loper's Island, and a day or so later to another island placed in latitude 7° 30′ S., longitude 178° 45′ E., named Tracy's Island.

These are the positions of Niutao, the northernmost of the Ellice Islands, and of Vaitupu, also in the Ellice Islands, which from these data and their relative locations in relation to Starbuck's course were plainly his Loper's Island and Tracy's Island respectively.

Starbuck's report of two islands in the main area of the Phoenix

[1] *Voyage of H.M.S. Blonde* (London, 1826), pp. 204–6.

[2] Stackpole, E. A., *The Sea-Hunters* (Philadelphia–New York, 1953), pp. 345–6, citing *Nantucket Inquirer*, 25 Nov. 1826; Reynolds, J. N., Report of 1828, in Doc. No. 105, House of Representatives, Navy Department, 23rd Congress, 2nd Session (Washington, 1835).

group are mentioned in section 106. For the reasons given in that section it is not possible to say whether these were original discoveries or rediscoveries.

Obed Starbuck must be credited with the discovery of Starbuck Island, Baker Island, and Vaitupu; and with the first firm report of Niutao, which may, however, have been Mendaña's Isle of Jesus (see section 10).

98. Otto von Kotzebue's Second Voyage

IN 1824 Otto von Kotzebue, on his second voyage, came through the Tuamotu Archipelago in the Russian vessel *Predpiatie*. He wrote a detailed narrative of this voyage.[1]

On 2 March 1824, while passing through the Tuamotus, Kotzebue discovered a low, thickly wooded, inhabited island, the position given being latitude 15° 58' 18" S., longitude 140° 11' 30" E. This island he called Predpiatie. He sailed round it but no landing could be made. In order to make sure that it was not Bellingshausen's Arakcheev Island, i.e. Angatau (see section 88), Kotzebue came west and found the latter in the position assigned to it by Bellingshausen and answering to his description.

Predpiatie was Fangahina, 40 miles east-south-east of Angatau, in the Tuamotu Archipelago. It may have been discovered by Magellan (see section 2), but Kotzebue gave the first firm record of it.

From Angatau Kotzebue came north-west past Takume to Tikei, on which he landed, noting that it had no lagoon. On 8 March he saw Takaroa and Takapoto lying close to each other, his position at this point being taken as latitude 14° 41' 36" S., longitude 144° 55' W. During the night they were becalmed. The next morning, 9 March 1824, he had adverse winds and was carried by a current to the south. As a result he came to an island estimated to be 10 miles in length from east to west and 4 miles broad. It appeared to consist of a narrow strip of land with a lake in the centre. The position of the middle of this island was latitude 15° 27' S., longitude 145° 31' 12" W. Kotzebue conjectured this was an island discovered by Roggeveen in 1722 (see

[1] Kotzebue, O. von, *A New Voyage* (London, 1830).

section 27). To the west of it he came to Cook's Palliser's Islands (see section 37).

This island was Aratika—a new discovery. It lies south-south-west of Takapoto, and to the east of Roggeveen's course from that island and west of Tikei, Roggeveen's previous discovery, the chance of encountering winds and currents which carried him to the south from Takapoto being the reason why Kotzebue came into waters which had not been previously traversed. On 9 October 1825 Kotzebue discovered the Eschholtz Isles in latitude 11° 40′ 11″ N., longitude 194° 37′ 35″ W., i.e. Bikini.

99. John Hall

In 1824 the French explorer Duperrey visited Truk in the Caroline Islands. In his geographical memoir of 1827 Duperrey cited references by one Captain Saliz, in the *Annales Maritimes* of May 1827, to a voyage from Calcutta to Mexico by Captain John Hall of the British vessel *Lady Blackwood*. Since Hall's latitudes and longitudes, and his references to large numbers of small islands, agreed with Duperrey's own observations, Duperrey realized that Hall, on the morning of 2 April 1824, had passed Truk. Later in the same day, 2 April 1824, Hall discovered a new group of islands, which he examined the following day, traversing the middle of them and fixing their positions as latitude 8° 45′ N., and longitudes 149° 53′ 40″ to 149° 19′ 40″ E. from Paris. Duperrey called these islands the Iles John-Hall.[1]

These were the modern Hall Islands, two closely contiguous atolls some 44 miles north of Truk. Of these Hall was the discoverer.

100. George Joy

The French explorer Duperrey recorded that on 30 May 1824 he spoke to an American whaling vessel named the *Boston*, commanded by Captain George Joy, close to the western islands of the Marshall group. Joy told Duperrey that on 25 May 1824 he had discovered eight small

[1] Duperrey, L. I., *Mémoire sur les opérations géographiques* (Paris, 1827), p. 68.

low islands on an extensive reef with an opening to the north-east, the position given being latitude 4° 45′ N., longitude 165° 50′ E. of Paris.[1]

Ebon, a detached atoll in the south-western sector of the Marshall Islands, is close to the stated position. The *Pacific Islands Pilot* says that there are islets on all sides of the reef enclosing the lagoon except the north.[2] Joy was thus its discoverer.

101. George W. Gardner

ON 19 December 1824 George W. Gardner, of the American whaling vessel *Maria*, discovered a small island, judged to be 6 or 8 miles in length and 3 miles across, in latitude 21° 45′ S., longitude 155° 10′ W.[3]

This is the position of the modern Maria Island, a detached atoll in the Austral Islands, which was no doubt the island discovered by Gardner.

102. Koerzen and Eeg

IN 1825 two Dutch naval vessels, the *Maria Regersbergen* and the *Pollux*, commanded respectively by Koerzen and Eeg, made a traverse of the Ellice Islands, during which they made contact with an island which was not yet on the charts, in latitude 7° 10′ S., longitude 177° 33¼′ E. They called it Nederlandsch Eyland. It was inhabited by a fierce and athletic race of men.[4]

This was Nui, of which Koerzen and Eeg thus gave the first firm report. It may have been Mendaña's Isle of Jesus (see section 10).

[1] Duperrey, L. I., *Mémoire sur les opérations géographiques* (Paris, 1827), p. 54.
[2] *Pacific Islands Pilot*, vol. ii, p. 458.
[3] Stackpole, E. A., *The Sea-Hunters* (Philadelphia–New York, 1953), p. 354, citing *Nantucket Inquirer*, 23 May 1825.
[4] Horsburgh, J., *India Directory*, vol. ii (London, 1827), p. 596; Findlay, A. G., *A Directory for the Navigation of the Pacific Ocean* (London, 1871), p. 667; Meinicke, C. E., *Die Inseln des Stillen Oceans* (Leipzig, 1888), vol. ii, p. 133.

103. George Anson Byron

GEORGE ANSON BYRON, of the British vessel *Blonde*, in 1825 came south from Hawaii. On 29 July 1825 he discovered an island, the position given being latitude 4° S., longitude 155° W., which he named Malden's Island. A landing party went ashore and found that it was uninhabited, but that there were ruins of previous structures.[1]

This was Malden Island, a detached island in the mid-Pacific area, the position of which is precisely that given by Byron, the identification being confirmed by the ruins. This was possibly seen by William Clark in 1823 (see section 96).

104. Prince B. Mooers

IN 1825 Prince B. Mooers, of the American whaling ship *Spartan*, saw an island, the position given being latitude 1° 10′ N., longitude 154° 30′ E.[2]

Since this is very close to the position of Kapingamarangi, the southernmost of the Caroline Islands, and a particularly isolated island, it can reasonably be concluded that this was the island reported by Mooers. It is possible, although not probable, that this was the Dos Pescadores reported by the survivors of Grijalva's ship (see section 6).

105. Laysan Island

IN 1827 Captain Stanikowitch, of the Russian vessel *Moller*, found a small, low, uninhabited circular island with a lagoon. It appeared to be about 6 miles in circumference. The position was given as latitude 25° 46′ N., longitude 171° 49′ W. The Russian hydrographer Krusenstern considered that this was the same as Laysan Island, a previous American whaling discovery, and it was named accordingly.[3]

This was the modern Laysan Island, in the north-western sector of the Hawaiian Islands.

[1] *Voyage of H.M.S. Blonde* (London, 1826), pp. 204–6.
[2] Stackpole, E. A., *The Sea-Hunters* (Philadelphia–New York, 1953), p. 372, citing *Nantucket Inquirer*, 3 Mar. 1827.
[3] Krusenstern, A. J., *Supplémens* (St. Petersburg, 1836), p. 110.

P

106. Early Encounters with the Phoenix Islands

IN 1794 the British ship *Arthur*, Henry Barber being the captain, made a trip from New South Wales to the north-west coast of America. An Arthur Island, seen in this passage, was in due course shown in nineteenth-century charts. As late as 1871, Findlay's *Directory* stated that Arthur Island, placed by Arrowsmith in latitude 3° 30′ S., longitude 176° 0′ W. required confirmation as to existence and position.[1]

No land in fact exists in the precise position given for Arthur Island. McKean Island in the Phoenix group, which is in the stated latitude but some 1¾° to the east of the stated longitude, is the most likely candidate for identification with this island.

The name Phoenix was given to the group by Wilkes of the U.S. Exploring Expedition of 1838–42 at a time when its geography was still imperfectly known,[2] a Phoenix Island having been reported in the area. The Russian hydrographer Krusenstern, in a note published in 1834, said on the authority of the French explorer Tromelin, who crossed the Pacific in the *Bayonnaise* in 1823, that the position of Phoenix Island was latitude 3° 42′ S., longitude 170° 43′ W., and that Arrowsmith's latitude for Phoenix Island was 0° 12′ too far north.[3] Jeremiah N. Reynolds, in his report of 1828 to the U.S. Navy Department on discoveries by American whaling vessels,[4] gives the position of a 'Phenix Island', described as small and sandy and 3 miles in circumference, as latitude 2° 35′ S., longitude 171° 39′ W. Records of American whaling voyages refer to American whaling ships called *Phenix* and *Phoenix* prior to Reynolds's report in 1828.[5] Reynolds also

---

[1] Stackpole, E. A., *The Sea-Hunters* (Philadelphia–New York, 1953), p. 375, citing *Albany Sentinel*, 29 Aug. 1797; Findlay, A. G., *A Directory for the Navigation of the Pacific Ocean* (London, 1871), p. 665.

[2] For references to Wilkes in this section, Wilkes, C., *Narrative of the United States Exploring Expedition* (Philadelphia, 1845).

[3] Royal Geographical Society, *Journal* (London, 1837), pp. 407–8; Krusenstern, A. J., *Supplémens* (St. Petersburg, 1836), pp. 158–9.

[4] For references to Reynolds in this section, Reynolds, J. N., Report of 1828, in Doc. No. 105, House of Representatives, Navy Department, 23rd Congress, 2nd Session (Washington, 1835).

[5] Starbuck, A., *History of the American Whale-Fishery*, in Appendix to the Report of the Commissioner for Fish and Fisheries for 1875–6 (Washington, 1878).

says that 'Birney's Island in lat 3° 30' long 171° 30' W and Sidney's Island in lat 4° 25' long 171° 20' W discovered by Captain Emmert will be found on the charts'. He gives this as a comment on a position for a Sidney's Island as latitude 4° 30' S., longitude 171° 20' W., which is listed by him in juxtaposition to two unnamed islands in latitude 3° 14' S., longitude 170° 50' W. and latitude 3° 35' S., longitude 170° 40' W. respectively. In another place he gives another position for a Sidney's Island as latitude 4° 29' S., longitude 171° 20' W. These positions for two unnamed islands and two Sidney's Islands were evidently derived by Reynolds from information secured by him about contacts by American whaling ships independently of Emmett. Captain Emmett, of the British vessel *Sydney*, was presumably associated with Captain James Birnie, a contemporary shipping man of London and New South Wales; Tromelin found Sidney's Island again in 1823 and gave its position as latitude 4° 26' 30" S., longitude 171° 18' W.[1] Two islands reputed to be rediscoveries of Emmett's islands but of doubtful longitude were seen by Obed Starbuck (see section 97).[2] Enderbury Island (a corruption of Enderby's Island), reported by Captain James Coffin of Nantucket in 1823 while in command of the British whale-ship *Transit*, is shown in early nineteenth-century charts in latitude 3° 10' S., longitude 171° 10' W.[3]

When these data are compared with the actual geography of the south-eastern sector of the Phoenix Islands, comprising Phoenix, Birnie, and Enderbury Islands, the impossibility of deciding who discovered which of these three islands, and when, becomes apparent. The positions of the modern Phoenix, Birnie, and Enderbury Islands, all of them small, are respectively latitude 3° 43' S., longitude 170° 44' W., latitude 3° 35' S., longitude 171° 32' W., and latitude 3° 8' S., longitude 171° 8' W. Tromelin's position for his Phoenix Island corresponds almost exactly with the position of the modern Phoenix Island, but whether Arrowsmith's data for the previously reported Phoenix Island are sufficient to differentiate it from Birnie is open to question. The position for Reynolds's 'Phenix Island' corresponds neither to the modern Phoenix nor the near-by Birnie or Enderbury, being in

[1] Krusenstern, A. J., *Supplémens* (St. Petersburg, 1836), pp. 4, 12; Appendix to Bigge's Report, in McNab, R., *Historical Records of New Zealand*, vol. i (Wellington, 1908), pp. 458–69.
[2] Stackpole, E. A., *The Sea-Hunters* (Philadelphia–New York, 1953), p. 375.
[3] Krusenstern, A. J., *Supplémens* (St. Petersburg, 1836), pp. 158–9; Bryan, E. H., *American Polynesia* (Honolulu, 1941), p. 58.

fact 11 miles north of Canton Island, the visible land of which is 8 miles long and over 20 miles in circuit, as compared with the description of 'Phenix Island' as small and sandy and 3 miles in circumference. The precise identification of the two unnamed islands listed by Reynolds in this area is also doubtful, as is the identification of the islands reported by Starbuck. One or other of the Sidney's Islands in these data may have been Hull, since Sydney and Hull lie east and west of each other in latitude $4\frac{1}{2}°$ S. and longitudes $171\frac{1}{4}°$ and $172\frac{1}{2}°$ W. respectively. All that can be said is that Emmett apparently discovered Sydney, and that the first firm reports of Phoenix and Enderbury would appear to have been made by Tromelin and Coffin respectively.

Wilkes established the locations of the modern McKean, Hull, Birnie, and Enderbury, seeing each of them in turn, and heard from a French turtle-hunter on Hull that Sydney was some 60 miles to the east.

Howland Island, the northernmost of the Phoenix group, is said to have been discovered by Captain George B. Worth, of the Nantucket whaling ship *Oeno*, about 1822, being called Worth Island.[1] It was placed on the charts under the name Howland Island following a contact in November 1827, by Daniel McKenzie of the American whaling vessel *Minerva Smith*, who placed it in latitude 0° 47′ N., longitude 176° 35′ W., and gave it its present name.[2]

New Nantucket, as we have seen (see section 97), was the name given to Baker Island by its discoverer Obed Starbuck, of the American ship *Hero*, in 1823.

Mary Balcout's Island is described in Reynolds's report as being in latitude 2° 47′ S., longitude 171° 58′ W., surrounded by a reef 20 leagues in circuit, with only four openings where boats could enter. The English hydrographer Norie, in his map of 1825, lists a Mary's Island,[3] which may be identical with Mary Balcout's Island, being virtually in the same position. Reynolds also gives the position of a Barney's Island as latitude 3° 9′ S., longitude 171° 41′ W., described as having a lagoon 20 miles in circumference. Several masters

[1] Bryan, E. H., *American Polynesia* (Honolulu, 1941), p. 46.
[2] Stackpole, E. A., *The Sea-Hunters* (Philadelphia–New York, 1953), p. 374.
[3] Ibid., p. 375.

and owners named Barney are listed in records of American whaling voyages.[1]

The position given for Mary Balcout's Island is precisely that of Canton Island, the north-easternmost of the Phoenix group. While nothing like the size indicated, Canton is larger than any of the other islands in the vicinity. Its sides are broached by several openings, although only one is in fact negotiable by boats.[2] Barney's Island, from the size of the lagoon, would also appear to have been Canton, although the stated latitude is somewhat south of Canton.

Late in 1825 Captain Joshua Gardner, of the American whaling vessel *Ganges*, found an island named by him Gardner's Island, the position given being latitude 4° 30′ S., longitude 174° 22′ W.[3] Wilkes found an island described by him as being in much the same position as the Kemin's or Gardner's Island of the charts.

The positions given for Kemin's or Gardner's Island are almost precisely that of the modern Gardner Island, a relatively detached member of the Phoenix group.

107. Curé Island

IN 1827 Captain Stanikowitch, of the Russian vessel *Moller*, found a small, low, dangerous island, placed by him in latitude 28° 27′ N., longitude 178° 23′ 30″ W. The Russian hydrographer Krusenstern suggested that this was the same as Curé Island, a previous vaguely reported discovery.[4]

This was the modern Kure Island, in the north-western sector of the Hawaiian Islands.

[1] Starbuck, A., *History of the American Whale-Fishery*, in Appendix to the Report of the Commissioner for Fish and Fisheries for 1875–6 (Washington, 1878).

[2] *Pacific Islands Pilot*, vol. ii, p. 472.

[3] Stackpole, E. A., *The Sea-Hunters* (Philadelphia–New York, 1953), p. 378, citing *Nantucket Inquirer*, 8 Dec. 1827.

[4] Krusenstern, A. J., *Supplémens* (St. Petersburg, 1836), pp. 109, 162.

108. Frederick William Beechey

FREDERICK WILLIAM BEECHEY, commander of the British naval vessel *Blossom*, while traversing the Tuamotu Archipelago in 1826, discovered several new islands.[1]

While coming from Wallis's Egmont Island, namely Vairaatea (see section 30), to Edwards's Carysfort's Island, namely Tureia (see section 47), Beechey, on 27 January 1826, found a very small island, the position at the north of it being taken as latitude 20° 45′ 7″ S., longitude 4° 7′ 48″ W. of Mangareva. This island he named Barrow's Island. It was considered by Beechey to be only 1¾ miles in length and 1³⁄₁₀ miles in width, and consisted of a narrow strip of land of oval shape with a lagoon in its middle. Beechey then beat to windward to Carysfort's Island, which agreed with Edwards's descriptions.

Barrow's Island was Vanavana, corresponding in all respects to Beechey's topographical descriptions and relative locations.

From Tureia Beechey came south in search of Weatherhead's 'Matilda Rocks' (see section 52) and Carteret's Osnaburgh Island (see section 31). At daylight on 28 January 1826 he came to a large island which he circumnavigated, and at daylight on 29 January 1826 he came to a small coral island near it to the south. He returned to the larger island, and entered the lagoon. At this island he found many signs of the wreck of a whaling ship which he concluded from various signs was the *Matilda*, the position of the island as observed by him being close to that given for Matilda Rocks. Beechey named the smaller island Cockburn.

These two islands were Mururoa and Fangataufa. The position of Mururoa agrees with Beechey's and with that of 'Matilda Rocks', and Fangataufa is a small island about 20 miles south-south-east of Mururoa. Mururoa is a large atoll with passages into the lagoon. Beechey was thus the discoverer of Fangataufa.

Beechey did not succeed in finding Carteret's Osnaburgh Island in or near the position assigned to it by Carteret. This is not surprising, since Carteret's stated longitudes in this area are two or three degrees too far east. Thus Tematangi, the only island identifiable with Osnaburgh in reference to Carteret's

[1] Beechey, F. W., *Narrative of a Voyage* (London, 1831).

course and sailing times, was well to the west of where Beechey was looking.

Beechey made one more discovery, namely of an island placed in latitude 19° 40′ S., longitude 14° 29′ W. Recognizing that it was not on the charts, Beechey called it Byam Martin's Island. The date of this discovery was not specified, but was early in February 1826.

This was Ahunui.

Frederick William Beechey, on 27 and 29 January 1826, and early in February, discovered Vanavana, Fangataufa, and Ahunui in the Tuamotu Archipelago.

109. Captain Clerk

IN 1826 Captain Clerk passed through the southern sector of the Gilbert Islands in the whaling vessel *John Palmer*. He reported seeing three islands which were shown in contemporary charts and hydrographic compilations under various names, e.g. Rotch or Rotcher, Clerk or Eliza, and Francis. When in due course the islands Tamana, Onotoa, and Beru were established as being in positions close to those given for Clerk's three islands, it was considered by later geographers that these were Clerk's three islands.[1]

The identification of Clerk's Island with Onotoa, which has no island close to it on the east or west, may be taken as reasonably clear. This was a new discovery. Both Tamana and Arorae to the south of Onotoa had been seen previously (see sections 72 and 78), so the issue of which was Rotch is academic so far as discovery is concerned. Whether Francis was Beru or alternatively Nukunau may be open to doubt, since they are both small islands lying some 22 miles east and west of each other. The discovery of these two islands is obscure, the reports of one or other of them by Byron (see section 29), Clerk, and later voyagers[2] being subject to

[1] Krusenstern, A. J., *Supplémens* (St. Petersburg, 1836), p. 19; Findlay, A. G., *A Directory for the Navigation of the Pacific Ocean* (London, 1851), vol. ii, p. 1055; Meinicke, C. E., *Die Inseln des Stillen Oceans* (Leipzig, 1888), vol. ii, pp. 319–20.

[2] Cf. Plaskett, W., Log of the *Independence II*, 1825–8, cited in Stackpole, E. A., *The Sea-Hunters* (Philadelphia–New York, 1953), pp. 343–4; Meinicke, C. E., *Die Inseln des Stillen Oceans* (Leipzig, 1888), vol. ii, p. 320.

uncertainty as to which of these islands was in fact encountered on these various contacts.

110. Jules Sébastien César Dumont d'Urville

THE French explorer Dumont d'Urville, who had accompanied Duperrey on the latter's voyage (see section 94), himself made an extensive exploration of the Pacific in the years 1826–8.

While traversing the Fiji Islands in 1827 d'Urville had with him some Fijians, who directed him to islands called 'Mouala', 'Totoua', and 'Motougou'. On 2 June 1827, having left these Fijians at 'Mouala', d'Urville approached within an estimated distance of 6 leagues of 'Totoua' and 'Motougou', which were high islands. In his accompanying Atlas d'Urville gives their positions as follows: The west part of 'Totoua'—latitude 18° 56′ 15″ S., longitude 177° 39′ 40″ W. (from Paris); the peak of 'Motougou'—latitude 18° 54′ 30″ S., longitude 177° 56′ W. (from Paris).[1]

'Mouala' was Moala, previously seen from the north by Bligh on his second voyage (see section 51). 'Totoua' and 'Motougou' were Totoya and Matuku in the Lau sector of the Fiji group. Of these two islands d'Urville thus gave the first firm record. It is possible these islands had been seen by Oliver (see section 47).

111. George Rule

J. N. REYNOLDS, in his report of 1828 to the U.S. Navy Department on discoveries by American whalers, says that Captain George Rule of Nantucket in 1827 discovered an uninhabited island in latitude 11° 48′ S., longitude 164° 47′ W., 1½ miles long from south-south-east to north-north-west, with a reef around it at 100 rods from the shore.

---

[1] Dumont d'Urville, J. S. C., *Voyage de la corvette L'Astrolabe* (Paris, 1830–3), vol. iv, pp. 424–30, and Atlas.

There was wood and fish in abundance, but no water was found. Rule named his discovery Lydra Island.[1]

These data conform in all respects with Nassau, an arid atoll in the northern Cooks.

112. Richard Macy

J. N. REYNOLDS, in his report of 1828 to the U.S. Navy Department, gives details of interviews with Richard Macy, an American whaling captain. Macy said that in 1827 he discovered a small group of islands in latitude 6° N., longitude 153° E. The islands were all enclosed in a reef and abounded in trees. He called the group by the name of his ship, the *Harvest*.[2]

Namoluk is an atoll consisting of four islands on a reef, the position being very close to that given for Macy's Harvest. The Nomoi Islands to the south-east of Namoluk do not correspond to Macy's description, consisting of a number of separate atolls. Namoluk may have been discovered by Saavedra (see section 5), but the first firm report of it must be credited to Macy.

113. Fedor Lütke

IN 1826–9 the Russian explorer Fedor Lütke made a voyage as commander of two vessels, the *Senyavin* and the *Moller*, during the course of which he made extensive explorations in the Caroline Islands.[3]

On 12 April 1828 Lütke discovered an island identified by him as that known to the Caroline Islanders as 'Eourypyg'. In an accompanying

---

[1] Reynolds, J. N., Report of 1828, in Doc. No. 105, House of Representatives, Navy Department, 23rd Congress, 2nd Session (Washington, 1835).

[2] Ibid.

[3] Lütke, F. P., *Voyage autour du monde* (Paris, 1835–6).

plan its position is shown as latitude 6° 39' 44", longitude 216° 49' 2".

The plan and location of this island as given by Lütke leave no doubt that it was Eauripik, in the western Caroline Islands. Lütke was thus its discoverer.

114. J. A. Moerenhout

J. A. MOERENHOUT, a Belgian national, made a number of voyages in the Tuamotu–Society Islands area in the early nineteenth century. During the course of these he made some contributions to discovery.[1]

In 1829 Moerenhout came from Chile to Tahiti in his vessel the *Volador*. On 1 March 1829, 3 days after leaving Pitcairn, he came to an island with reefs on which the sea was beating with great violence, the position given being latitude 22° S., longitude 135° 50' W. (from Paris), to which he gave the name Bertero. This was presumably Minerva Reef, which is in about that position. Continuing on for Marutea in the Tuamotu Archipelago, known from Edwards's report of it (see section 47), Moerenhout came to an island without an entrance to the lagoon, which he at first thought was Marutea, the position given being, however, latitude 22° S., longitude 137° 50' W. (from Paris), which was south of the position of Marutea. When Moerenhout later made contact with Marutea, he realized the previous island was smaller. In an accompanying chart it is called Moerenhout.

The positions, relative locations, and descriptions as detailed by Moerenhout make it plain that Moerenhout Island was the atoll Maria, in the Tuamotu Archipelago, which was thus discovered by Moerenhout in March 1829. It is a small atoll with no entrance to the lagoon, situated 40 miles south-west of Marutea.

In the accompanying chart two islands are shown as having been seen by Moerenhout in 1832, the positions being given as doubtful, one in about latitude 23° 10' S., longitude 139° 35' W. (from Paris), the other in about latitude 25° 55' S., longitude 140° 20' W. (from Paris).

[1] Moerenhout, J. A., *Voyages* (Paris, 1837), vol. i, pp. 133–4, 156; vol. ii, Chart.

The first position is very close to that of Morane, a small atoll in the Tuamotu Archipelago. No island or reef exists in or near the position given for the other island. In view of this fact, coupled with the doubtful position of the first island, it cannot be assumed that the latter was in fact Morane.

115. Captain Ireland

ON 1 October 1831 Captain Ireland of the British vessel *Adhemar* encountered an island of which the native name was Raraka, in the north-western sector of the Tuamotu Archipelago. It was a low wooded atoll with a lagoon communicating with the sea by a narrow channel. It was calculated to extend 19 miles in an east and west direction, and the lagoon appeared to be 10 or 12 miles long in a north and south direction.[1]

This was Raraka in the north-western Tuamotus, which conforms well with Ireland's description, including having an entrance to the lagoon.[2] Ireland was thus its discoverer.

116. Nathaniel Cary

IN April 1832 Nathaniel Cary, of the American whaling vessel *Gideon Barstow*, coming south and east from the Society Islands, found a low island which was not on his charts. It was judged to be about 15 miles long and very narrow, with a dangerous reef from north-west to west-north-west, and only 25 feet above sea-level. Cary placed it in latitude 23° 13′ S., longitude 137° 24′ W. It was named Barstow Island.[3]

Barstow Island was evidently Morane, a long, narrow island close to the stated position. It had probably been seen by Moerenhout (see section 114).

[1] Findlay, A. G., *A Directory for the Navigation of the Pacific Ocean* (London, 1851), vol. ii, p. 868, citing *Bull. Soc. Géog.* of 1832.
[2] *Pacific Islands Pilot*, vol. iii, p. 113.
[3] Stackpole, E. A., *The Sea-Hunters* (Philadelphia–New York, 1953), p. 383, citing *Nantucket Inquirer*, 12 Jan. 1833.

117. D'Wolf Island

STEPHEN R. CROCKER, of the American whaling ship *General Jackson*, on 28 January 1839 visited a low, well-wooded island where the natives were friendly. When 5 miles to the south-east of it he took his position as latitude 9° 26′ S., longitude 171° 7′ W. Crocker says in his log that this island was D'Wolf Island, discovered on 14 February 1835, William De Wolf of Bristol being the owner of the ship.[1]

The position given is that of Fakaofo, in the Tokelau Islands. The existence of Nukunonu (some 35 miles west-north-west of Fakaofo), which had been discovered by Edwards in 1791 and named Duke of Clarence's Island (see section 47), would presumably be known to Crocker and his contemporaries from the charts. D'Wolf Island can therefore reasonably be taken to be Fakaofo, of which there is no previous direct record.

118. Robert Fitz-Roy

ROBERT FITZ-ROY, a British naval captain, in command of the *Beagle*, while passing from Pukapuka to Fakarava in the Tuamotu Archipelago, discovered two uncharted islands on 13 November 1835, 4 days after leaving Pukapuka. He said in his narrative of the voyage[2] that their native names were 'Tairo' and 'Cavahi', this knowledge being apparently derived from indirect native information, since he passed the islands without visiting them. 'Cavahi' was seen a few hours after leaving 'Tairo'. 'Tairo' was an islet, 'Cavahi' consisted of a number of islets surrounding a lagoon.

Taiaro and Kauehi are two atolls lying on a westerly course from Pukapuka, so placed that a sailing time of four days from Pukapuka to Taiaro, during which no islands were seen, and then of a few hours to Kauehi, is realistic. Taiaro is a small circular islet only about 3 miles wide. Kauehi is a much bigger atoll. It is evident that Taiaro and Kauehi, in the Tuamotu Archipelago, were discovered by Fitz-Roy on 13 November 1835.

[1] Stackpole, E. A., *The Sea-Hunters* (Philadelphia–New York, 1953), p. 282, citing log of the *General Jackson*.
[2] Fitz-Roy, R., *Narrative of the . . . Beagle*, vol. i (London, 1839).

119. R. L. Hunter and Captain Grimes

CAPTAIN R. L. HUNTER, of the British vessel *Marshall Bennett*, on 25 December 1835, while coming from New Georgia to the Banks Islands, saw, while travelling east in the parallel of 14° S., the 'Torres islands' to the northward, and other islands to the east which, from his descriptions, were Vanua Lava and Gaua in the Banks group.[1]

The southernmost of the modern Torres Islands, a group of five islands to the north-west of the Banks Islands, is 896 feet high and lies 34 miles north of the 14th parallel. It is not clear whether the 'Torres islands' seen by Hunter included any of the Torres Islands of today or were confined to the northern islands of the Banks group discovered by Quiros (see section 14), namely Vanua Lava and Ureparapara.

When Hunter referred to the 'Torres islands' he no doubt got the name from the contemporary charts. Thus Arrowsmith in his chart of 1798 showed islands called by him Banks Islands in consequence of Bligh's reports of islands in the area, with islands to the north-west of them called Torres, supposed to have been discovered in 1606, no doubt in consequence of the islands reported in that year by Torres of Quiros's expedition (see section 14).[2] The discoveries both of Quiros's expedition and Bligh, however, were confined to the Banks Islands as they are known today. It was by a mere coincidence that the Torres Islands of the nineteenth-century charts lie in somewhat the same relationship to the Banks Islands as the Torres Islands of today, which were in fact unknown.

Hunter on another occasion encountered an island which was not on his charts. In September 1836, while coming from Laughlan's Islands, i.e. the Nada Islands to the north of the Louisiade Archipelago (see section 81), he went north and then west-south-west, and so came to a large inhabited island, estimated to be about 40 miles in extent, nearly east by south, and west by north, of moderate elevation with some hills in the interior, the highest being of a remarkable sugar-loaf shape. Hunter made the eastern end of the island in latitude 9° 9' S., longitude 153° 5' E., and the western end in latitude 8° 53' S., longitude 152° 24' E. Hunter commented that three small, high islands could be

[1] In *Nautical Magazine* (London, 1840), p. 468.
[2] Arrowsmith, A., *Chart* (London, 1798).

seen to the west from the western end, not four, as in some charts. He said he made no claim to the discovery of the large island, as it was first pointed out by Captain Grimes of the *Woodlark* of Sydney, which ship he saw in Sydney later. The island in question was therefore named Woodlark Island.[1]

Woodlark was the island usually known as Murua today, some 33 miles west of the Nada Islands. Grimes was the first clearly established discoverer, at a date prior to September 1836.

The islands seen by Hunter to the west of Woodlark were those still sometimes called the Marshall Bennett Islands after Hunter's ship. Of these, Gawa is the chief. Whether these islands were in fact discovered by Hunter is, however, dubious, since he himself refers to islands charted in that location, and to the track of one Bristow in that area as shown in the charts.

120. Captain Swain

CAPTAIN HUDSON, of the U.S. Exploring Expedition of 1838–42, visited the Tokelau Islands in 1841. The master of a whaling ship, Captain Swain, had informed Hudson of the direction of another near-by island, called by Hudson Swain's Island. Hudson visited it, and placed it in latitude 11° 5′ S., longitude 170° 55′ 15″ W. It was of coral formation but no lagoon was seen. It was nearly round and appeared to be only a few miles in circumference, and was about 15 to 25 feet above the sea. There was no safe landing place. The island appeared to be uninhabited.[2]

This was Swains Island, some 180 miles north-north-west of Savaii in the Samoa group. It is not clear when Swain discovered it.

[1] In *Nautical Magazine* (London, 1840), pp. 465–7.
[2] Wilkes, C., *Narrative of the United States Exploring Expedition* (Philadelphia, 1845), vol. v, p. 18.

121. John Elphinstone Erskine

It has been seen that Captain R. L. Hunter, when coming to the islands of Vanua Lava and Gaua in the Banks group in 1835 (see section 119), may have had a distant sight of the Torres Islands to the north-west of the Banks Islands. It was explained that the Torres Islands were placed on the early charts to the north-west of the Banks Islands by a mere coincidence and not from knowledge of the existence of the Torres Islands of today.

The first firm record of the Torres Islands was given by John Elphinstone Erskine of the British naval vessel *Havannah*, in 1850. In a chart published in 1853, Erskine showed the track of his voyage in 1850 from Espiritu Santo in the New Hebrides northward to Vanikoro in the Santa Cruz Islands. This chart shows four islands close to the track on the west side, the Banks Islands being shown to the south-east. Erskine names these four islands, which are shown close to one another in a chain from south-east to north-west, as 'Quiros or Torres Is', and gives accompanying legend saying that they were seen by the *Havannah* on 13 September 1850.[1]

These islands were unmistakably the Torres Islands. There are actually five islands, separated by channels which are in some cases narrow.[2]

122. Midway Island

The first firm record of the modern Midway Island, an atoll in the northern sector of the Hawaiian Islands, appears to have been that of Captain Brooks, of the United States vessel *Gambia*, in 1859. Brooks fixed its position, and described its topography in some detail. Several islands in that vicinity, one or other of which was probably this island, had, however, been reported previously.[3]

[1] Chart accompanying Erskine, J. E., *Journal of a Cruise among the Islands of the Western Pacific* (London, 1853).
[2] *Pacific Islands Pilot*, vol. ii, pp. 233–5.
[3] Meinicke, C. E., *Die Inseln des Stillen Oceans* (Leipzig, 1888), vol. ii, pp. 313–14.

BIBLIOGRAPHY

THE following is a list of the publications cited in this book:

AMHERST, LORD, and THOMSON, B. (eds.), *The Discovery of the Solomon Islands* (London, 1901, 2 vols.).

Anon., *Journael vande Nassausche Vloot* (Amsterdam, 1626).

—— *Suite du Neptune françois* (Amsterdam, 1700, 2 vols.).

—— *The Voyage of Governor Phillip to Botany Bay* (London, 1789).

—— *The World Encompassed by Sir Francis Drake* (2nd ed., London, 1854).

—— *Voyage of H.M.S. Blonde* (London, 1826).

ARROWSMITH, A., *Chart* (London, 1798).

BARROS, J. DE, *Asia*, Decade 3 (Lisbon, 1563), Decade 4 (Madrid, 1615).

BEAGLEHOLE, J. C., *The Exploration of the Pacific* (London, 1934).

—— (ed.), *The Journals of Captain James Cook*, vol. i (Cambridge, 1955).

BEECHEY, F. W., *Narrative of a Voyage* (London, 1831, 2 vols.).

BLIGH, W., *A Voyage to the South Sea* (London, 1792).

BOUGAINVILLE, L. A. DE, *Voyage autour du monde* (Paris, 1771).

BROSSES, C. DE, *Histoire des navigations aux terres australes* (Paris, 1756, 2 vols.).

BRYAN, E. H., *American Polynesia* (Honolulu, 1941).

BUCK, P. H., *Explorers of the Pacific* (Honolulu, 1953).

BURNEY, J., *Discoveries in the South Sea* (London, 1803–17, 5 vols.).

CANTOVA, J., In *Choix de lettres édifiantes et curieuses écrites . . . des missions étrangères* (Paris, 1770).

CARRINGTON, H. (ed.), *The Discovery of Tahiti* (London, 1948).

COLLINS, D., *An Account of the British Colony in New South Wales* (London, 1798, 1802, 2 vols.).

COOK, J., *A Voyage towards the South Pole* (London, 1777, 2 vols.).

—— and KING, J., *A Voyage to the Pacific Ocean* (London, 1784, 3 vols.).

COOKE, E., *A Voyage to the South Sea* (London, 1712, 2 vols.).

CORNEY, B. G. (ed.), *The Quest and Occupation of Tahiti by Emissaries of Spain* (London, 1913–18, 3 vols.).

COUTO, D. DO, *Asia*, Decade 4 (Lisbon, 1602).

CROZET, J., *Nouveau Voyage*, ed. Rochon, A. (Paris, 1783).

DAHLGREN, E. W., *The Discovery of the Hawaiian Islands* (Uppsala, 1917).

DAMPIER, W., *A Collection of Voyages*, vols. i, ii, iii (London, 1729).

DEBENHAM, E. (ed.), *The Voyage of Captain Bellingshausen* (Engl. ed., London, 1945, 2 vols.).

DUMONT D'URVILLE, J. S. C., *Voyage de la corvette L'Astrolabe* (Paris, 1830–3, 5 vols. and Atlas).

DUPERREY, L. I., *Mémoire sur les opérations géographiques . . . Coquille* (Paris, 1827).

EILERS, A., *Ergebnisse der Südsee-Expedition 1908–1910. II. Ethnographie B Mikronesien*, vol. ix, part 1 (Hamburg, 1935), part 2 (Hamburg, 1936).

ENGELBRECHT, W. A., and HERWERDEN, P. J. van (eds.), *De ontdekkingsreis van Jacob Le Maire en Willem Cornelisz. Schouten* (The Hague, 1945, 2 vols.).

ERSKINE, J. E., *Journal of a Cruise among the Islands of the Western Pacific* (London, 1853).

ESPINOSA, J., *Memorias* (Madrid, 1809, 2 vols.).

FANNING, E., *Voyages round the World* (New York, 1833).

FIGUEROA, C. S. DE, *Hechos de D. Garcia, Marques de Cañete*, vol. vi (Madrid, 1613).

FINDLAY, A. G., *A Directory for the Navigation of the Pacific Ocean* (London, 1851, 2 vols.).

—— *A Directory for the Navigation of the Pacific Ocean* (3rd ed., London, 1871).

FITZ-ROY, R., *Narrative of the . . . Beagle*, vol. i (London, 1839).

FORNANDER, A., *An Account of the Polynesian Race*, vol. ii (London, 1880).

FUNNELL, W., Narrative in *A Collection of Voyages*, vol. iv (London, 1729).

GALVANO, A., *Tratado* (republication of Hakluyt's edition of 1601, London, 1862).

GILBERT, T., *Voyage from New South Wales to Canton* (London, 1789).

GILL, W., *Gems from the Coral Islands*, vol. ii (London, 1856).

GILL, W. W., *Life in the Southern Isles* (London, 1876).

GOBIEN, C. LE, *Histoire des Isles Marianes* (Paris, 1700).

HAWKESWORTH, J., *Voyages* (London, 1773, 3 vols.).

HEERES, J. E. (ed.), *Abel Janszoon Tasman's Journal* (Amsterdam, 1898).

HENDERSON, G. C., *The Discoverers of the Fiji Islands* (London, 1933).

HORSBURGH, J., *India Directory* (3rd ed., London, 1826–7, 2 vols.).

HUNTER, J., *An Historical Journal* (London, 1793).

HUNTER, R. L., 'Note of new discoveries in the Pacific' in *Nautical Magazine* of 1840, pp. 465–8.

HYDROGRAPHIC DEPARTMENT, ADMIRALTY, *Pacific Islands Pilot* (London, 1931–57, 3 vols. and supplements).

KOTZEBUE, O. VON, *A New Voyage* (Engl. ed., London, 1830, 2 vols.).

—— *A Voyage of Discovery* (Engl. ed., London, 1821, 3 vols.).

KRÄMER, A., *Ergebnisse der Südsee-Expedition 1908–1910. II. Ethnographie B Mikronesien*, vol. iii, part 1 (Hamburg, 1917); vol. xi, part 1 (Hamburg, 1938).

KRUSENSTERN, A. J., *Atlas de l'Océan Pacifique* (St. Petersburg, 1824, 1827, 2 vols.).

—— *Receuil de mémoires hydrographiques* (St. Petersburg, 1824, 1827, 2 vols.), *Supplémens* (St. Petersburg, 1836).

LABILLARDIÈRE, J. J. DE, *Relation du voyage à la recherche de La Pérouse* (Paris, 1800, 2 vols. and Atlas).

LEE, I., *Captain Bligh's Second Voyage* (London, 1920).

LISIANSKI, U., *A Voyage round the World* (London, 1814).

LÜTKE, F. P., *Voyage autour du monde* (Paris, 1835–6, 3 vols.).
MACGREGOR, G., *Ethnology of Tokelau Islands* (Honolulu, 1937).
MCNAB, R., *Historical Records of New Zealand*, vol. i (Wellington, 1908).
—— *Murihiku and the Southern Islands* (Invercargill, 1907).
MARCHAND, É., *Voyage autour du monde* (Paris, 1798–1800, 4 vols.).
MARETU, Engl. trans. of manuscript reference, in *Journal of the Polynesian Society*, vol. xx, p. 192.
MARKHAM, C. (ed.), *The Voyages of Pedro Fernandez de Quiros* (London, 1904, 2 vols.).
MASSACHUSETTS HISTORICAL SOCIETY, *Collections*, vol. ii (Boston, 1810).
MAUDE, H. E., 'In Search of a Home', *Journal of the Polynesian Society*, vol. lxvii, pp. 104–31.
MEARES, J., *Voyages* (London, 1790).
MEINICKE, C. E., *Die Inseln des Stillen Oceans* (2nd ed., Leipzig, 1888, 2 vols.).
MEYJES, R. P. (ed.), *De reizen van Abel Janszoon Tasman* (The Hague, 1919).
MILET-MUREAU, M. L. A. (ed.), *Voyage of La Pérouse* (Engl. ed., London, 1798, 2 vols.).
MOERENHOUT, J. A., *Voyages aux îles du Grand Océan* (Paris, 1837, 2 vols.).
MULERT, F. E. Baron (ed.), *De reis van Mr. Jacob Roggeveen* (The Hague, 1911).
NAVARRETE, M. F. (ed.), *Colección*, vols. iv, v (Madrid, 1837).
NEVERMANN, H., *Ergebnisse der Südsee-Expedition 1908–1910. II. Ethnographie A Melanesien*, vol. ii (Hamburg, 1933); vol. iii (Hamburg, 1934).
PACHECO, J. F., CÁRDENAS, F. DE, and MENDOZA, L. T. DE (eds.), *Colección de documentos inéditos relativos al descubrimiento . . . sacado . . . del Real Archivo de Indias*, vol. v (Madrid, 1866); vol. xiv (Madrid, 1870). Continuation: *Colección de documentos inéditos . . . de ultramar. Segunda serie*, vol. ii (Madrid, 1886); vol. iii (Madrid, 1887).
PURCHAS, S., *Purchas his Pilgrimes*, vols. i, iv (London, 1625).
PURDY, J., *The Oriental Navigator* (London, 1816).
RAMUSIO, G. B., *Delle Navigationi e Viaggi* (Venice, edition of 1588).
RECHE, O., *Ergebnisse der Südsee-Expedition 1908–1910. II. Ethnographie A Melanesien*, vol. iv, part 1 (Hamburg, 1954).
REYNOLDS, J. N., Report of 1828, in Doc. No. 105, House of Representatives, Navy Department, 23rd Congress, 2nd Session (Washington, 1835).
ROGERS, W., *A Cruising Voyage* (London, 1712).
ROSS, J. C., *A Voyage of Discovery* (London, 1847, 2 vols.).
ROSSEL, E. P. E. (ed.), *Voyage de Dentrecasteaux* (Paris, 1808, 2 vols.).
ROYAL GEOGRAPHICAL SOCIETY, Editor's notes in *Journal*, vol. vii (1837).
SCOTT, E., *Life of Matthew Flinders* (London, 1914).
SHARP, A., *Ancient Voyagers in the Pacific* (2nd ed., Penguin Books, 1957).
STACKPOLE, E. A., *The Sea-Hunters* (Philadelphia–New York, 1953).
STANLEY, LORD (ed.), *The First Voyage round the World, by Magellan* (London, 1874).

STARBUCK, A., *History of the American Whale-Fishery* (in Appendix to the Report of the Commissioner for Fish and Fisheries for 1875–6, Washington, 1878).

STEVENS, H. N. (ed.), *New Light on the Discovery of Australia* (London, 1930).

THOMSON, B. (ed.), *Voyage of H.M.S. Pandora* (London, 1915).

TURNBULL, J., *A Voyage round the World* (London, 1805, 3 vols.).

VANCOUVER, G., *A Voyage of Discovery* (London, 1798, 3 vols.).

WAFER, L., *A New Voyage*, ed. L. E. Joyce (republished from 1699 and 1704 eds., London, 1934).

WALTER, R., *A Voyage* (London, 1748).

WIEDER, F. C. (ed.), *De reis van Mahu en de Cordes*, vol. i (The Hague, 1923).

WILKES, C., *Narrative of the United States Exploring Expedition* (Philadelphia, 1845, 5 vols.).

WILLIAMS, J., *Missionary Enterprises* (London, 1837).

WILSON, W., et al., *A Missionary Voyage to the Southern Pacific Ocean* (London, 1799).

ZARAGOZA, J., *Historia* (Madrid, 1876), vol. i.

INDEX

Abaiang, first firm report of, by Gilbert and Marshall, 153; probable discovery of, by Grijalva's ship, 24–26.

Abemama, discovery of, by Gilbert and Marshall, 153.

Abgarris, 200.

Abgarris Island, 200.

Abriojos, 29.

Acapulco, 40.

Acea, 153, 202.

Actaeon Islands, group, discovery of, by Quiros, 57–60.

Adams, William, authority for voyage of *Hope* and *Charity*, 55–56.

Adams's Island, 166–7.

Adhemar, 219.

Admiral Greig Island, 197.

Admiralty Islands, group, discovery of Manus and others, by Saavedra, 19–20; ethnology of, 19; first firm report of south-eastern sector of, by Le Maire, 77–78; seen by Carteret, 112, Maurelle, 147.

Adventure, 128–30.

Adzes, at Hawaiian Islands, 144.

Africaansche Galey, 95, 97, 102.

Agiguan, possible discovery and first firm report of, 9–10, 29–30, 86–87.

Agrigan, possible discovery and first firm report of, 9–10, 86–87.

Aguila, 124–7.

Ahe, possible discovery of, by Le Maire, 73–74, Roggeveen, 97–98.

Ahunui, discovery of, by Beechey, 214–15.

Ailinginae, discovery of, by Saavedra, 17–18.

Ailinglapalap, first firm report of, by Dennet, 177–8; probable discovery of, and Jabwot, by *San Jeronimo*, 40–41; seen by Patterson, 191.

Ailuk, discovery of, by Legaspi, 37–38.

Aitutaki, discovery of, by Bligh, 158; ethnology of, 158.

Akiaki, discovery of, by Bougainville, 114–15; seen by Cook, 120.

Alamagan, possible discovery and first firm report of, 9–10, 86–88.

Albo, Francisco, authority for Magellan's expedition, 5–6.

Alexander, 156.

Alexander Turnbull Library, 2.

Allen, Joseph, discovery by, of Gardner Island (in Hawaiian Islands), 196.

Alofi, discovery of, by Le Maire, 75; ethnology of, 75–76.

Amango, 81–82.

Amanu, discovery of, by Quiros, 57–60; seen by Andia, 125.

Amargura, 148–9.

Amatafoa, 81–82.

Ambrim, discovery of, by Cook, 132–3.

America, North, South, 4, 8, 9, 17, 18, 27, 32, 36, 39, 43, 47–48, 56, 66, 79–80, 87–88, 102, 124, 126, 189, 210.

Amsterdam, 81–82.

Anaa, discovery of, by Bougainville, 114–16; not seen by Quiros, 59; seen by Boenechea, 124–6, Cook, 120.

Anachorètes, 119, 147.

Anamocka, 81–82.

Anatahan, possible discovery and first firm report of, 9–10, 29–30, 86–87.

Andia y Varela, Joseph, traverse by, of Tuamotus, 125; record by, of Bonacorsi's observations at Raivavae, 125–7.

Aneityum, discovery of, by Cook, 133–4.

Angatau, first firm report of, by Bellingshausen, 196; possible discovery of, by Magellan, 5–6; seen by Kotzebue, 206.

Aniwa (Immer), discovery of, by Cook, 133; ethnology of, 135.

Annatom, 133.

Annublada, 68.

Anonima, 183.

Anson, George, capture by, of Spanish chart, 67–69.

Ant, discovery of, by Saavedra, 19–20; possibly seen by Ysabel Barreto, 54.

Roggeveen, Jacob (*cont.*)
Easter Island, 95–96, Manua Islands, 99; possible discovery by, of Ahe, 97–98, 100, Manihi, 97–98, 100.
Rondacor Reef, first firm report of, by Maurelle, 148; possible discovery of, by Mendaña, 43–44.
Rongelap, discovery of, by Saavedra, 17–18; seen by Wallis, 108.
Rongerik, discovery of, by Wallis, 108.
Rose, 188.
Rose Island, of James Cary, 188.
Rose Island (in Samoa group), discovery of, by Roggeveen, 99.
Ross, J. C., authority for Bristow's discovery, 189.
Ross Island, 177–8.
Rossel, E. P. E., authority for d'Entrecasteaux's expedition, 173–4.
Rossel Island, first firm report of, by Bougainville, 117–18; possible discovery of, by Prado and Torres, 64, 118; Rossel, of d'Entrecasteaux's expedition, source of name of, 118; seen by d'Entrecasteaux, 174.
Rota, discovery of, by Magellan, 5–6; possibly visited by *Florida*, 19–21, visited by Dampier, 92, *San Jeronimo*, 41–42.
Rotch, Rotcher, 215.
'Roterdam', Rotterdam, 123, 81.
Rotuma, discovery of, by Edwards, 164; ethnology of, 164; not seen by Bougainville, 116–17.
Roux, Jean, authority for Duclesmeur's voyage, 122–3.
Royal Admiral, 173.
Rule, George, discovery by, of Nassau Island, 216–17.
Rurick, 193.
Rurutu, discovery of, by Cook, 121–2; people of, 122.
Russell Islands, discovery of, by Shortland, 156–7.

Saavedra, Alvaro de, discovery by, of Ailinginae, 17–18, 23, Ant, 19–21, 23, Eniwetok, 19–23, Manus, 19–20, 23, Ponape, 19–21, 23, Rongelap, 17–18, 23, Taka, 17–18, 23, Ujelang, 19–21, 23, Utirik, 17–18, 23; ethnological observations by, at Eniwetok, 21–22, 'Los Reyes', 18, Manus, 19,

Ponape, 20; possible discovery by, of islands to west and south-east of Manus and in vicinity of Ponape, 19–23. *See also* Aua, Hermit Islands, Kaniet, Liot, Losap, Manu, Mokil, Nama, Namoluk, Ngatik, Ninigo Islands, Nomoi Islands, Pingelap, Sae, Wuvulu.
Saddle Island, discovery of, by Bligh, 160.
Sae, first firm report of, by Bougainville, 119; possible discovery of, by Saavedra, 19–20, Retes, 30–32, Vries, 86; seen by Maurelle, 148.
Sagitaria, La, 58–60, 62.
Saint-Aignan, 174.
St. Antony, 11.
St. George's Bay, 92, 112.
St. George's Channel, discovery of, by Carteret, 112.
S. Jans, 76, 84.
Saint John, St. John, 11, 111–12.
St. Philip and St. James, 63.
St. Stephen's Day, 27.
Saipan, possible discovery and first firm report of, 9–10, 86–87.
Sala y Gomez, 89–90.
Salazar, Toribio Alonso de, discovery by, of Taongi, 9, 12–13.
Salcedo, Felipe de, discovery by, of Parece Vela, 39.
Saliz, Captain, record by, of reference to Hall's voyage, 207.
Salmon Sweers Cape, 84.
Samal, 50.
Samoa, Samoa Islands, group. See Apolima, Manono, Manua Islands, Rose Island, Savaii, Swains Island, Tutuila, Upolu.
San Agostino, S. Agostino, of Maurelle, 150; of Tompson, 128, 189.
San Ambrosio and San Felix, Carrington's identification of, with land seen by Davis, 89–90.
San Anton, 27.
San Bartolomé, San Bartolomeo, 12, 47.
San Bernardo, 52–53.
San Christoval, 46–47.
San Cristobal, 27, 29.
San Cristobal, discovery of, by Henriquez, 46–47; seen by Shortland, 156.

PRINTED IN GREAT BRITAIN
AT THE UNIVERSITY PRESS, OXFORD
BY VIVIAN RIDLER
PRINTER TO THE UNIVERSITY